THR

CW00733038

THREE COMEDIES

The Bereaved Family
"Dr"
Mrs Minister

Branislav Nushich

Translated by Geoffrey N. W. Locke

A S W A

Published in 2001 by *ASWA*
(The Association of Serbian Writers Abroad)
PO Box 20772
London E3 5WF

Copyright © G.N.W. Locke 2001

All rights reserved. No part of this work may be reproduced,
stored in a retrieval system, or transmitted in any form or by
any means, electronic, electrostatic, magnetic tape, mechanical,
photocopying, recording or otherwise, without the prior
permission in writing of the publisher.

ISBN 0-9541777-1-1

CONTENTS

FOREWORD – TRANSLATING NUSHICH

by Geoffrey N. W. Locke

In 1954 I was an impecunious regular subaltern of artillery. To avoid a dull posting, and to obtain a career "good mark", I volunteered to attend an interpreters' course, of which a number of languages were on offer. I have to admit that I chose to learn Serbo-Croat partly because it sounded exotic, partly because it was one of the very few courses in which one was sent to the actual country to learn the language, and, perhaps not least, because that language was officially classified as "difficult" with the result that the award for qualifying as an interpreter amounted to almost a year's pay!

So the following year, after an intensive nine months at London University grappling with the grammatical foundations of the language, I found myself in Belgrade lodging with a Serbian family, none of whom spoke any English, with my head stuffed so full of declensions and conjugations that I could hardly utter a word without stumbling. Communication was, shall we say, limited. However after a month or two of this "total immersion", things started to come together and, one evening, the family invited me to go to the theatre with them to see Nušić's play *The Bereaved Family (Ožalošćena Porodica)*. This was a turning-point. Of course, I missed much of the repartee and many of the nuances, but I easily caught the main thread of the story and immensely enjoyed the performance, which was played by an excellent cast (of which the principal character was ad-libbing hilariously) to a packed and highly appreciative house. It was a short step to reading the book and that, together with some formal tutoring, much evening conversation with total strangers in cafés and restaurants (frequently very entertaining: the Serbs love talking as much as the Irish do, and have a rumbustious and ironic sense of humour), daily reading of the newspapers, and occasional visits to the cinema (where I once sat through four hours of a film of Stendhal's *Le Rouge et le noir* in Hungarian with Serbian cyrillic subtitles!), enabled me to return to England some six months later sufficiently fluent in the language to satisfy the Civil Service examiners and to qualify as an interpreter.

As anyone acquainted with the normal ways of armies (or any governmental institutions) will expect, I was never afterwards called upon to use the qualification – indeed, my next posting was to Singapore! However, my experiences had left me with an abiding interest in Yugoslavia and the Balkans generally and, over my remaining years in the army, and subsequently as a barrister, I spent much spare time reading Serbian and Croatian literature, including several more of Nušić's plays, with increasing confidence and pleasure. I make no pretensions to being a literary critic, but it seemed to me from the start that this was a major twentieth-century dramatist comparable to, and in some ways an amalgam, of the likes of Oscar Wilde, G.B.Shaw, and J.B.Priestley, for, like them, Nušić writes fluently and with style, deploying superb characterisation, wit, humour, and irony within an expertly constructed dramatic framework. His works are not confined to comedies – indeed, some of his plays are rather dark – but I think that it is in the comedies that his genius reached its full flowering. His use of language is wide-ranging and ideally suited to the various characters into whose mouths he puts the words, but it all translates comfortably into English with a minimum of adaptation because his plays are so timeless and universal and, above all, entertaining. It is this which makes them such a joy to see on the stage, to read, and to translate.

It is clear that Branislav Nušić was a man of many parts. He was born in 1864 in Belgrade and read law at the Universities of Graz and Belgrade, where he graduated in 1886 after a tour of active service as a volunteer in the Bulgarian war. A year later, at the age of 23, he was sent to prison for a year for "writing an anti-dynastic poem", but this did not prevent his being appointed to the Diplomatic Service immediately after his release in 1888, in which year also his first, still highly regarded play, *The Suspect*, was produced. Although by 1902 he had progressed to senior rank, he resigned from government service to pursue careers variously as a prolific writer, dramatist, theatre director, and editor of newspapers and periodicals. In 1915 (aged 51) he took part in the Serbian army's epic withdrawal to Corfu, and until the end of the war lived in Italy, France, and Switzerland. Returning in 1919 to Belgrade, he became Head of the Arts Department of the Ministry of Education and, later, Director of the Sarajevo Theatre, amongst other varied appointments, before finally retiring on pension in 1929. He died in Belgrade in 1938.

It was in his years of retirement that he wrote, and saw produced to great acclaim, the three comedies in this book, *Mrs Minister* (1931), *The Bereaved Family* (1934), and *"Dr"* (1936). Of all his plays these were the ones that I enjoyed the most and which I read again and again, with increasing familiarity bringing increased pleasure. It therefore seemed natural for me to set about translating them as a retirement project, not only for my own satisfaction, but particularly also from the wish to put before the English-speaking world three superb plays which would, I have not the slightest doubt, delight any modern audience. Those of a serious bent who seek sociological comment will find it here, and those who appreciate a subtle but brilliant satirical exposure of pomposity, of political chicanery, of lust for power and the abuse of it, of immorality in high places, of media-mischief, and of the corrosive effect of snobbery and of family feuds, which are so acutely observed in these plays, and all of which are immediately recognisable in any country in any era, will find it here. Above all, those whose only desire is to be richly entertained will assuredly not be disappointed.

I have, throughout, transliterated the names of places and people (including that of the author) into a convenient English form. The Serbian language is not difficult for English-speaking people to pronounce but, unfortunately, the original spelling, with diacritic signs on the consonants, "looks" so foreign as to cause endless confusion.

These are free translations, which inevitably implies occasional compromise. I have, throughout, attempted to give priority to the thought behind the words, rather than to literal construal of them. Of course, some passages contain plays on words or "in" jokes about contemporary personalities which would have been appreciated by a 1930's Yugoslav audience, which cannot be transcribed satisfactorily. Little can be done about these, but I have made sparing use of footnotes where they appear to be essential. Finally, I am must express my sincere gratitude to Mr Dušan Puvačić of London University for his meticulous examination of my work and for his invaluable correction of my errors, gross and minor, and particularly for his suggestions as to the best way to transcribe some nuances of meaning which I had mistaken or missed. If faults remain, they are mine.

G.N.W.L.

Poole, Dorset

November 2001

The Bereaved Family

Ožalošćena Porodica

A Comedy in three Acts

CAST

AGATON ARSICH *A Retired Rural District Administrator*

TANASIYE DIMITRIYEVICH *A merchant*

PROKA PURICH *A local government servant*

TRIFUN SPASICH *A citizen of private means*

MICHA STANIMIROVICH

DR PETROVICH *A lawyer*

SIMKA *Agaton's wife*

VIDA *Tanasije's wife*

GINA *Proka's wife*

SARKA *A widow*

TETKA (AUNT)

DANITSA

The action takes place anywhere, and at any time.

Translator's note: The title of the play derives from the standard subscript to the black-bordered notice which, in Serbia, is traditionally posted up outside the house of a deceased person by his relatives.

Act One

*A wide hall with a staircase leading upstairs. Heavy leather
furniture. Dominating the scene is a large painting of the deceased
Mata Todorovich hanging on the wall in a gilded frame. Doors left
and right and French windows at the rear.*

SCENE 1

Enter THE FAMILY *(ALL except Dr* PETROVICH, AUNT, *and*
DANITSA*)*

*(The stage is at first empty. Then the French windows are opened
and a crowd of men and women enters. This is the family of the
deceased Mata Todorovich, just returning from the cemetery
after the funeral service.[1] They sit down in various places in
silence. After a short pause the men light cigarettes, whilst the
women gaze curiously at the furniture, whisper to each other, or
simply exchange glances).*

AGATON: *(Typical old-fashioned type of Rural District
Administrator. A large man, wearing a wing collar, striped
trousers, and a black coat. He slowly taps a cigarette on his knee,
puts it into a holder, lights it and, as he exhales the smoke looks
about at all the others):* That's it, then – it's all over! It's as if he
had never lived.

PROKA: That's right, Agaton. Here one moment, gone the next.

---

1. Funeral service. The original is *Parastos*, which is actually a service held
   seven days after the burial.

VIDA: Well, it is law of God, Proka, and there's no way round it.

PROKA: No way round it, for sure.

AGATON: You say it's the law – I know it's the law, but at least there ought to be some sort of justice in the law. How can it be a just law that takes away such a man?

TANASIYE: Such a wonderful man …

AGATON: They don't make men like him any more.

TANASIYE: Honest, respected …

AGATON: He wasn't only honest and respected – he was a man of huge generosity. A philanthropist, that's what he was, a genuine philanthropist.

SIMKA: He helped so many people.

PROKA: There was no one too wretched for him to help.

GINA: He helped everyone, left, right, and centre!

TANASIYE: It's a tragedy that he's gone.

AGATON: And what an honest man he was!

TANASIYE: He never tricked anyone – he never did anyone down.

PROKA: Tricked? – Did anyone down? – what are you talking about? He was a giver!

VIDA: He gave with both hands!

MICHA: What a dreadful loss he is to our family!

AGATON: What a dreadful loss, indeed!

SARKA *(to GINA, who is crying)*: For goodness' sake, Gina, stop snivelling! It's one thing crying at the funeral – there were people watching, and somebody had to cry for the sake of decency – but you don't have to keep on doing it here, where there's only Family around.

GINA *(still crying and dabbing her eyes with a handkerchief)*: I can't help it. As they said, a week ago he was here, alive, in this house – and now, today .. ?

SIMKA: And now, today, we've all been to his funeral.

VIDA: That's true. And now that you mention it, I have to say that I was disgusted to see that there was only the one priest at the service. The dear departed deserved better than that, considering how much it all cost.

TANASIYE: There should have been at least three.

VIDA: Three priests, at the very least.

MICHA: That would certainly have been proper, for a man of his standing..

SARKA: It was disgraceful – his funeral service, and only one priest officiating!

GINA: Agaton, dear, did you arrange it?

AGATON: What, me? Nobody asked me. The lawyer was in charge – he must have arranged it.

VIDA: What more do you expect when it's strangers making the arrangements and giving the orders on the family's behalf – they just don't care.

AGATON: Well, what can you do? The dear departed wanted it done like that.

TANASIYE: He was a good and honest man but, I have to say, he was rather inclined to avoid the family. He might at least have invited one of us round occasionally for a bit of a chat.

AGATON: Actually, I came to see him just before he died. I sat here, on this very chair, and he was very happy to see me. He said: "I'm really glad to see you, Agaton! There's no one closer to me than you are!"

TRIFUN *(Coughs)*: Er .. really?. . I wouldn't have thought you were all that close to him, were you, Agaton?

MICHA: Yes, I was just going to say that myself.

AGATON: I'm not saying that we were like brothers born, but we *were* family. You see, he could, on that occasion, have said: "My dear Agaton, there's lots of Family, but they're all so .. I don't know .. the thing is, my dear Agaton, you're so … well, you spent so many years as the District Administrator, organising people and arranging everything, that you're just the man to administer my estate when I'm gone."

TRIFUN *(expressing the general air of protest apparent amongst everyone)*: Well, he *could* have said that, I suppose. But, you know, Agaton, the dear departed was an educated man who read the newspapers, and he *could* have thought to himself:

"Agaton – oh yes, he was indeed the District Administrator, but most of his activities left a rather nasty smell behind them."

AGATON (*furious*): It's all lies! That's what the opposition papers said. You can't expect the gutter Press to say that I always smelled of roses!

TANASIYE: Anyway, apart from that, Agaton, there's a lot of difference between bossing people about as District Administrator, and handling an estate.

AGATON: Oh no there isn't, Tanasiye, they're just the same. For both things, you've got to have wisdom and experience. Come on, now, who's the best man for the job amongst all of us here? Can anyone say that Tanasiye is? If he'd been any good he would have looked after his own affairs and not gone bankrupt.

TANASIYE (*angrily*): Well what if I did go bankrupt? These days far bigger fish than me go bankrupt, so why shouldn't I?

VIDA: And even if he did, Agaton, he never cheated you.

AGATON: No, I don't say you did, Tanasiye. If you'd gone bankrupt and then bought a brand-new car, I'd have taken my hat off to you, but you didn't. You just aren't up to it, it's obvious. Anyway, they found that you'd been fiddling the books.

TANASIYE: That wasn't me, that was the accountant.

AGATON: The accountant was it? Well, we don't need to go into that – I only mentioned it in passing. We can forget about you. The next question is, is Proka up to handling the estate?

PROKA (*angrily*): Really!

GINA: If you could do it, Agaton, so could he – just as well.

AGATON: Maybe he could, I don't say he couldn't. But, I ask you, look at him! After working for thirty years in the Borough archives he's so dried up that he looks like a starving beetle that's just crawled out of an old file of documents.

GINA: Oh!

AGATON: To handle an estate you've got to have *presence*! You've got to have a loud voice! When you're dealing with lawyers, and tenants, and contractors, you've got to have a big fist that you can bang on the table

GINA: I beg your pardon, Agaton, but I don't think we've come
here to quarrel. We've come to pay our respects to the dear
departed in a decent manner, as a family ought to …
(She starts crying again).

SARKA: For goodness' sake, Gina, are you snivelling again?

PROKA: Leave the woman alone, let her cry! He was kin, and
she's sad.

SARKA: Aren't I kin, then?

TRIFUN: She's a woman with a soft heart perhaps.

PROKA: That's right – soft-hearted

SARKA: When it comes to that, Trifun, *I've* got a soft heart.
Everyone knows how soft-hearted I am – but I'm not crying.

AGATON: My dear Gina, don't take offence at what I said about
Proka. That was just by way of example. If you're going to take
it to heart then there's no more to be said about Proka. Let's
take Trifun, for instance.

TRIFUN: Hey, what's all this?

AGATON: 'Hey, what's all this?' – I ask you, how could he manage
an estate? 'Hey, hey ..!'

TRIFUN: I don't see why not.

AGATON: Don't be offended, but I think that here, within the
family, we can be frank. The reason why you couldn't handle
the estate is because your hands are so constantly handling
playing-cards that you simply haven't got the time.

TRIFUN: Agaton, you know I've never gambled a penny of your
money!

AGATON: No, you haven't, that's true. And I don't say for a
moment that you'd *intend* to gamble a penny of the dear
departed's estate. The trouble is, you know what happens –
you get some rent money, you put it in your pocket, you sit
down with some friends, the cards get dealt and you find
you've got an ace. And so you dip into the rent money, don't
you?

TRIFUN: Never!

AGATON: The trouble is, I don't say that you'd do it intentionally, but you know how it is – when you've got an ace in your hand it'd be such a shame to waste the opportunity! And even if it isn't like that, even if you haven't got an ace, still, my friend, you know yourself that it wouldn't be right and proper.

TRIFUN: I don't know why you say that.

AGATON: Because, my dear chap, you've got no occupation. You've always been a layabout – 'Trifun Spasich, local layabout'. You've never done a day's work in your life.

TRIFUN: I don't need to.

AGATON: Don't need to? It's not a question of 'need'. Work is only one of life's burdens. The point is, my dear fellow, if you haven't got any recognizeable occupation you can't administer an estate. It's simply not on. So that cuts you out, you see. Now, who's left?

MICHA: Who's left? What about me – don't I exist?

AGATON: Of course you exist. No one says you don't exist – but you do exist rather .. up in the air, as it were, don't you?

MICHA: What d'you mean – 'up in the air'? What are you talking about?

AGATON: Well, you know, it's difficult for you to pin anything down …

MICHA: I don't see what 'pinning anything down's' got to do with it.

AGATON: It's simply the fact that things seem to .. slip away from you – like your inheritance, for instance. Your father left you plenty of money but, somehow, the whole lot just slipped through your fingers, didn't it?

MICHA: My education was paid for out of that money.

AGATON: Yes, it was, I agree, and a damned expensive education it was. But, you know, the trouble is, I can't see what you've gained from it. You've got no job, no qualifications, no practical advantage at all.

MICHA: No, I haven't, I agree. But a chap doesn't go to college just to get some practical advantage, but so that he can become a rounded, educated man.

AGATON: That's the whole point, and that's why you couldn't manage an estate. Book-learning's one thing: running an estate's another. At college you may learn all about chemistry, but you don't learn how to get the rent in when one of your tenants does a midnight flit and takes all the furniture with him.

TRIFUN: This is a lot of nonsense! "This one's no good and that one's no good." "This, this and that, that!" In other words, however much you shuffle the cards, it always turns out that Agaton's the only one fit to be in charge of the estate!

AGATON: Well, you said it, Trifun! Don't you understand what it means to have been the District Administrator of a Borough of 52,374 inhabitants? 52,374 inhabitants, and when I called them to "Attention!" every single one of those 52,374 inhabitants came to attention, stood still, looked me in the eye, and trembled! That's what 'being in charge' means, Trifun!

TRIFUN: Yes, if your tenants were willing to stand to attention.

AGATON: Don't worry, I had ways of making sure they were.

SCENE 2

Enter DANITSA. *(As soon as she appears everyone stops talking. They all exchange glances and indicate by signs that no one should say anything while she's in the room. She is carrying a large cake on a tray[1] and she starts serving them).*

SIMKA *(Who, even before* DANITSA's *entrance, was nudging* VIDA *with her elbow. She now whispers to her)*: Well, thank goodness somebody's remembered that refreshments are in order.

AGATON *(crosses himself and takes some cake)*: May God have mercy on his soul!

TANASIYE *(crosses himself and takes some cake)*: May he rest in peace!

---

1. Cake on a tray. The original is zhito (*žito)*, which is a traditional soft wheaten cake always served after the *Parastos*, and on other ceremonial occasions, and eaten communally with spoons.

VIDA *(crosses herself and takes some cake)*.

GINA *(starts crying when offered cake)*.

SARKA: For goodness' sake stop, Gina! It's not as though you'd been paid to cry!

GINA: I'm just so sad. *(Crosses herself and takes some cake)*: God rest his soul!

MICHA *(stands up, obviously attracted, as* DANITSA *approaches him)*: Who would have thought to see, in a house so full of grief and sadness, such a fresh and charming sight! *(Takes a piece of cake)*

AGATON *(to* DANITSA, *while she serves the others)*: Where's your Aunt? Is she unwell?

DANITSA: No, but she's an old lady and I'm doing this for her.

AGATON: Yes, yes. And, of course, you're very young …

*(*SIMKA *interrupts him by jealously tugging the back of his coat)*
(After she has served everyone, ***exit*** DANITSA*)*.

SCENE 3

MICHA *(whose eyes had followed* DANITSA *as she left)*: My word, that's a pretty girl!

SIMKA *(to* AGATON*)*: And what, may I ask, were you going to talk to her about?

AGATON: I was just going to ask her a few questions.

SIMKA: What questions? You're not in the Town Hall now, you know: you're at a funeral wake. What questions could you possibly have wanted to ask her?

VIDA: But you know, Simka dear, I really do think that we ought to have some answers from her. The whole situation seems to me to be quite disgraceful. Here we all are, Family, his proper Family, in the dear departed's house, and yet we find ourselves being received and served by a total stranger.

AGATON: My dear Vida, what can we do? These were the dear departed's last wishes, and we can't go against them.

SARKA: And to whom, pray, did he reveal these last wishes?

TANASIYE: Yes, who indeed? His last wishes must be in his Will, and the Will hasn't been opened yet.

AGATON: And it won't be opened until forty days after he passed away.

PROKA: But Agaton, only yesterday I was reading up the law on this, and I asked a lawyer friend of mine about it, and one or two legal experts in the Town Hall as well, and they all told me that there's no law which says that a deceased's Will can't be opened until forty days after his death.

AGATON: And do you think I haven't looked into this?

TANASIYE: We've all enquired about it.

AGATON: Of course we have! How the devil can we put up with a delay of forty days? I'm counting every day on my fingers, and I can't sleep at night for thinking of numbers with five noughts after them.

TRIFUN: Well, Agaton, those five noughts are all in your imagination, and, as for the Will, frankly, I've no objection to waiting for forty days.

AGATON: No, you're enjoying it, aren't you?

TRIFUN: Yes, I am.

PROKA: Shut up, Agaton! – let him enjoy it if he wants to. More to the point – you say you've been looking into this?

AGATON: Yes, I have.

PROKA: And what did you find out?

AGATON: Well, I dug about a bit, and even had a word with the judge of the Trustee Court , and I asked him whether we, the family, could demand that the Will be opened immediately.

TANASIYE: And what did he say?

AGATON: He said: "You could, but it would be better if you waited. The deceased's wish was that you should be patient."

SARKA: It's easy for him to be patient: he's dead.

PROKA: Sarka's right. It's no problem for him to wait for forty days in his grave, but it's too much to ask of us – we're still alive.

TANASIYE: It certainly is! I can't wait that long. And even if I could, I wouldn't.

– 23 –

AGATON: Well, we're just going to have to wait, because he didn't just *say* that his Will was not to be opened for forty days. He had it all written down and drawn up as a legal document as well.

SARKA: May we enquire why he did that?

SIMKA: I was going to ask the same question.

AGATON: How on earth should I know? He knew exactly what he wanted. Oh yes – he was respected, and philanthropic, and honest, and all the rest of it, but it has to be said that he was also a bit of a practical joker. He knew what he was doing, all right! You can almost hear him saying: "I'll keep them all waiting for forty days, so that for all that time they'll have to keep on saying how sorry they are, instead of slagging me off the moment I'm in my grave."

SARKA: Oh! Who'd speak ill of him?

AGATON: We'll damn soon find out – that was his whole idea. He said to himself: "They can go on mourning until I'm cold in my grave. Agaton will have to dig his old black coat out of the chest, shake out the mothballs, and hang it up to get the creases out. Tanasiye can get out the old black suit which he had made for his wedding, and which he wears for funerals and national holidays. Proka can borrow a black tie off some committee member at the Town Hall, and a black coat from an undertaker. Trifun can pull a long face as if his jack's just been trumped by an ace; and my dear friend Micha can preen himself in mourning – the latest fashion, of course. The wives can wear black. The widow Sarka can put on her posh black dress – the one she usually wears for burying her husbands. And Gina can snivel for forty days without stopping."

(GINA *bursts into tears*).

SARKA: Oh, Gina, Agaton only meant 'for example'!

AGATON: Yes, yes, of course – I only meant 'for example'.

PROKA: He certainly tied it all up, God rest his soul!

AGATON: Didn't he just! He said to himself: "Let them all flog themselves through forty whole days, dressed up like tailors' dummies, playing at being 'The Bereaved Family' like a bunch of actors; let them trail bare-headed after my coffin; let them come to all the Services and light candles, and only then, when *I'm* completely cold, can *they* cool off!"

TANASIYE: Well, all right then, if it must be, it must be. We'll just have to wait, like it or not. But why does there have to be a stranger looking after the estate for these forty days?

AGATON: Simply because the dear departed said, in that document, words to the effect that until his Will is opened his entire estate is to be administered by the lawyer who is holding the Will and who is also to see to it that his last wishes are respected. *(All make various noises and gestures of protest)* And the lawyer, thank you very much, has it all signed and sealed, and has put the Aunt in as housekeeper here, because the dear departed's wish was that the house should not be closed up.

VIDA: Agaton, tell me, just who is this 'Aunt'?

AGATON: How should I know? I know that there's a small cottage on the estate with two rooms and a kitchen, which Mata had built about eight years ago. I know that the 'Aunt' has lived in it all that time. And that's all I know.

SARKA: And just whose Aunt is she, for goodness' sake?

AGATON: She's the Aunt of that girl who brought us the cake just now. She's her Aunt, and everybody just calls her 'Aunt'. Even the dear departed Mata used to call her 'Aunt'.

VIDA: But why did the lawyer put her in charge of the house? I don't suppose she's the lawyer's Aunt as well, is she?

AGATON: Not as far I know. But she was already here, in the house. She looked after Mata; he was in her arms when he passed away – she was on the spot.

SARKA: All right, that's the Aunt. But what about the girl? She troubles me, that girl.

MICHA: Me too!

SARKA: The way she troubles you, my dear Micha, is not the same as the way she troubles me.

AGATON: Why should you be troubled by her, Sarka? She's only a girl, like any other.

MICHA: But you've got to admit that she's a damned good-looker!

SARKA: All right, that's quite enough of that! But tell me, Agaton, how did she come to be here in the first place?

AGATON: I don't know. All I know is that the Aunt brought her up and that she's still at college – doing philosophy or something like that .. and that's all I know.

SARKA: If she's still at college, well and good, but isn't it practically time she finished there?

PROKA: I get the impression, my dear Sarka, that you're digging for dirt.

SARKA: Well, if we're going to face the facts and speak plainly, the dear departed was rather inclined to .. to .. what's the word I'm looking for?

TRIFUN: He was rather inclined to stray.

SARKA: That's it! "Stray"! That's what I meant to say. He wasn't exactly faithful, God rest his soul!

TANASIYE: That's true, it has to be admitted.

MICHA: That simply means that he was a very modern man.

SARKA: Modern or not, that's how he was. I know. There was one occasion when I came round to see him .. but that's enough of that! God will pardon his sins.

TRIFUN: Go on .. tell us!

SARKA: It's not right to speak ill of the dead.

SIMKA: Quite honestly, Sarka, I can't believe that sort of thing of him. In any case, the girl's much too young for an old man like him.

SARKA: You know how it is, Simka, you can graft a new shoot on to old wood.

SIMKA: It could be quite different: perhaps the girl has an elder sister, or maybe the Aunt has a younger sister.

MICHA: Yes, one must take such possibilities into account.

SARKA: Anyway, I'll tell you what I think. When one looks at her closely, one can see a definite resemblance to the dear departed Mata.

TANASIYE: Sarka! Really! How can you say such a thing?

VIDA: There's no need to say it again, but ... now that you mention it, when I looked at her a bit more closely I couldn't help noticing her nose. She's certainly got Mata's nose.

SARKA: You're right, Vida. If nothing else, the nose is the same, but .. come to think of it, Mata didn't have a nose.

GINA: Oh, Sarka, how can you say he didn't have a nose?

SARKA: Of course he had a nose, but ...

PROKA *(crossly)*: Stop chattering on about his nose, as if it was of any importance! Think about what really matters, and forget his nose. *(To* AGATON*)*: Well, Agaton, tell us what you've been able to find out about the Aunt.

AGATON: Nothing much – I really can't make it out at all. As I see it, she was there when he fell ill and she looked after him – right! He passed away – right! She was there at the time – right! So why not pay her off, say: "Thank you" to her, and "Goodbye"? I can't see why she's become the lawyer's agent, as it were. The lawyer took on the estate as a trustee: I understand that – that's legal, after all. But I don't see why he put her in here as housekeeper.

VIDA: And all done so openly!

TANASIYE: Well of course it was done openly – it was all signed, sealed, and delivered.

AGATON: And how do we know how much of the stuff is missing? The house is full of valuables, solid silver ...

PROKA: And just some 'Aunt' looking after it all.

SIMKA: It's disgraceful! Here we are, the Family, and we've no idea what we've got.

TANASIYE: It's bad enough that we don't know what we've got – we don't even know what the house is like inside. I've only ever seen this room. I talked to Mata in here once or twice, but I've never seen the rest of the place.

AGATON: Nor have I, to tell you the truth. Well – I've been upstairs once, when Mata was ill, but I've never seen the rest of the house.

PROKA: None of us have. The dear departed wasn't very sociable.

GINA: The fact is, he couldn't stand the Family!

SARKA: He could stand the 'Aunt' all right!

TRIFUN: He could stand her because she *wasn't* Family!

SARKA: Going back to what Tanasiye said, suppose someone said to me: "Sarka, you were a close relative of Mata's, weren't you?" I'd say: "Yes" – "Well, in that case, you must know what his house looks like." – I'd have to say: "No, I don't" – "How many rooms are there?" – "I don't know." – "What's the furniture like?" – "I don't know." – it'd all be horribly embarrassing.

VIDA: I don't see any reason why we shouldn't have a look round and see for ourselves.

TANASIYE: I don't see why not, either. Let's have a look round, Agaton. We can at least do that.

SIMKA: We are Family, after all!

AGATON: Yes, I suppose we can, why not? – But on one condition: that we all stay
together. Nobody's to go sloping off and snooping on their own …

PROKA *(insulted)*: The very idea! You don't think we'd …?

AGATON: I think what I think. Just let's not have anyone going off on their own.

TANASIYE: All right, then, we'll all stay together.

AGATON: I'll lead the way, because I know it better than you.
(They all gather round him). Right, then, this room first. This is a sort of ante-room, you see, but it's not actually an ante-room. It's more like an ordinary room, but it's not a bedroom, because it's a hallway. From here, the staircase leads upstairs *(indicating the staircase).* Upstairs is where the deceased passed away. We'll go first to the room where he died.
(He starts to climb the stairs, with the others following).

SARKA *(to GINA, who has started to cry again)*: What on earth are you crying for now?

GINA: I can't help crying, Sarka. We're going to see the room where he died.

SARKA: Wait till you get there, and then do your blubbing, if you must. We don't need an advance instalment, thank you very much!

SCENE 4

They all go upstairs, AGATON *leading and* MICHA *bringing up the rear.* MICHA *has only reached the first or second step when* DANITSA **enters** *through the French windows. She is carrying a tray full of cups of coffee, and is surprised to see that everyone is leaving. As soon as* MICHA *sees her he comes back down into the room.*

MICHA: Aha! Coffee! I don't usually take it, but since it's you …

DANITSA: Where are all the ladies and gentlemen going?

MICHA: They want to look round the house.

DANITSA: Oh, I see.

MICHA: It's a big house and there's a lot of furniture. Do you have to look after it all?

DANITSA: Not me – my Aunt. But, of course, I help her because she's an old lady.

MICHA: It must be hard work for you.

DANITSA: It's only for a few days, until the house is handed over to whoever inherits it.

MICHA: Only until then? Hadn't you thought of staying longer?

DANITSA: Of course not.

MICHA: Not even if the person who inherits it asked you to?

DANITSA: I don't know. That would be for my Aunt to decide.

MICHA: Why your Aunt? You could decide for yourself. Supposing I inherited it – and I certainly hope I will – I'd very much like *you* to make the decision.

DANITSA: What decision?

MICHA: To stay in your cottage. Why not? It would be very convenient for you, because you've obviously got used to living there and, so far as I'm concerned, to tell you the truth I would very much like to have a pretty little creature like you about the place. Why not?

DANITSA: Thank you. That's very kind of you, but I think my Aunt wants to move away.

MICHA: For goodness' sake, why? It would only make things difficult for you both. You've been living here rent-free, and you could go on doing so. Surely that would be better for you?

DANITSA: Yes, it might, but ...

MICHA: And what is most important, I'm not thinking of getting married in a hurry, but you could certainly stay on until I do.

DANITSA *(astonished)*: Why only until then?

MICHA: I'm afraid my wife might get jealous... and she might have reason to!

DANITSA: Reason to .. ?

MICHA: Yes, indeed. You are such a sweet, gorgeous little thing! I like you very, very much indeed ... *(He tries to kiss her)*.

DANITSA *(outraged)*: Sir!

MICHA: There, there, you mustn't be angry.

DANITSA *(very upset)*: What makes you think ... ?

(At this point THE FAMILY *all start coming down the staircase and **enter** into the room)*

MICHA: I told you, I like you very much indeed. I'm allowed to say that, aren't I, to such a pretty young woman? In any case, when I get the opportunity, I'll make it all quite clear to you. You'll see: it's all very simple, really.

SCENE 5

AGATON *(Leading the others)*: Ah, coffee! A bit late, but we can manage standing up.

(He takes a cup, drinks it in two swallows, puts it down, and starts to walk out of the room LEFT, *continuing the tour of the house)*

TANASIYE *(Behind* AGATON, *takes a cup and sips it)* I can only manage a sip. *(He puts the cup down and follows* AGATON*)*.

SIMKA *(Comes after* TANASIYE*)*: Thank you, I never take coffee in the morning. *(Moves away after* TANASIYE*)*.

PROKA *(Comes after* SIMKA*)*. Thank you, I don't drink coffee. *(Follows* SIMKA*)*.

VIDA *(Takes one sip and puts the cup down)*: Ugh! It's as cold as ice. *(Follows* PROKA*)*

TRIFUN *(Takes a cup)*: I'll take this and drink it on the way. *(Goes out with it)*

GINA *(Sighing)*: Thank you, coffee's not for me. *(Follows* TRIFUN *out).*

SARKA *(Following* GINA*)*: Thank you, I daren't drink coffee – my nerves, you know! *(She follows* GINA *out).*

MICHA: *(To* DANITSA, *as he follows* SARKA *out)* You'll see, it's all very simple!

*(**Exeunt** FAMILY, continuing their tour).*

SCENE 6

DANITSA *stays in the middle of the room holding the coffee tray and looking at the departing Family.*

*After the family have all left **enter** Dr* PETROVICH, *the lawyer.*

PETROVICH: Good morning! Oh, what a shame: you've got your hands full.

DANITSA: Well, of course, I've got a houseful of visitors. *(She puts the tray down on the nearest table).*

PETROVICH: What visitors? Who are they?

DANITSA: They're the family of the deceased gentleman, on their way back from the funeral service. You told us, me and my Aunt, that we should be attentive and polite to them.

PETROVICH: At least politeness doesn't cost anything.

DANITSA: Oh, yes it does: it's cost me a lot.

PETROVICH: What d'you mean?

DANITSA: It's cost me humiliation.

PETROVICH: Have they been insulting you?

DANITSA: Oh, I don't care about their winks and whispers and their disdainful glances – that's one thing, but I've just had a very nasty experience …

PETROVICH: What?

DANITSA: One of the gentlemen, who says he's the one who's going to inherit the property, impudently asked me to stay on in the cottage, rent-free, but only until he gets married.

PETROVICH: Some gentleman! And what did you say to him?

DANITSA: If you hadn't told us to be polite to them, I don't know what I would have said!

PETROVICH: It's as well you held yourself back, because perhaps he didn't mean to insult you.

DANITSA: What do you mean?

PETROVICH: Perhaps his intentions were serious.

DANITSA: But what if his intentions were serious?

PETROVICH: Well, for instance, suppose that he does turn out to be the one who inherits.

DANITSA *(angrily)*: Do you really think as little of me as that?

PETROVICH: Please don't think I'm insulting you. Wealth can change things, you know.

DANITSA: Oh really? Does that mean that you'd weaken for money?

PETROVICH: I didn't say that.

DANITSA: It sounded like it.

PETROVICH: In any case, lawyers and doctors don't necessarily themselves abide by the opinions and advice that they give to their clients.

DANITSA: Don't you think you'd be tempted to trim a little for a person who'll be as rich as the one who's going to inherit here?

PETROVICH: No, I wouldn't, believe me, even if it for was a woman I loved, because I know that she'd ever afterwards be suspicious of the sincerity of my motives.

DANITSA *(During this conversation she has been feeling in her pocket, looking for a slip of paper, which she now produces)*: Anyway, what about this? You always talk so much that you make me forget important things. I'd forgotten this note from my Aunt: it's an account of the expenses she's paid out of the money you gave her.

PETROVICH: Oh, another time will do.

DANITSA: No, I want to settle it now. My Aunt particularly asked me to.

(VOICES ARE HEARD APPROACHING)

PETROVICH: That's them , I suppose? I don't want them to find me here.

DANITSA: Why not?

PETROVICH: I'm not keen on seeing them at all. They're always on at me, whether I'm in my office or at home.

DANITSA: So you've met them, then?

PETROVICH: Oh yes, I've met them. I'd never met any of them before. They were simply private individuals of no particular concern to me, but when this rich man's last Will and Testament came to light they all started raising Cain, going round all the lawyers' firms, and hanging about the District Court all day.

DANITSA: It seems that they were all his close relatives?

PETROVICH: Yes, probably, but after the Will is opened we'll see just how "close" they were by how much he's left to each of them! *(SOUNDS OF RAISED VOICES)*. That's them. I shall make myself scarce. Good bye!

DANITSA: But what about my Aunt's account?

PETROVICH: I told you before – another time! *(Exit)*

(DANITSA picks up the tray again as the FAMILY enters).

SCENE 7

(AGATON comes out of a room, LEFT, followed by all the others. They cross the hall and exeunt into a back room from which they are going to continue their inspection of the house, so that, later, they will be seen through the glass of the French windows passing along the outside passageway. On this occasion they all pass without taking any notice of DANITSA. As TRIFUN passes DANITSA he puts the coffee cup which he took earlier back on the tray that she is holding).

MICHA *(as he passes DANITSA)*: You're still here, then: that's nice. *(Exit with the others)*

SCENE 8

Enter AUNT *(through the French windows, rear)*

AUNT: What's happening, child? Why have you been so long?

DANITSA: I haven't even been able to serve the coffee yet.

AUNT: Why, where are all the visitors?

DANITSA: Going round the house, looking at everything.

AUNT: Didn't they want coffee?

DANITSA: I offered it to them.

AUNT: Has the lawyer been?

DANITSA: Yes, he has.

AUNT: And did you show him my account?

DANITSA: I tried to, Auntie, but he's a very strange man. He keeps on talking about other things.

AUNT: You know how I hate holding other people's money without accounting for it properly.

DANITSA: Yes, I know. Auntie, may I ask you a question?

AUNT: Of course!

DANITSA: When this place is handed over to whoever inherits it, we shan't stay in the cottage, shall we?

AUNT: No, we shan't.

DANITSA: Where shall we go?

AUNT: We'll have to see.

DANITSA: I'd so much like to go back to our old house. It was only small, I know, but we had a little garden, and I liked it so much – perhaps because it was where I spent nearly all my childhood.

AUNT: Oh, they knocked that house down almost immediately after we left – and that was eight years ago.

DANITSA: Where did we live before that?

AUNT: Surely you remember?

DANITSA: I do remember, but like in a dream. I remember a small paved courtyard with a tree in it, and … that was when my mother was still alive, wasn't it?

AUNT: Yes.

DANITSA: And my father?

AUNT: My dear, he died long before: you couldn't possibly have known anything of him. Anyway, why all these questions now?

DANITSA: I just thought about it. One of the gentlemen spoke to me about our cottage, and it made me think of our old house.

AUNT: Don't worry about it, my dear, we've got other things to do. Now, take that tray and off you go! The coffee's all got cold: nobody will want to drink it now.

DANITSA: All right. There's no point in waiting for them.

(DANITSA *takes up the tray, and she and* AUNT **exeunt** *together*).

SCENE 9

(**Enter** *the* FAMILY *through the French windows, led by* AGATON).

AGATON: Right, you've seen it all now.

VIDA: A palace – a real palace!

TANASIYE: He knew how to live, all right.

SARKA: Oh, that silver alarm clock!

SIMKA: And those candlesticks! What did you think of those silver candlesticks?

SARKA: I liked the alarm clock. I'm used to alarm clocks. I've never had one in the house, but I'm used to them.

TRIFUN: How the devil can you be used to them when you've never had one?

SARKA: My first husband used to sleep like a top, God rest his soul, but my second was always waking me up during the night, just like an alarm clock. That's how I'm used to them.

GINA: But, Simka, what did you think of that cutlery set – twenty-four place settings, and all solid silver?

SARKA: Yes, you certainly cried when you saw that, didn't you, Gina!

VIDA: It's dreadful! All these lovely things, and the whole lot's in the hands of a complete stranger – some old Aunt!

MICHA: And her niece.

VIDA: All right, 'and her niece'. Agaton! There's something I've got something to say.

AGATON: Go on.

VIDA: I have to say that I think that we, the Family, should be looking after this house and all the things in it, not some total stranger.

TANASIYE: That's right! May I ask, Agaton, who has vouched for this 'Aunt'?

GINA: I wonder how many things have gone out of the house already …

VIDA: And how many more things will go before the forty days are up!

SARKA: Oh, my alarm clock!

TRIFUN: What do you mean – "my"?

TANASIYE: There are a lot more valuable things here than that alarm clock.

VIDA: I suggest, Agaton, that one of us should move in to look after everything.

SARKA: Good idea! It had better be me.

VIDA: Why you?

SARKA: I'm a widow, I'm on my own; it's easier for me than for you.

SIMKA *(aside, to* AGATON*)*: D'you hear what they're saying, Agaton?

AGATON *(aside, to* SIMKA*)*: I hear it. *(They continue to talk in whispers)*

SIMKA: Well, you're not going to let those others move in, are you? If anyone moves in, it ought to be you.

AGATON: I'm thinking about it.

SIMKA: Don't just think about it – do something, or they'll get in before us!

AGATON: All right.

SIMKA: Don't just say "All right", say "Come on!" – or that Gina will beat us to it!

AGATON: Very well – come on, let's get on with it! *(Aloud, to the others)* Simka and I are going. There's nothing more to do here. We've been served, we've had some coffee, and we've looked round the house – no point in staying any longer.

Come on, Simka, let's go. Goodbye, everyone!

SIMKA: Good bye!

*(**Exeunt** AGATON and SIMKA).*

SCENE 10

SARKA: Did you see that! First they were whispering, those two, whispering, and then they both left in a hurry!

GINA: I noticed that, too.

VIDA *(aside, to* TANASIYE*)*: Look, I may be seeing too much into it, but I've got a good idea what Agaton and Simka were whispering about.

TANASIYE *(aside, to* VIDA*)*: Yes, I think I know, too.
(They continue to whisper).

VIDA: It's obvious – they're planning to move in here.

TANASIYE: Well, that's all right. It'd be better if someone from the Family did move in.

VIDA: If any of us is going to move in, in ought to be you!

TANASIYE: Well, I don't know … if Agaton has already …

VIDA: Oh, you silly man – you let Agaton walk all over you. You can do what you like, but I'm going home, I'm going to pack a few things while this lot are still dithering, and *I'm* going to move in here, with you or without you. Come on! *(Aloud, to the others)* Agaton's right, there's no need to stay here any longer. Come on, Tanasiye, we're going! I'm longing to get home and have a rest. Good bye, everyone!

TANASIYE: Yes, I feel like a rest. Good bye!

*(**Exeunt** TANASIYE and VIDA).*

SCENE 11

SARKA: What are they up to? Why are they all whispering?

GINA: I wondered about that. I don't like it.

SARKA: I don't like all this whispering in the Family.

GINA: No, it's not very nice.

SARKA: They should talk out loud. And if they start swearing, or havings rows, or calling each other names, one can

understand it – it's just expressing family love and togetherness
– but when they start whispering …

MICHA: You're right, Sarka, I can't stand whispering, either.
It's not decent.

SARKA: It certainly isn't. It was whispering like this that nearly
made my first husband divorce me. And it wouldn't have been
decent if he'd divorced me, would it?

TRIFUN: Even if we'd known what it was they were whispering
about?

GINA: We don't know that.

TRIFUN: You may not know, but I do.

GINA: Go on, then tell us, then.

TRIFUN: They're going to get their things and move in here.

GINA: What?

TRIFUN: What I said.

PROKA: Trifun's right. That's exactly what they're going to do.
I'll bet Agaton moves in here.

TRIFUN: Well, if Agaton's going to, so am I, by God!

SARKA: Why you?

TRIFUN: Because if Agaton reckons he's going to move in here
"to guard the property and see that things don't go missing or
get stolen", then I reckon *I'm* going to move in and guard the
property from Agaton – I know him only too well!

PROKA: He's right.

TRIFUN: And he won't get in before me, either – I'll be here first.
I'm off!

(Exit TRIFUN*)*

SCENE 12

GINA: It looks as if everyone's going to move in.

SARKA: I wouldn't be surprised if you did too, Micha dear!

MICHA: Well, I might. If it's my duty to act as a caretaker, I'll do it
willingly.

SARKA: What are you thinking of taking care of – the property, or
the niece?

MICHA: You have to admit, Sarka, she really is a good-looker!

SARKA: Huh! Oh, yes, indeed!

MICHA: I'm going to get my suitcase. I'll be back before those others. *(Exit)*

SCENE 13

GINA: Well, I never! The whole family's going to move in, then!

SARKA: Yes, the lot.

GINA *(to* PROKA*)*: But what about us? – we're the closest relatives, after all.

PROKA: I think we'd better move in as well, dear.

GINA: All right, then, Proka dear, we'll move in too, even though it'll be rather upsetting for me because, after all, I'll be thinking about the dear departed all the time. *(She starts crying)*.

SARKA: Gina, why on earth does moving in set you off crying? Anyway, while you're wasting time blubbing Agaton will come and grab all the best rooms.

GINA: You're right! Come on, Proka! What about you, Sarka?

SARKA: I won't intrude. I may come, but later, and only if there's room for me. If there isn't any room I'll go back home. I don't need to worry if *you're* all here, do I?

GINA: That's right. Good bye!

(Exeunt PROKA *and* GINA*)*.

SCENE 14

*(*SARKA, *left alone, goes to the right-hand room, looks inside, then turns, walks across to the left-hand room and goes inside. On the way she takes off her hat and coat)*.

(Enter DANITSA *who, finding the room empty, breathes a sigh of relief)*.

SARKA *(reappearing in the doorway, relaxed, and with her formal clothes unbuttoned)*: I wonder if there's a pair of slippers in the house?

DANITSA *(startled)*: I didn't know you were still here!

SARKA: Oh yes, I'm still here all right. I've chosen this room and

I've moved in, but I can't go about the house without some slippers on my feet.

DANITSA *(wringing her hands)*: Oh my God!

Curtain

Act Two

The same room, later in the day.

SCENE 1

*(*SARKA *is sitting on a sofa, smoking a cigarette and looking through a photograph album. She is wearing a man's dressing-gown and has an enormous pair of mens' slippers on her feet).*
Enter MICHA, *carrying a suitcase.*

MICHA: Oh, are you here already, Sarka?

SARKA: I'm not just 'here already' – I've never been away.

MICHA: What, you stayed?

SARKA: Yes, I stayed. If I hadn't, someone else would have taken this nice room with a balcony. I like looking at what's going on outside.

MICHA: I had to go home to fetch the things I need.

SARKA: What things? I don't intend to spend my life here. I looked about a bit in the house and found Mata's old dressing-gown and slippers. What more do I need?

MICHA: Has anyone else come yet?

SARKA: They're all here.

MICHA: What, all of them, already?

SARKA: Yes, all of them.

MICHA: Are they using all the spare rooms?

SARKA: They certainly are! Agaton and Simka are in that room over there. I'm in this one.

MICHA: And the others?

SARKA: Tanasiye and Vida are in that one there.

MICHA: And Proka?

SARKA: He's in there, over by the courtyard, and Trifun's in the small room above.

MICHA: Well where can I go?

SARKA: Nobody's using Mata's room, the one he died in.

MICHA: I'll go in there, then. I like that room. It should be mine, anyway.

SARKA: You can if you want, as long as you're not easily scared.

MICHA: Why should I be scared?

SARKA: You might be scared of Mata's ghost appearing to you in a dream.

MICHA: Let him appear! I'd be glad if he did. I'd rather like to have a talk with him, face to face.

SARKA: Well, if you do, Micha, I've got one small request. If his ghost does appear, would you please ask him how in God's name Agaton and Simka came to be related to him at all? I'm getting rather sick of the way they've been boasting about their "close" relationship.

MICHA: Don't worry, Sarka, I'll ask him about Agaton, and about some of the others, too. *(He starts to go up the stairs)* They all seem to think that they're closer to him than me – as if I didn't exist. *(**Exit** upstairs)*.

SCENE 2

Enter GINA, *from outside. She comes in furtively, looking to left and right, but not noticing Sarka. She walks across the room on tiptoes, carrying a large black box under her arm. (It contains the silver cutlery set).*

SARKA *(looking round and seeing her)*: Where've you been, Gina?

GINA *(She starts violently, then immediately puts the box behind her back and presses it and herself against the wall, so as to leave her hands free)*: Oh dear!

SARKA: What are you doing?

GINA *(very upset)*: Oh, you did give me a fright!

SARKA: What have you got to be frightened about? – I'm not

Mata's ghost! Anyway, where have you been, for goodness'
sake?

GINA: Outside .. it was a bit .. I went out for a bit of a walk, and
then I went into the dining room to give it a bit of a dusting..

SARKA: But Gina dear, why should you go and dust the dining
room? Surely there's someone in this house who does the
dusting?

GINA: Of course there is, and it has been dusted, really it has, but
I'm so used to doing the dusting myself, you know!

SARKA: Yes, you're right, me too. When I'm in someone else's
house I always like to go round dusting it!

GINA: Well, you know then – and while I was doing it I saw those
things and they all reminded me of Mata. I saw the chair where
he used to sit, and his plate, and his knife and fork, and I got all
choked. Then I saw his salt-cellar and I thought: "Oh, dear
God, he's dead, and last week he was shaking that very salt-
cellar .. " *(She bursts into tears)*.

SARKA: Oh, not again! You don't have to cry about him shaking a
salt-cellar.

GINA: I know I don't have to but, when I remember him, it makes
me so sad.

SARKA: Leave off, for goodness' sake! Anyway, what are you
doing, woman, stuck to the wall like a postage stamp?

GINA *(confused)*: Well, the fact is .. I, er .. I'm not *stuck* to the
wall, I'm just *resting* against it. My legs were feeling a little
weak, and I'm just resting for a bit.

SARKA: Go to your room and lie down, then.

GINA: I can't, I can't move just at present.

SARKA: I'll help you.

GINA: There's no need. You go to your room, and I'll go to mine.
I'll be all right in a minute – really!

SARKA *(approaches* GINA*)*: How could I possibly go to my room
and leave you there, leaning helplessly against the wall like
that? *(She makes to put her arms round* GINA*)*: Come on, lean
on me, I'll help you.

GINA *(desperately)*: No! No! For God's sake don't!

SARKA: Well now, Gina dear, what's that behind your back, I wonder?

GINA *(frightened)*: What are you talking about?

SARKA *(pulling away the box)*: This!

GINA: Oh, that! It looks like some sort of box.

SARKA: I don't think it's just a box, Gina. I think it's a silver cutlery set.

GINA: It might be … it could be, I suppose … if you say so … I really don't know.

SARKA *(opening the box)*: Well, fancy that, it *is* a silver cutlery set!

GINA: Oh my! Oh my! Who'd have thought it?

SARKA: Yes, I wonder who.

GINA: I thought it was just some old box.

SARKA: Never mind what you thought; only couldn't you have taken something a bit smaller than a whole set of silver cutlery?

GINA: In God's truth, Sarka, I took it for a memento of Mata. You know how deeply I mourn for him.

SARKA: Oh yes, I know all about that!

GINA: I thought that, because of all my grief, I could take a tiny little something to remember him by.

SARKA: If you'd wanted a tiny little something you could have taken his salt-cellar. Wouldn't that have consoled you enough, rather than a whole set of silver cutlery?

GINA: To tell you the truth, Sarka, I took it so that I could hide it. I've seen that Agaton snooping round the house with Simka, sniffing into all the corners. I thought to myself, if Agaton finds this cutlery set … you know how he is, he's got a weakness for silver things.

SARKA: That's true! *(Thinks)* My goodness, he might take a fancy to that alarm clock.

GINA: Which room is it in?

SARKA: It's in his room.

GINA: Well, you can be quite certain that that alarm clock's already inside his suitcase.

SARKA: What are you saying?

GINA: What I say.

SARKA: Thank you. I'll not let him get his hands on *that* without a struggle. Did you say that he and Simka were somewhere else in the house now?

GINA: Yes, I saw them.

SARKA: Right then, Gina! *(Gives her back the box)* Take your tiny little something and hide it in your suitcase so that Agaton won't find it. I know what I'm going to do.

GINA *(going towards her room)*: Sarka, I don't think we ought to talk to the others about this.

SARKA: Don't worry. I know what a family secret is.

GINA: Yes, let's keep it between ourselves. *(Exit, into her room, carrying the box)*.

SCENE 3

SARKA *looks to left and right and, when she is sure that there is nobody about, she goes quietly into Agaton's room. Moments later* AGATON *and* SIMKA **enter** *from the side.* AGATON *is walking awkwardly because he has stuffed a large silver salver up the back of his coat and is holding the bottom of it (which protrudes beneath his coat) with one hand. When they reach mid-stage,* SARKA **re-emerges** *from their room holding an object wrapped in a large handkerchief (it is the alarm clock). She is startled to see Agaton and Simka, and hastily puts the object inside her dressing-gown.*

AGATON *(to* SARKA, *and facing her)*: Hey, what are you doing in our room?

SARKA: Oh, I was just doing a bit of dusting .. er, no, what am I saying? No .. er .. I'm looking for my slippers.

AGATON: You've got them on your feet.

SARKA *(looking down)*: Oh, so I have!

SIMKA: Yes, you certainly have and, anyway, I can't understand why on earth you should be looking for your slippers in *my* room.

SARKA: Really, Simka! We're not exactly strangers: I don't see anything wrong with dropping in to see you. I can come to your room and you can come to mine.

SIMKA: No, we're not strangers, but I'd be obliged if you'd only come to my room when I'm in it, and not go poking about in there when I'm not.

SARKA: Oh, Simka! You're surely not suggesting that I'd go into your room for any improper reason?

SIMKA: No, but … what about that thing you're holding?

SARKA: Oh, I . . er . . felt a little peckish, and I went and got a couple of bread rolls.

AGATON: Well, why did you stick them into your dressing-gown when you saw us?

SARKA: You sound very suspicious. I wouldn't have expected it of you, Agaton. You know very well that I'm not that sort of person. Rather than touch anything that wasn't mine I'd let my hand be cut off! *(At this moment the alarm clock inside her dressing-gown starts ringing loudly. She pales, takes fright, becomes confused, upset, and considerably rattled)* Oh dear! Oh dear!

SIMKA: What on earth … ?

AGATON: Sarka, I get the distinct impression that you're ringing!

SARKA *(fiddling desperately, but unsuccessfully, with the alarm clock)*: What d'you mean 'ringing'? How can I be 'ringing'?

AGATON: You *are* ringing, Sarka!

SARKA: Nonsense! How could I be ringing? I'm not an electric doorbell.

AGATON: There! Listen to that, Simka!

(SIMKA pretends to put her head near SARKA, as if listening).

SARKA *(attempting to drown the noise of the alarm clock by singing)*: Tra la la . . ! tra la la . !

SIMKA *(crossing herself)*: God forgive you, Sarka, *singing* in this house of sorrow!

SARKA *(extremely rattled)*: Oh my God! *(She looks all round and finally, in desperation, throws the alarm clock, still wrapped in the handkerchief, on to the sofa and, dejected and exhausted, sits on top of it in an effort to drown the noise. At that moment, the alarm clock stops ringing. She calms down and looks desperately at Agaton and Simka)*: Well, I wonder what on earth *that* was!

AGATON: Sarka, you *were* ringing. There's no doubt about it, you were ringing!

SIMKA: And singing!

SARKA *(crossing herself)*: It must have been ghosts – God preserve us from them!

AGATON: It wasn't ghosts, Sarka, it was an alarm clock.

SARKA: What alarm clock?

AGATON: The one you're sitting on.

SARKA: Why on earth should I be sitting on an alarm clock? I've never sat on an alarm clock in my life – why should I start now?

AGATON: I'm talking about the silver alarm clock which you took out of our room.

SARKA: Oh!

SIMKA: God moves in a mysterious way. Only yesterday I said to Agaton: "Why don't you wind up that alarm clock so that we can hear how it rings?"

SARKA: Well, there you are – now you've heard it.

SIMKA: Oh, we've heard it, all right.

AGATON: This is disgraceful, Sarka, I must say – disgraceful! We didn't come to the house to steal things, but to guard the dear departed's property, and now you …

(He moves angrily, turning his back on Sarka and forgetting that he is still holding the silver salver under his coat).

SARKA *(seeing the salver)*: Just one moment, my dear Agaton! I was going to ask you – but you kept interrupting me – just why are you standing there so awkwardly? You look like a naughty schoolboy who's trying to hide something.

AGATON: Oh, it's nothing, just a bit of rheumatism in my back.

SARKA: I can see that it's rheumatism, but I'd have said it was 'silver rheumatism'.

AGATON: Well, if it is silver, at least it doesn't ring.

SARKA: Maybe it isn't ringing now, but I reckon that if it had a clapper and I pulled the rope it would ring like four cathedral bells.

AGATON: Be quiet, woman!

SARKA: Oh, I'll be quiet, but I did want to remind you of what you said a few moments ago, about us 'not being here to steal things, but to guard the dear departed's property!'

AGATON: But we are guarding it, for goodness' sake! That's why I'm looking after this, why else?

SARKA: Why else, indeed!

AGATON: I haven't been deliberately taking things out of other people's rooms: I just happened to come across this.

SARKA: A likely story!

AGATON: Simka and I decided to go into the garden to pick some flowers, so we went for a stroll round and on the way we happened to go through the dining room and I noticed this salver in there. So I said to Simka: "Why bother to go into the garden to pick flowers? It would be better to take this salver instead."

SARKA: Oh, much better, I'm sure!

AGATON: Yes, indeed! I said: "Simka, it would be better to take this salver." And I'll tell you why it was better. I wouldn't tell just anybody, but I'll tell you. It's that Trifun, you see. If he sees it he's quite capable of taking it straight to the pawnbroker's, just to raise some cash to gamble with. So, you could say that by taking this salver I'm protecting it.

SARKA: Oh, naturally! Just like I'm protecting the alarm clock.

AGATON: All right, all right! But let's keep this to ourselves, Sarka, otherwise they'll all start protecting things …

SIMKA: Knowing them, they'd soon 'protect' the whole house.

AGATON: Right, then, let's go to our rooms and unload.

SARKA *(who has been sitting on the alarm clock throughout, now gets up)*: Yes, let's! This damned thing's been digging into my backside something cruel!

Exeunt *to their various rooms.*

SCENE 4

MICHA *now* **enters**, *coming down the stairs. At the same time*
DANITSA **enters** *through the French windows.*

MICHA: What a pleasant surprise! Here I am in my new
    accommodation, and you're the first person I meet!

DANITSA: What new accommodation?

MICHA: Well, I've just moved in.

DANITSA *(astonished)*: What, you too?

MICHA: What d'you mean 'You too'? I'm the first: I'm ahead
    of all the others.

DANITSA: Oh, my God, what's going on? It's like open house
    in here!

MICHA: Yes it is – they're all coming.

DANITSA: My poor aunt is so angry it's made her ill, and I …

MICHA: I don't see why that should that make her ill?

DANITSA: Well, really! It's .. I simply cannot understand how all
    you ladies and gentlemen are able to move in. Has anyone
    asked the lawyer whether you're allowed to? What about you –
    have you asked him?

MICHA: What, me? – ask the lawyer? Why on earth should I ask
    the lawyer? If he wants to, he can ask me: "Would you care to
    move into the house, Sir?" Lawyers ask me: I don't ask
    lawyers.

DANITSA: Well, did he ask you?

MICHA: No, he didn't. Anyway, there's nothing that either of us
    have got to ask of each other.

DANITSA: I just don't know what to do!

MICHA: Keep calm, my dear. A pretty girl like you shouldn't get
    excited.

DANITSA: You can't expect me to be indifferent to all that's
    going on.

MICHA: Indifferent, no. Nor can I be, when I'm near you! Just
    give me half a chance, and you'll soon find that I'm not at all
    indifferent towards you!

DANITSA: Sir, I've already warned you once! If that wasn't

enough I'll have to find some other way of making things clear to you.

MICHA: Oh dear! How can such a pretty girl be so hard? Listen to me – you and I need to understand each other if we're going to be together, in the same house, under the same roof, as it were.

DANITSA: You're wrong, sir, there's no question of us ever living under the same roof.

MICHA: Are you thinking of moving, then?

DANITSA: I certainly will, if I have to, but before that I'm going to see the lawyer and tell him what's been going on here.

MICHA: What's it got to do with him?

DANITSA: All I know is that he's the executor and he's responsible for this house. He'll know whether you're allowed to turn the place into a camping site. *(Exit)*.

SCENE 5

(MICHA watches her go out. He sits down and lights a cigarette).
AGATON *and* SIMKA **enter** *from their room.*

AGATON: Oh, you're here, are you?

MICHA *(offended)*: What d'you mean – "Oh, you're here, are you"? I could ask the same question of you two.

AGATON: Oh, no you couldn't! Simka and I have every right to be here, but actually the whole damned family's moved in.

MICHA: What, all of them?

AGATON: The lot! Sarka's there, in that room. She sits on her balcony all day long, and when she does come out she makes ringing noises. Tanasiye and Vida are in that room: they sit there all day trying to work out which of us is Mata's nearest relative. Proka and Gina are over there. They chose the room which has Mata's safe in it, and Gina spends the whole day sitting by the safe and crying. Trifun's upstairs: he found an old pack of cards in the dining room and spends his time playing Patience – and cheating at it.

SIMKA: And which room have you taken?

MICHA: Me? I'm in my proper place: in Mata's bedroom.

SIMKA: But the candle's still burning in there!

MICHA: Oh, I put it out.

SIMKA: You put the candle out! But it's supposed to be burning for the soul of the dear departed!

AGATON: It would have been rather a waste to leave it burning all week.

MICHA: Absolutely! That's just what I thought.

SCENE 6

(Enter GINA)

SIMKA: Oh, hallo Gina! I was just saying to Micha that you'd shut yourself up in your room all day, crying.

GINA: Well, who's going to do some proper mourning if I don't?

AGATON: Where's Proka?

GINA: He's gone to the Town Hall to ask the lawyers there whether we have the right to move into this house.

AGATON: What does he want to do that for?

MICHA: Isn't it obvious?

SIMKA: Why didn't he ask Agaton? Agaton knows the law.

GINA: But you don't know the whole story. You were all able to move in easily, but only because Proka had actually taken over the house earlier.

MICHA: What d'you mean 'taken over'?

GINA: We were the first to arrive, and that Aunt woman was waiting for us.

SIMKA: What on earth had it got do with her?

GINA: She was waiting for us as if we were enemy invaders, not the Family. She wasn't going to let us in at all: she said that she was in charge of the house and it was her responsibility to look after it.

SIMKA: I ask you! The cheek of it – a complete stranger playing at being the lady of the house!

GINA: She locked the door and wouldn't let us in.

SIMKA: Well, how did you get in?

GINA: Thank goodness, Sarka was already in the house, and she let us in from the inside. Then Proka, I'm afraid, shoved the Aunt aside, and she went off saying she was going to call the police. So Proka's gone off too, to make enquiries.

SIMKA: Well, Agaton, at least you know the law. Can she complain to the police?

MICHA: Surely we, as the Family, have the right to move in?

AGATON: Well, how shall I put it? The law in this area is somewhat uncertain. It could be this way, or it could be that way.

MICHA: I don't understand that. How can the law be 'this way or that way'?

AGATON: Oh, the law can be like that, I assure you.

SCENE 7

*(**Enter** TANASIYE and VIDA).*

VIDA *(recoiling)*: What's all this, some sort of conference? We'll go if we're disturbing you.

SIMKA: You're not disturbing us. What concerns us concerns you too, because it looks as if the police are going to throw you out as well as us.

TANASIYE: What are you talking about? How can the police throw us out? What for?

MICHA: On account of 'uncertainty'.

TANASIYE: What 'uncertainty'?

MICHA: On account of the uncertainty of the law, on account of it being 'this way or that way'. If you want to know the details, ask Agaton.

TANASIYE: Well, what do you say, Agaton?

AGATON: What d'you want me to say? If it turns out that we have occupied the house illegally, they can eject us.

SIMKA: The Aunt warned us that she was going to get the police to throw us out.

VIDA: Well, that's nice! D'you mean to say that we, the Family, have no rights?

TANASIYE: It seems to me, Agaton, that you know more about the law than any of us.

AGATON: Of course I do!

TANASIYE: Well then, if you moved in …

AGATON: Oh, no, that's quite different. Don't bring me into it. If it had just been me who had moved in that could have been justified in law, but you lot moved in as a mob, and occupied the whole house.

SIMKA: Yes, exactly! If it were just you, Tanasiye, and you, Vida, and perhaps even Micha, that would have been enough. But what's Trifun doing here, and Sarka, come to that? And then the rest of them, all over the place. Oh, here is Sarka! What's she up to, I wonder?

SCENE 8

(Enter SARKA, dressed).

SARKA: I thought I might come out for a while to see what's going on. My lips got rather dry in that room.

AGATON: Lick them, then.

SARKA: I must say, I really do enjoy having a room with a balcony. I sit on the balcony, and, do you know, I feel completely at home there. People pass by, to and fro … I tell you, it's very enjoyable.

SCENE 9

(Enter TRIFUN, coming down the stairs).

TRIFUN: Is this some sort of meeting? Agaton, the next time you decide to hold a family meeting you'd better blow trumpets and beat drums to let us know.

AGATON: It is right and necessary that we hold a family meeting now, because we have to discuss a problem that concerns us all.

TRIFUN: Oh, yes? What's that?

AGATON: The problem is that you lot have all moved in here. If you'd let me move in alone .

TRIFUN: If, if! It's far better that we stay together.

AGATON: Hah! We'll see whether it's better or not!

SCENE 10

(Enter PROKA from outside).

PROKA: Is everybody here?

SIMKA, GINA, TANASIYE, and MICHA: What happened?

PROKA: It's no good!

GINA: What's no good?

PROKA: I've been to see the Town Clerk, and he told me that we have moved into the house illegally.

AGATON: Well of course *you've* moved in illegally, that's what I said all along.. If you'd let *me* move in alone, it would have been different.

PROKA: Yes, it would have been very different.

TANASIYE: All right, then, Agaton – tell us, what are we going to do now?

TRIFUN: We move out the same way as we moved in.

GINA: Oh, what a scandal this will cause!

PROKA: It'll be a disgraceful scandal, Agaton, you must go and see the lawyer.

AGATON: What lawyer?

PROKA: The one who's in charge of the estate, of course – and make it absolutely clear to him that we moved in here with the best of intentions.

AGATON: As far as I'm concerned, I've always had the best of intentions.

SARKA: And haven't I?

AGATON: You too, if you say so.

GINA: Why only you? We all came with the best of intentions.

SARKA: Gina's right. We all came here in good faith.

PROKA: Never mind who came and why. Agaton, are you going to go and see him?

(SEVERAL VOICES) Yes! You must!

AGATON: All right, if you want me to, I will.

MICHA: It occurs to me, Agaton, that while you're talking to him you might be able to find out from him what's in the Will.

(SEVERAL VOICES) Yes! Yes! That would be good!

AGATON: I've already tried, indeed I have, but he won't budge. He won't say a word about it: he says he doesn't know.

PROKA: How can he say he doesn't know, when it was he who drew up the Will?

AGATON: Oh, he knows, all right, but you can't screw a word out of him.

TRIFUN: Well, Agaton, you're always boasting about what an expert interrogator you were: now you can prove it.

AGATON: I don't want to boast, but I have always considered myself to be a most expert interrogator. As a magistrate I could always extract a confession from the most hardened criminal. Oh yes, I had my own special methods. Say I'd spoken gently to the accused, humanely even, but the wretch still wouldn't confess – very well! – I'd order him down to the cells and after the prison staff had worked him over a bit he'd confess, all right! What else could he do but confess? I tell you, I had my own methods and I was certainly a very expert interrogator, but that's altogether another matter. I can't order this lawyer to be taken below and beaten up to make him confess what's in the Will.

TANASIYE: Oh really? How surprising!

PROKA: Don't listen to all this chatter: we're wasting time. Agaton, you must go and see the lawyer.

VIDA: Tell him that we've moved in because we're Family: we're not just people who've come in off the street.

SIMKA: And we've got more right to be here than that 'Aunt'.

MICHA: My dear Agaton, point out to him that we are Mata's heirs.

PROKA: And tell him that we respect the law and have no wish to break it.

GINA: And tell him that we moved in to make sure that nothing went missing.

TANASIYE: And tell him that we are all decent, respectable people.

TRIFUN: And tell him that we're going to seek a second opinion!

AGATON: Don't try to teach me my business! I've had plenty of dealings with lawyers: I know what needs saying.

PROKA: Well, go on, get on with it, then!

MICHA *(who has been constantly looking out of the windows, hoping to catch a glimpse of Danitsa)*: There's no need for you to go and see him, Agaton – here he comes.

ALL *(Surprised)* He's coming?

MICHA: Yes, with her.

GINA: Who, the Aunt?

MICHA: Not with the Aunt, with *her*.

SIMKA: Who, that girl?

MICHA: Yes, she told me a little while ago that she was going to complain to him that we'd all moved in.

AGATON: That alters the situation. Look, we can't all talk to him. The best thing is for you all to make yourselves scarce and leave it to me.

PROKA: Yes, he'd better not see so many of us here.

AGATON: And I'll just slip into my room, so that it doesn't look as if I was expecting him. I'll, sort of, walk in here casually after he arrives..

TANASIYE: Yes, yes, come on, everybody!

*(**Exeunt**, all dispersing to their various rooms)*

SCENE 11

Enter Dr PETROVICH *and* DANITSA, *from outside.*

PETROVICH: Well, where are they all, then?

DANITSA: In their rooms.

PETROVICH: Which rooms?

DANITSA: All of them: they've taken over the whole house.

PETROVICH: Hm! A most interesting family!

DANITSA: Do you think this is a laughing matter?

PETROVICH: Well, it is rather amusing, isn't it? It's certainly not a tragedy.

DANITSA: It isn't a bit amusing! It's upset my aunt so much that it's made her ill.

PETROVICH: Calm down! It will be all right in the end.

DANITSA: God willing!

PETROVICH: I shall deal with this immediately, only, to tell you the truth, I'm not quite sure which is the best way of going about it. The simplest thing would be to call the police and have them all thrown out.

DANITSA: Oh, no! Not the police, please. That would cause a public scandal.

PETROVICH: I rather agree with you. It would certainly be most unpleasant to have to throw out a bereaved family. It wouldn't look good in the newspapers: people are so sentimental.

DANITSA: No, don't call the police. Isn't there another way?

PETROVICH: Well, another way of dealing with it might be for me to apply to the Court for leave to open the Will immediately.

DANITSA: I thought that it wasn't to be opened for forty days.

PETROVICH: Yes, that's what the deceased wanted, but his wishes aren't legally binding.

DANITSA: But surely it would be better to respect his wishes?

PETROVICH: I do respect them, but in fact the deceased himself foresaw that there might be problems. In the document containing the direction that his Will should not be opened for forty days he added words to the effect that this could be altered if the executor decided it was essential to do so. I'm entitled, therefore, to decide that the situation makes it essential to open the Will now, and I intend to obtain leave to open it tomorrow.

DANITSA: What good will that do?

PETROVICH: Well, we'll all know then who is to inherit the property, and the rest of them can clear off.

DANITSA: In that case, will my aunt and I have to move out of the cottage tomorrow?

PETROVICH: I don't think it will have to be as sudden as that. Anyway, it's possible that you won't have to move out at all.

DANITSA: Why not?

PETROVICH: Well, the person who inherits may not want you to go.

DANITSA: But in that case, we'd have to start paying rent from tomorrow. You know that we didn't have to pay any rent to the deceased gentleman. My aunt looked after the house in return for having the cottage rent-free. The deceased gentleman was really very kind to us, especially to me. He'd often give me little presents, and would sometimes talk to me for hours. Once, when I was ill, he never left my bedside. He was such a nice, kind man.

PETROVICH: Yes, I know that, and that's why I think the person whom he's named as his heir will be very considerate towards you.

DANITSA: You're wrong! They're hostile and disdainful: all of them. They make me feel very uncomfortable. It's got so bad that I wanted to leave immediately, even though it would have made things very difficult for me and my aunt.

PETROVICH: Why? It's not difficult to find somewhere to live.

DANITSA: No, but ... my aunt only has a tiny pension, and her income's not enough to cover the rent as well as our living expenses. I'd have to earn some money. I wonder if you'd consider giving me a job as a clerk in your office? I know the pay would only be small, but at least I'd be earning something.

PETROVICH: I'll give you a job with the greatest of pleasure.

DANITSA *(delighted)*: Will you? Oh, that's marvellous! And my aunt will be so pleased! Honestly, all this trouble has made her ill. She says that she's sick with frustration over all that's been going on in the house, but I think it's really from worrying about what will happen to us in the end. Can I go and tell her the good news – that you'll give me a job in your office? That'll do her better than any tonic. Can I go?

PETROVICH: Of course you can. And I'll stand by my word.

DANITSA *(excited and happy)*: Excuse me, then, for the moment. I'll come straight back, but I must run and tell her now. I'll be back very soon. **(Exit).**

SCENE 12

(AGATON *now peeps out from his room and, when he has made sure that Petrovich is alone, he* **enters**).

AGATON: Ah! I was hoping to see you alone. I've got something rather important to talk to you about.

PETROVICH: So much the better – I've got something important to talk to you about.

AGATON: That's good. We two need to talk, because we're the only ones who are men of the law.

PETROVICH: Are you a man of the law, then?

AGATON: I certainly am! I was a District Administrator for twenty-seven years.

PETROVICH: Better still. You can give me some very serious advice.

AGATON: Willingly!

PETROVICH: When you were a District Administrator did you ever come across the situation where animals, say, horses or pigs, cows or donkeys, had strayed on to somebody else's land?

AGATON: Certainly! I'd simply fine the owner of the animals and tell the owner of the land that they'd strayed on to beat them with sticks and drive them out.

PETROVICH: Very well, but that's animals – dumb creatures without understanding. But how would you have dealt with people, intelligent human beings, who had trespassed on someone else's property?

AGATON: Ah! Now I see what you're driving at. Yes, you're right. I'd say to them: "You mustn't do this, it's against the law", but this lot's swarming all over the place.

PETROVICH: They might be forgiven, perhaps. But what about you – you're here, and you say you are a man of the law?

AGATON: I certainly am. Believe me, I'd never do wrong – I'd never break the law, never! But what happened here was that a whole crowd of people moved into this house, and there was nobody to keep order, so what could I do? I had to move in myself, simply to keep order.

PETROVICH: I see. But if you were still, shall we say, the District Administrator, in charge of the Police Force as you used to be, and if, by chance, today, for instance, I were to come to you and tell you that a lot of people had moved into a house that I'm responsible for – what would do?

AGATON: Do? I'd send for a bailiff, and a policeman to go with him, and order him to go straight round and eject the trespassers!

PETROVICH: Well, isn't that what I've got to do here?

AGATON: Probably, I can't argue with that.

PETROVICH: But supposing I don't want to do that?

AGATON: Well, don't do it, then!

PETROVICH: Supposing I had a better idea?

AGATON: I'd like to hear it.

PETROVICH: I'm thinking of going to the Court and obtaining permission to open the deceased's Will tomorrow.

AGATON: Is that possible?

PETROVICH: Why shouldn't it be possible?

AGATON: But what about the deceased's last wishes – the forty-day delay?

PETROVICH: They were only wishes, and he himself foresaw that there might be circumstances in which, if I as executor thought it essential, the Will could be opened earlier.

AGATON: But do you think it's essential?

PETROVICH: Surely you agree that it's essential to do something, when the whole family is illegally occupying this house?

AGATON: Of course. And, in any case, it would be much better to open the Will tomorrow.

PETROVICH: Well, I'll do that, then.

AGATON: What about us? Can we stay here until tomorrow?

PETROVICH: It's not proper, but, just for one day …

AGATON: That's right. There's no point in us moving out just for one day and, anyway, it could cause a public scandal.

PETROVICH: All right, then, stay until tomorrow.

AGATON: That really is very kind of you. I can assure you that I've already said to the others: "That lawyer is an exceptionally intelligent person, you know: he's not the sort to go to extremes." I myself realised that all along, of course! So, in the name of the family, I'd like to thank you very much indeed!

PETROVICH: Thank you. Please tell the others, then, that I shall open the Will tomorrw.

AGATON: I certainly will, don't worry. But, if you'll allow me, there is one other small, rather indirect matter that I'd like to ask you about.

PETROVICH: Ask away!

AGATON: Well, we shall know tomorrow, shan't we, so it doesn't really make any difference whether we know today or tomorrow, but, you know, there's one thing that I'm so curious about that I can hardly wait until tomorrow.

PETROVICH: What's that?

AGATON: I'd very much like to know what I'm going to inherit.

PETROVICH: Well, since you ask me such an indirect question, I must give you an indirect answer. I don't know what it says in the Will.

AGATON: How can you not know, when you wrote it out?

PETROVICH: It's precisely *because* I wrote it out that I don't know what's in it. If someone else had written it out, I would have known what it said, but as it is …

AGATON: You know, I've great hopes of that Will. All the others have great hopes, too, but I think …

PETROVICH: And you're all expecting to inherit something?

AGATON: Yes, all of us, and each of us thinks that he's going to be the principal heir.

PETROVICH: Well, why don't you come to some agreement amongst yourselves?

AGATON: What d'you mean?

PETROVICH: If each of you thinks that he's going to be the principal beneficiary, that means that you all have equal rights. In those circumstances, there'd be nothing to prevent you from agreeing to divide up the estate between the members of the family in a fair and friendly way.

AGATON: Of course, that would be possible. And if were able to say tomorrow that we'd already agreed amongst ourselves how to divide up the inheritance between us, do you think it would be accepted?

PETROVICH: In the end, the Court will accept only what's written in the Will.

AGATON: Well, does the Will say that we can make an arrangement like that?

PETROVICH: I don't know, do I? You'll just have to wait until tomorrow, and if it says that in the Will, then you can do it. There's no point in doing it before.

AGATON: No, you're right.

PETROVICH: Don't forget to tell the family that I am going to open the Will tomorrow.

AGATON: I certainly won't forget. But I must tell my wife first. You can't imagine how impatient she'll be to hear about our conversation. I must tell her first.

PETROVICH: Fine! Do!

*(**Exit** AGATON to his room).*

SCENE 13

PETROVICH *(To DANITSA, whom he sees as she **enters** throught the French windows)*: Well, have you spoken to your aunt? Was she pleased?

DANITSA: She certainly was!

PETROVICH: Only, have you thought carefully about coming to work for me?

DANITSA: I don't see that there's anything to think about.

PETROVICH: You know, I'm a very strict employer.

DANITSA: And I'm a very conscientious worker.

PETROVICH: I'm pretty pernickety, as well.

DANITSA: And I'm very attentive to my duty.

PETROVICH: I get upset and bad-tempered sometimes.

DANITSA: And I know how to be sympathetic and patient.

PETROVICH: I must tell you that I take my work very seriously.

DANITSA: I'm glad: that impresses me.

PETROVICH: It's really rather amazing how well we suit each other.

DANITSA: Well, that means that you needn't have any doubts about taking me on.

PETROVICH: I should tell you that there's one thing about me – a failing – which you might find disturbing ...

DANITSA: What?

PETROVICH: I can get very jealous.

DANITSA *(astonished)*: Jealous! *(She looks him directly in the eye)*: I don't understand.

PETROVICH *(trying to play down the situation)*: Anyway, that's of no importance: it needn't affect you at all.

DANITSA: I still don't understand.

PETROVICH: Well .. I .. Look! I've told the family that I'm opening the Will tomorrow, so there's nothing more for you to worry about.

DANITSA: Oh yes, of course. I was so excited that I forgot to tell my aunt.

PETROVICH: You'd better go and tell her now.

DANITSA: I will.

PETROVICH: Tell her straightaway. I must go now: I've got to make arrangements for the Will to be opened tomorrow. Good bye! *(Exit PETROVICH).*

DANITSA: *(Exit, following Petrovich out)* Good bye!

SCENE 14

Enter AGATON and SIMKA, from their room.

AGATON: We'll have to call them all together.

SIMKA: We can go round their rooms and call them.

AGATON: Wait, I'll call Sarka – she can do it. *(He knocks on SARKA's door. She opens it and comes out). Enter SARKA.*

SARKA: Did you call me, Agaton?

AGATON: It's not just you. I have something very important to tell the whole family and and I'm trying to think how to call them all to a meeting.

SARKA: Well, you don't imagine that *I'm* going to call them, do you? I'm not the Town Crier.

AGATON: No, of course not. But you could set the alarm clock off: that would bring them.

SARKA: They wouldn't be able to hear it. It would probably be better, Agaton, if you were to bang on that silver salver. They'd be able to hear *that* all right.

AGATON: Yes, they would, but I'd rather not.

SARKA: Well, if you'd rather not, don't. Anyway, you've been in a powerful position and you've got a loud voice. When you were the Administrator the whole District could hear your bellowing, and everyone will be able hear you now if you just shout.

AGATON: You're right. *(He puts his hands to his mouth, trumpet-fashion, and shouts)* Hey! All of you! Proka, hey, Proka! Tanasiye! Trifun! Micha! Come here!

SCENE 15

(Enter the Family, one at a time, all from their various rooms. They gather round AGATON).

PROKA: What is it, Agaton?

AGATON: Wait until everyone's here.

TANASIYE: We are all here.

AGATON: Right, then. Sit down, and I'll tell you what's happened.

PROKA *(as he sits down)*: Have you spoken to him?

AGATON *(waits until they are all seated, but remains standing himself)*: Oh, I've spoken to him all right! And *this* time there was no beating about the bush. I said to him: "You may know the law, laddie, but so do I, so you've got nothing to be stuck up about!" Then I said to him straight: "In the name of the Family, I *demand* that you open the Will *immediately!*"

PROKA and TANASIYE: What did he say?

AGATON: Well, of course, he was pretty shaken by that. I hadn't just asked, I had *demanded!* He started trying to hedge, mumbling away about the deceased's wishes, the forty days, and so on and so on. But I wouldn't listen. I said: "There's no law which says I have to wait forty days, and I'm not going to!" I shouted him down, that's what I did!

VIDA and SARKA: And what did he say?

AGATON: He kept on trying to sneak out of it. He started babbling about paragraph seventy-two, and paragraph fifty-six, but I stopped him dead. I said to him:"And what about paragraph one hundred and forty-seven, sir? What about paragraph one hundred and forty-seven, eh?" – and he practically fainted.

(VARIOUS VOICES): And then . . ?

AGATON: Then he saw that there was no way he could get round me, and that there was no point in trying to confuse the issue any more. So he agreed.

(ALL) *(excitedly)*: Agreed what?

AGATON: He agreed to open the Will.

(ALL): Oh!

AGATON: Yes. He agreed to open the Will.

(ALL): When?

AGATON: He even tried to prevaricate about that. "All right, Mr Agaton," he said, "In a few days' time, perhaps." But I wasn't having that. I shouted, right in his face: "I *demand* that you open it *tomorrow!*"

(ALL): Tomorrow!

AGATON: Yes, tomorrow. *(Proudly)* There you are! That's how I deal with lawyers!

PROKA: And what did he say about us moving in here?

AGATON: There again, it was quite a struggle. He tried to say that we had no right to be here. He said: "Of course, it would have been a different matter if you had just moved in yourself, Mr Arsich, but the whole family . . ?"

TRIFUN: Never mind about all that – what did you actually say?

AGATON: I said to him: "There is nothing in the law to prevent it, and there's no law which regulates whether his family may or may not move into the house of a deceased person. And since there is no specific, written law on this subject, one is entitled in these circustances to rely upon natural law, according to which, when a family member dies the family has the right to look after his property."

(VARIOUS VOICES): That's right!

AGATON: Yes, of course it is. But – well, you know what lawyers are like – he started trying to argue again, but I shouted at him: "I'm not moving out of this house, and you have no power to make me!"

PROKA: Exactly!

AGATON: When he heard that he gave in and started simpering like a widow: "Oh, please, Mr Arsich, forgive me! I do beg your pardon! Please don't be angry! Of course you can stay!"

MICHA: And stay we shall!

SARKA: So we'll hear no more about having to move out!

AGATON: You again! Do you want to spend your whole life sitting on that balcony? We only have the right to stay until the Will is opened, and after that only the one who's inherited the estate will be able to stay here.

MICHA: Obviously.

SARKA: I did like that room.

TANASIYE: Well, Agaton, if you were able to beat the lawyer down like that, surely you could have asked him about the other thing?

AGATON: What 'other thing'?

TANASIYE: What the Will says, of course.

PROKA: Oh, that! You'll know tomorrow.

VIDA: Who can wait till tomorrow, for God's sake?

AGATON *(to* TANASIYE*)* As it happens, I did ask him about that, too.

(ALL): Oh?

AGATON: Yes, I interrogated him about that.

PROKA: Really? Well, tell us, Agaton, tell us!

AGATON: Yes, he may be one hundred percent a lawyer, but I'm an expert interrogator: he couldn't evade my questioning.

PROKA *(crossly)*: Get on with it, for God's sake!

AGATON: I started talking to him about the Will, but indirectly, you know, and skilfully, so that he wouldn't notice what I was leading up to. I said to him: "Since you drew up the Will, it would seem, in all the circumstances, that you know what's in it."

(SEVERAL VOICES): What did he say?

AGATON: He only looked down at the floor and said nothing. He dared not look me in the face, because he knew that, if he did, I would be able to read the Will in his eyes. But I'm an expert interrogator: once I've got a grip I don't let go. I kept on asking him indirect questions, and indirect questions, and indirect questions, again and again.

PROKA *(bursting with impatience)*: Well, what did he say?

AGATON: He did say something but he was only shilly-shallying, so I started hitting him again with indirect questions, and indirect questions, and more indirect questions.

PROKA *(desperately)*: For God's sake stop going on about your indirect questions!

SARKA: Well, did he at least give you an indirect answer?

AGATON: The fact is that he didn't *actually* answer me. I can't say that he answered me, but I *was* able to screw one single word out of him. One word is enough for me, of course, as an expert interrogator – I don't need any more. They've only got to say: "Our Father", and that's quite sufficient for me to sentence them to penal servitude for life! I've often reached a conclusion on the basis of a single word.

TANASIYE: Well, at least tell us what it was!

AGATON: Shall I tell you?

PROKA *(shouting)*: For God's sake, man, tell us!

AGATON: He didn't speak directly, only indirectly, but, of course,

I was able to catch the drift of it at once. It seems that the Will leaves the estate to the whole family, and it's up to us to come to an agreement as to how we divide it up between us.

(ALL) *(astonished)*: Ah!

AGATON: He didn't say so in as many words, but it was perfectly clear to me.

TANASIYE *(worried)*: What are we going to do now?

AGATON: I think, my friends, that we should be prepared for this possibility.

TANASIYE: How?

AGATON: By coming to an amicable agreement. I propose that we convert this gathering into a proper formal meeting, here and now.

TRIFUN: And no doubt you'll be the chairman!

AGATON: I don't have to be, why me? Why shouldn't Trifun preside? *(He sits down)* He thinks he knows best about everything, so let him preside.

PROKA: No, you, Agaton!

(ALL): Yes! Yes!

AGATON: Why me? Trifun's here: let him do it!

TRIFUN: Don't be silly! You know more about it than I do.

AGATON: Right, then! If I know best, don't be hindering me. *(He gestures importantly)* Well, members of the family, we have to be prepared for the Will to say that we are to divide the inheritance between ourselves, fairly and by agreement. When the Will is read out tomorrow, and it gets to the words 'I leave all I possess to my family, on condition that they agree amicably how to distribute it amongst themselves', we must be ready to say immediately: "We have already so agreed".

(ALL): Yes! That's right!

AGATON: Very well, then. We must come to an agreement now.

TANASIYE: And how do you think we can do that?

AGATON: Like this: first of all we shall have to agree, in a friendly, civilised manner, which of us are the closest relatives of the deceased, and which are more distant.

SARKA: How can we do that when we're all close relatives?

AGATON: No, we're not. For a start, you're not a close relative.

SARKA: What! How can you say that?

AGATON: I can say it because it's true – you're not.

SARKA: And are you?

AGATON: Certainly I am.

SARKA: If you are, so am I.

AGATON: No, you're not, Sarka. You're not a close relative, nor is Proka, nor is …

PROKA *(angrily)*: I certainly am a close relative!

SIMKA: How, Proka? You're only related through your first wife.

PROKA: If I was only related to him through my first wife, my second wife wouldn't have spent so much time weeping for him, would she?

VIDA: Well, frankly, Proka, we've all been wondering why your Gina has been making such a meal of it.

GINA: If you want to know, it's because I truly mourn for him, not like you.

SARKA: And not like us?

GINA: The only reason you're all dressed up in black is because of the Will: not one of you has shed a single, solitary tear for poor Mata.

SIMKA: We don't need to, Gina, dear: he's had a bucketful of *your* tears.

GINA: Oh! What a thing to say!

TRIFUN: Look, Agaton, are you the chairman of this meeting or aren't you? If you're going to let the women argue like this we'll never get anywhere.

AGATON: You're right, this conference is turning into a chattering session at the Womens' Institute. Come to order! Where had we got to?

PROKA: I hadn't finished what I was saying.

AGATON: Well, get on with it, then!

PROKA: I can't say off the top of my head how close my relationship is, but I have the proof of it here. *(He takes a large*

folded sheet of paper out of his pocket). This is a Document:
a vital Document.

AGATON: What is it, a Baptismal Certificate?

PROKA: It is not a Baptismal Certificate. Here, see for yourself!
(He unfolds it and passes it to AGATON:*).*

AGATON *(looking at the paper)*: It looks like some sort of diagram.

TRIFUN: Proka's the Town Hall archivist, so he knows how to
make diagrams.

AGATON: It's like a cadastral register.

PROKA: It's not a cadastral register, it's a family tree. Do you see
the tree-trunk?

AGATON: Yes, what of it?

PROKA: That's the deceased.

AGATON: What, the deceased Mata?

PROKA: Yes.

AGATON: Well, maybe – but, actually, Mata wasn't quite as
straight as that.

PROKA: And you see this branch here?

AGATON: Yes.

PROKA: That's an uncle, Rista Nikolich, deceased.

AGATON: Whose uncle Rista?

PROKA: The uncle of the deceased Mata.

AGATON: Oh, him! So?

PROKA: Now look, this uncle Rista had four sons: Spira, Boshko,
Tasa, and Mika. They are the four branches coming down
from there, see?

AGATON: I see.

PROKA: And you see this branch which hangs down from Mika?

AGATON: Yes, what of it?

PROKA: That's me.

AGATON: What, you?

PROKA: Yes, I'm Mika's son.

AGATON: If you were what's hanging from that branch, you'd
have fallen off by now.

PROKA: There, isn't it as clear as daylight? This is a Vital

Document, my friend!

SARKA: As far as that goes, Proka, I must be hanging off one of those branches, too.

TRIFUN: And how would it be if Agaton were to explain how he comes to be the nearest relative?

AGATON: It's obvious.

GINA, PROKA, VIDA, TRIFUN, and SARKA: Oh, yes? Tell us!

AGATON: Look, if we start going into such petty details we'll never get anywhere. Now, let's get down to the most important business, which is that we agree to share out the estate in a fair and civilised way, as befits a respectable family like ours.

PROKA: Well, what do you propose: let's hear it!

AGATON: All right. Let's start with Sarka.

SARKA: Why do you always start with me?

AGATON: Well, largely because I'm always finding you under my feet. Anyway, starting with Sarka. What does she need – a single soul with no other mouths to feed?

SARKA: Don't you go counting how many souls or how many mouths I've got to feed – I want my just dues!

AGATON: We must take needs into account. Your needs, for instance, are different from mine.

SARKA: How, may I ask?

AGATON: It could be said, for instance, that you need something to make you marriageable, but the fact is you've already had two husbands, and that's enough for anyone.

SARKA: What do you mean, 'enough'? Who are you to say what's enough for me and what isn't? I'll decide what's enough for me!

AGATON: It would be another matter if you had any children, but you weren't able to, were you?

SARKA: There you go again! Why d'you drag up whether I've had children or not? And why do you say I couldn't?

AGATON: Well, you've had two husbands, but no children.

SARKA: Yes, I have had two husbands, that's true, but is it my fault that there were no children? How long did I live with my first husband? – two years, that's all, and with my second three years and seven months. The time passes and if children don't come that's that. It wasn't that I didn't want children – I just didn't have time. Anyway, what about you? – you haven't got any children either!

AGATON: I'm not reproaching you, Sarka, I'm just stating a fact. If you'd had any children you could have had a bigger share but, as it is, five thousand dinars in cash and a set of kitchen utensils is enough for you.

SARKA: What!! That's disgraceful, Agaton! How dare you treat me like a beggar? I'm not here to beg: I want what's properly due to me.

AGATON: All right, then, we'll throw in the silver alarm clock as well.

SARKA: You can have it – and stick it on the silver salver: it'll look better!

TANASIYE: Agaton, you can't just measure everything up by eye, like this.

AGATON: Hold on! I only mentioned that by way of a proposal. We can discuss it, of course – trim it a bit, add a bit here or there, perhaps. Be patient!

VIDA: All right, let's go on.

AGATON: Proka and Gina can have the meadows at Mali Mokri Lug[1] which the deceased owned, and ten thousand dinars in cash.

PROKA *(Jumps up)*: Oh no! You can forget that! I want my proper share!

AGATON: That is your proper share.

GINA: What, that rotten little place that isn't worth a row of beans! You can't be serious!

PROKA: I want Agaton to tell us what he reckons *his* share is: what's he going to get?

---

1. *Mali Mokri Lug:* (Literally "Small Damp Wood") – an oddly-named small village on the outskirts of Belgrade.

(ALL, except SIMKA): Yes! Yes! Tell us!

AGATON: I'll tell you all in good time.

(ALL): No! No! Tell us now!

PROKA: We want to know now what you what you think your
share is going to be.

AGATON: I think it would be better, my friends, if we settled all
your shares first, and I'll take what's left.

PROKA: Oh yes – what's left! Hah! We get fobbed off with some
fields at Mali Mokri Lug, a set of kitchen utensils, and two or
three thousand dinars each, and you take what's left – not
likely! First, we want to hear what you think your share is
going to be.

(ALL): Answer! Answer!

AGATON: Very well, I'll tell you. Taking into account the fact that
I am the closest relative ..

(SEVERAL VOICES): That's what you say! Prove it!

AGATON: All right, then, how's this? Taking into account that I
am related to Mata, and taking into account the fact that I am
the head of the family …

TRIFUN: Who says you're the head of the family? Why are you?

AGATON: I say I'm the head of the family because it was me who
dealt with the lawyer, not you! Right, I'll go on. Taking into
account my relationship to Mata; taking into account that I am
the family's representative; taking into account my personal
and general public needs; taking into account all the relevant
factors and circumstances pertaining at this moment in time,
I say that, in the first place, I get this house …

(ALL) *(General uproar)*: Oh! Oh!

AGATON: Hold on! … this house and everything in it, including
the alarm clock …

SARKA: And the alarm clock, and the silver salver, and all
that's left!

AGATON: Yes, *and* all that's left. And, on top of that …

TRIFUN: What, more yet?

AGATON: Yes, certainly.

PROKA *(To* TRIFUN*)*: Let him speak: let's hear it all!

AGATON: And, as well, those shops in the Terazije.[1]

(ALL): Oooh!

AGATON: And that's not all!

TANASIYE: Isn't it, by God?

PROKA: You just can't be serious!

AGATON: I also get the villa with the vineyards at Topchider Hill.[2]

(ALL): Oooh!

TRIFUN: And all the shares in the National Bank, no doubt?

AGATON: *And* all the shares in the National Bank, certainly!

PROKA: And all I get is a few fields at Mali Mokri Lug!

SARKA: And all I get is a set of kitchen utensils!

MICHA: And what about me – don't I exist?

AGATON: No, my friend, you don't!

TRIFUN *(to* MICHA*)*: Of course you don't exist. Hadn't you realised that the only one here who does exist is Agaton?

TANASIYE: But I'm probably a closer relative than Agaton is.

SIMKA: Shut up, Tanasiye!

VIDA: Who are you telling to shut up?

PROKA: Everybody! Don't you see? This isn't a conference for the family to agree on sharing out the estate – it's robbery!

SARKA: Daylight robbery! He gets all the shares in the National Bank, and I get a set of kitchen utensils!

TRIFUN: We aren't 52,374 peasants to stand looking to our front and trembling just because Agaton shouts: "Attention!"

(From here on to the end of the scene there are heated remarks and exchanges, everybody talks at once, the temperature rises as they all get more and more excited and angry, until it finishes in complete uproar).

TANASIYE: We're all equal here!

---

1. *The Terazije:* The main wide avenue, with shops, offices, and hotels, in central Belgrade.
2. *Topchider Hill:* A very fashionable suburb of Belgrade.

PROKA: I don't recognize this conference, I don't accept that he's the head of the family, I don't accept the Will, I don't accept anything at all!

AGATON: And nobody recognizes you!

TRIFUN: This is robbery!

MICHA: It's robbery all right, and it's aimed at me!

GINA: He wants the house and the shops in the Terazije as well!

SARKA: Fat cat!

VIDA: Mata never even looked at him!

SIMKA: No, but he looked at you, didn't he, Vida?

PROKA: We do not accept this agreement!

TANASIYE: Every man for himself!

AGATON: So, I'm giving you lot nothing!

(ALL) *(furiously)*: Who's giving us nothing? Who d'you think you are?

AGATON *(seizing a chair)*: Keep away from me!

PROKA: He just wants a fight! *(Also seizes a chair)*

TRIFUN: Let's give him one! No surrender!

The men grab chairs and various other objects and take up threatening attitudes towards AGATON. *The women all start screaming.* MICHA *jumps up on the table and starts waving his arms about …*

Curtain

Act Three

The same room, the next day.

SCENE 1

THE FAMILY *(all except* AGATON *and* SARKA*) are in the room. There is a general air of depression and hopelessness. They are dispersed, mostly sitting about singly, with their backs turned to each other.* PROKA, *with a look of despair on his face, is nervously pacing up and down with his hands behind his back.* GINA *has wrapped a shawl round her head.* SIMKA *is holding her head in both hands.* VIDA *has turned her back on everyone and is talking to herself as if she was telling someone off.* MICHA *is curled up on the sofa, with his arms wrapped round his knees, looking blankly into space.* TRIFUN *is sitting astride a chair with his forehead resting on its back.* TANASIYE, *looking despairing, is scribbling on a piece of paper.*

PROKA *(After a pause)*: Oh dear! Oh dear! Who would have thought it?

SIMKA: To have played such a mean trick on the family!

TANASIYE: Trick? Trick? It wasn't just a trick, it was a swindle! Mata's cheated us!

VIDA: Even while we were standing ouside the judge's chambers my left eyelid was twitching, and for me that's always a sign of trouble. And when the judge started to break the seal on the Will I felt a sort of sharp pain, and I said to myself: "This is going to turn out badly."

GINA: Badly! – it was catastrophic!

MICHA: And nobody said a word, there, in the judge's chambers.

TRIFUN: What was there to say?

MICHA: You could have protested, like I did.

TANASIYE: What did you do?

MICHA: I said out loud: "I don't accept the Will."

TANASIYE: And then what?

MICHA: And then I said: "We protest, and we shall take legal action to overturn the Will."

TRIFUN: Yes! What sort of a family would we be if we didn't have this Will overturned?"

TANASIYE: No stranger's going to get it overturned, are they?

MICHA: We shouldn't hesitate – we should lodge a complaint at once, and get the proceedings started today.

PROKA: We'd better wait until Agaton gets here. He stayed behind to make a copy of the Will.

TANASIYE: What do we want a copy for? We all know exactly what we're getting.

PROKA: Not for us, but for the lawyers. He's going straight from there to speak to Dr Stoyanovich, who is a real expert in these matters. He'll tell him to get the appeal started but, obviously, Dr Stoyanovich can't act without having a copy of the Will.

TANASIYE: Yes, I've heard of that Dr Stoyanovich.

PROKA: He's the best man there is for overturning Wills. A first-class lawyer, he is. Either he'll prove that the deceased was of unsound mind when he made the Will, or he'll invent some legal technicality that will overturn it, or he'll simply see that it disappears. I tell you, he's a first-class lawyer.

TANASIYE: The best thing would be for him to prove that Mata was mad. He must have been mad, mustn't he? – all he left me was 5,000 dinars. I ask you, five thousand dinars!

VIDA: As if we were mere beggars!

TANASIYE: 5000 dinars! How marvellous! – five thousand miserable dinars! Didn't he know perfectly well that in my bankruptcy proceedings the Commercial Court calculated my debts at over 460,000 dinars? – those are the sort of sums I deal in.

TRIFUN: It's as if Agaton had dictated the Will.

SIMKA: Don't deceive yourself, Trifun, my friend! If Agaton had dictated it he'd have put in a damned sight bigger figure than 5,000 dinars for himself.

TANASIYE: That's quite enough for Agaton.

SIMKA: And how is it enough for him, but not enough for you?

TANASIYE: Agaton's circumstances and mine are quite different.

SIMKA: In what way, pray?

TANASIYE: This inheritance was my last hope. My entire fate hung on this one card.

TRIFUN: One should never bet everything on just one card.

TANASIYE: I reckoned I'd be able to discharge my bankruptcy. I'd told my creditors to be patient, and that I'd see them right after Mata died – and all I get is five thousand dinars!

PROKA: Well, it's a nice round sum.

TANASIYE: Nice round sum be damned! Hah! Five thousand dinars – a nice round sum!

PROKA: It's not so bad. What about me? – 3,000, that's all! Three thousand – it's scandalous!

GINA: It'll hardly pay for all the candles we've lit.

MICHA: Who's complaining? Look at me – two thousand dinars! The Court janitors get more than that in tips! It's an insult!

SIMKA: And who did he leave it all to? Who? To that .. that .. I don't know what to call her ..!

GINA: Go on, dear, try!

SIMKA: … to that illegitimate daughter!

TRIFUN: He did leave something to the Church and Educational Charities..

SIMKA: He only did that to try and cover up his disgrace. She gets the lot – the house, the villa with a vineyard, the shops, the Bank shares, the cash – everything!

GINA: The whole lot.

VIDA: Proka, how can it possibly be legal to leave everything to an illegitimate child?

PROKA: You see – he even cheated us over that. Fancy having an illegitimate child, and the family not knowing anything about it!

SIMKA: And wasn't it utterly disgraceful how he openly admitted in his Will that she was his illegitimate daughter!

GINA: And didn't you notice how that girl behaved in front of us!

TANASIYE: Oh, come now, Gina. She didn't know anything about it. You saw what happened – she fainted away when she heard.

GINA: I'd have fainted, too, if I'd been left everything!

MICHA: I'm sure she didn't know anything in advance.

VIDA: Hah! Maybe! But, my word, didn't he cover it all up cleverly!

SIMKA: It must be possible to get that Will overturned: she's an illegitimate daughter and we're legitimate relatives.

VIDA: That must be right, if there's any justice in heaven or earth!

TANASIYE: And, anyway, it's all very well him leaving so much to the daughter, if that's what she is, and so much to the Church and the Educational Charities. But wasn't it more important to get me out of being bankrupt? The Church and the Educational Charities aren't bankrupt.

GINA: That's true, Tanasiya. Actually, I think it would have been better if he had left everything to the Church and the Educational Charities, rather than to that illegitimate child.

MICHA: It never entered my head that that girl (who is very pretty, I must say) would suddenly become a rich heiress, and that I'd finish up with a legacy of two thousand dinars.

VIDA: I told you! I said: "That girl looks like Mata", and you all just scoffed. Gina even burst into tears because she said I'd insulted the dear departed.

GINA: Of course she looks like him. I saw that from the moment I first set eyes on her, but I didn't like to say anything, out of respect for poor Mata.

PROKA: A fat lot of good your respect did you! 'Out of respect' he left you three thousand dinars, as if you were a mere beggar.

GINA: He can keep it for his next Memorial Service.[1] It might just pay for a decent turnout of priests, instead of only the one, like the lawyer arranged for the funeral.

SIMKA: What! Aren't you going to take the three thousand?

GINA: Oh, I'll take it all right, but I shan't say "Thank you"; I shan't go to the Memorial Service, and I shall not say "Rest in Peace!"

VIDA: Nor I!

GINA: Besides, I'm not too upset, actually. I'm afraid I'm not really related to Mata.

TRIFUN: Not related to him?

GINA: No, it was Proka's first wife who was related to him, not me.

SIMKA: Then, for goodness' sake, why were you crying so much?

GINA: For Proka's sake.

TRIFUN: Well, what was that diagram of yours all about, Proka – the tree trunk, and the branches?

PROKA: That diagram, actually, was drawn by a Russian emigré, a draughtsman in the Land Registry. He drew his own family tree, because he's a great-grandson of Prince Belyayeva and I used his family tree. I rubbed out the name of Prince Belyayeva and put in Mata's name instead. The branch that I hung from was really the branch of Prince Belyayeva' grandson.

TRIFUN: See what comes of letting yourself hang from foreign branches.

PROKA: It might have worked! If only it had!

TRIFUN: Well, you know, Mata probably thought: "That Prince Proka Belyayeva is only worth 3,000 dinars" – and that's why that was all you got!

1. *Memorial Service:* The second Orthodox Funeral Service *(Parastos)* normally takes place forty days after the day of death.

SCENE 2

Enter SARKA *(She is wearing a conspicuous red dress with a floral design, and a hat elaborately decorated with flowers and ribbons).*

SARKA: Hullo there, bereaved family! Good morning! How are you all?

SIMKA, VIDA, and GINA: Oh, Sarka!

VIDA: What's all this, Sarka?

SARKA: What d'you think? Let that Aunt wear mourning, not me! I've spent a whole week wearing black for Mata and that's all he's going to get for two thousand dinars!

GINA: You're right, Sarka. I don't know why I bothered to dress up in black just for his measly 3,000 dinars. I must be potty … *(She takes off the black head-scarf which she had been wearing, then takes a flower out of a vase and puts it in her hair).* Sarka's right – let the Aunt do the mourning!

TRIFUN: Aren't you getting a bit ahead, ladies? Aren't we expecting Agaton to arrive and tell us that the lawyers are going to overturn the Will?

SARKA: Well, if that happens I can just nip home and change back into something black, can't I?

TRIFUN: And you, Gina, you've only got to take the flower out of your hair, and you can start crying again.

GINA: That's right!

SARKA *(To the other women)*: To tell you the truth, I'm not very keen on wearing black. People assume that you're in mourning, and they show you a certain amount of respect. But what do I care about being respected?

VIDA: What indeed!

SARKA: You know, when I was widowed from my first husband and was wearing black, a young lecturer came hovering round me, and he said: "Oh Mrs Sarka, there's something I want to say to you, but I can't, out of respect for your grief!" What the devil 'respecting my grief' had to do with it I can't imagine. But it was nice to be shown respect 'for my grief' by such a nice, well-brought-up young man.

SCENE 3

Enter AGATON

ALL (*Crowding round* AGATON *excitedly, and all speaking at once*): Have you been? What happened? What did he say?

AGATON: Settle down! I'll tell you.

ALL: Quickly! Tell us!

AGATON: Right. It's all over.

ALL *(despairingly)*: Oh no!

AGATON: That's what I said.

PROKA: What, we're finished?

AGATON: Yes, finished.

ALL *(in utter despair)*: Ooh!

MICHA: Why are we finished? How are we finished?

AGATON: There's no way that we can overturn the Will.

PROKA: I don't understand it. Why can't we?

AGATON: Because, Proka, the Will is legally valid and because there is a legitimate descendant.

SARKA: How can an illegitimate daughter be a legitimate descendant?

AGATON: The lawyer said: "You should be thankful for the small legacies that he did leave you, because he had the perfect right to leave you nothing at all."

MICHA: All right, but I still don't see why we can't challenge the Will in Court.

AGATON: We could. We could also pay the lawyers, and the taxes, and the Court costs, but Dr Stoyanovich says that we have no chance of overturning the Will, and that means that we are finished.

PROKA: Frankly, Agaton, I can't make head or tail of this. How is it possible that the family can't overturn the Will? I don't understand it.

AGATON: The lawyer said that we're not direct descendants of the deceased: if one of us was a direct descendant it might be possible.

TANASIYE: I'm a direct descendant, surely?

AGATON: No, Tanasiya, you're not. Nor am I. None of us are. Take Sarka there: she's not a direct descendant, only an indirect one.

SARKA: What am I, then?

AGATON: An indirect descendant.

SARKA: Agaton, please stop saying these things. I know perfectly well whether I'm a direct or an indirect descendant.

AGATON: You don't understand: those are legal expressions.

SARKA: If they're legal expressions, why just pin them on me? What about Simka and Gina and Vida?

PROKA: Agaton, did the lawyer read the copy of the Will?

AGATON: Yes, every word of it.

PROKA: Couldn't he find a single word that could be challenged?

AGATON: No, he couldn't. He said: "You'll just have to hold your hands up."

PROKA: So Mata's beaten us, has he?

TANASIYE: He's more than beaten me – he's seen me dead and buried. You can come to my funeral if you like.

VIDA: And to think, Agaton, how you went on about 'what an honourable and decent man he was!'

AGATON: I said that when I still had expectations – and so did you.

TRIFUN: Honourable, eh? Now I know what his idea of honour was.

TANASIYE: The fact is, he was simply a usurer. Think of it – he charged *me* interest!

AGATON: And in your case he didn't get paid! Anyway, he didn't charge *you* more than twenty percent. He *flayed* other people – flayed them alive.

TANASIYE: He short-changed and robbed the poor.

PROKA: Anyone who had any dealings with him went through hell.

VIDA: He had no heart: no heart at all.

GINA: No heart and no soul.

TRIFUN: Frankly, he was a complete swindler.

AGATON: A swindler, yes, a swindler – may God forgive him! I remember how he made that poor fellow Sima Yovanovich pay him twice over. Sima had sent him a cheque, but he pretended he hadn't received it. Sima begged him and implored him – "22,000 dinars is no joke," he said. He said he'd already paid, he wept, he pulled his hair, but Mata wouldn't listen. All he said was: "Pay up!"

TANASIYE: I know. I once came to him, man-to-man, as a relative, and said: "I can't pay just at the moment," but he shouted at me like a bank-robber: "Pay up!"

MICHA: He was only too ready to refuse a favour. There was one occasion when I badly needed three or four thousand dinars. I asked him for help, but all he said was: "Not a penny!"

TANASIYE: Here we are today, running him down. Yesterday we were praising him.

PROKA: Yesterday was yesterday: today's different.

TANASIYE: I don't see why – Mata's just the same today as he was yesterday.

PROKA: Maybe he is, but yesterday *we* were different.

TRIFUN: I wonder why we let ourselves become so hopeful when we all knew that he was such a complete swine. We shouldn't have expected anything of him.

TANASIYE: That's true: we knew he used to rob us.

TRIFUN: If he robbed *you* he only did it while he was alive, but he's still robbing me even though he's in his grave. Dead and buried, he's *still* robbing me. He's left me a legacy of 3,000 dinars, and he had the damned cheek to write in his Will: "To my relative Trifun Spasich, the sum of 3,000 dinars, which he has already received according to a receipt dated the 14th of February last year." I'd asked him, man-to-man, to lend me 3,000 dinars, and now he simply writes off that debt by leaving it to me as a legacy!

VIDA: I ask you – wasn't it it absolutely shameful that he could brazenly admit that he'd had an illegitimate daughter – it's as bad as insulting the dead.

SARKA: As far as that's concerned he had no shame – may God

forgive him – and, to speak frankly, he was a complete swine.

SIMKA: Oh! Sarka!

SARKA: Oh, yes he was. There was one thing that I wasn't going to tell you, but immediately after I was left a widow by my first husband he started making advances to me. I said to him: "Really, Mata, how could you even think of such a thing, seeing that we are related?" And do you know what he said? He said: "What do you mean – 'related'? Your family connection with me is about as remote as the ninth hole in a tin whistle!" Just think of it – the sheer brass neck – calling me a 'ninth hole'!

MICHA: Yes, that's certainly some insult!

PROKA: Here we are, a respectable family, and he robs us in favour of an illegitimate child!

GINA: We can never forgive him – never!

SARKA: For goodness' sake, Agaton, is it really the case that the law recognises illegitimate children? I know that illegitimate children are inclined to happen, as it were, casually . . like . . how shall I put it? … like when a man has a hole in his trouser pocket and some pennies fall out of it. It's not that he actually *wanted* to leave his money lying in the road – it just fell through a hole in his pocket.

AGATON: In the good old days illegitimate children were regarded as illegal.

SARKA: Well, why are they regarded as legal now, for God's sake?

AGATON: They're not, but times change and attitudes change. I had a young clerk once – he'd just left school – and when a baby was found under a hedge where its mother had abandoned it, do you know what he said about that illegitimate child? He said: "Well, it's a member of society!"

GINA: What society?

AGATON: How should I know?

SARKA: Not a choral society, I'll be bound.

AGATON: Probably not, but, that's what people say nowadays: "Even a bastard is a member of society."

SARKA: And this one of Mata's?

AGATON: She's a member of society.

SARKA *(crosses herself)*: God-save-us-all!

VIDA: And does that mean that we have to consider that girl as one of our relatives?

SIMKA: What! An illegitimate child!

PROKA: She's a disgrace to the family.

GINA: She's someone we should all despise.

VIDA: As far as I'm concerned, I shall cut her dead if I meet her.

AGATON: And as far as I'm concerned, I shall spit when I meet her. I give you my word, I shall spit, on behalf of the whole family!

MICHA: And yet, you know, when one thinks about it carefully, she's not to blame.

SARKA: What do you mean – 'not to blame'? She's illegitimate, isn't she? If she was a decent woman she'd be legitimate!

GINA: Exactly!

AGATON: As a family we are expected, at least in the eyes of the world, to preserve and protect our honour and our reputation, and I propose that we adopt, here and now, a formal resolution that henceforward we dissociate ourselves from that girl.

SARKA: Why should *we* dissociate ourselves? We're not illegitimate – let *her* dissociate herself.

AGATON: You don't understand, Sarka, we're not just going to dissociate ourselves from her, we're going to repudiate her.

SARKA: Oh, that's different.

AGATON: We shall make it absolutely clear that we do not consider her to be part of the family, but that we scorn and despise her.

ALL: That's right! Yes! Agreed!

AGATON: And we all take a solemn oath to cut her dead when we meet her.

ALL: That's right! Yes! Agreed!

AGATON: And I therefore suggest that, as a sign of our disapproval, we all now, straightaway, leave this house.

SARKA: I shall miss my nice room.

AGATON: You don't want to let *her* throw you out, do you –
that girl?

GINA: Oh! She couldn't, could she?

AGATON: She certainly could! She's the heiress: it's her property.

VIDA: To think that it has come to this!

PROKA: Come along, Gina! I'm not going to stay here to be
thrown out by an illegitimate female.

GINA: Let's go and get our things. *(She moves off behind Proka)*
And I tell you, the next time any of our relatives dies I shall
damned well find out in advance what he's left me before I start
crying. Not like here, where I've been doing it all for nothing!
(Exeunt GINA followed by PROKA into their room)

TRIFUN: I've only got a few things, but I'll go and get them
(He starts going up the stairs) I've paid back everything I owed
Mata, After this, if he sees me at the Memorial service he can
light a candle for me – I shan't light one for him! *(Exit TRIFUN
up the stairs)*

VIDA *(to Tanasiye)*: Shall we go?

TANASIYE: All right. But there is one thing that I've just
thought of.

AGATON: What?

TANASIYE: Agaton, tell me, is there any actual *proof* that she's his
illegitimate child?

AGATON: You know how it is, Tanasiye, in these matters the child
is the proof. An illegitimate child is, in itself, a 'corpus delicti.'

TANASIYE: 'Corpus delicti?'

AGATON: Yes.

TANASIYE: And you mean to say that this 'corpus delicti' can
throw me out of the house?

AGATON: Yes.

PROKA *(turning to look at Mata's picture)*: Phew, Mata! Shame
on you!

VIDA: Come on, Tanasiye! We don't want to see that monster's
portrait any more.

TANASIYE: We certainly don't! *(Exeunt TANASIYE and VIDA
to their room)*.

SARKA: Well, there's no point in my staying. I'm not going to sit here and just look at Mata's picture.

AGATON: You're right, Sarka. We'd all better go.

SARKA: I'll just go and get my things. *(**Exit** SARKA to her room).*

AGATON *(to* MICHA*)*: What about you, young fellow? What are you thinking about?

MICHA *(looking at a piece of paper on which he has been writing)*: I've just been totting it up, and I reckon that I'm seven times removed from Mata.

AGATON: Like Sarka put it – the 'ninth hole' of the tin whistle, eh?

MICHA: So, I could legally marry the girl.

AGATON: What, with her being born out of wedlock?

MICHA: If I married her, she'd be *in* wedlock.

AGATON: What about our resolution to dissociate ourselves from her?

MICHA: You married people can stick to your resolution, but … to tell you the truth I look at it this way – why should so much wealth go out of the hands of the family? Wouldn't it be better if it stayed in the family?

AGATON: Yes, it would. And it would be very convenient for you, wouldn't it, if the property could somehow pass into your hands?

MICHA: And, anyway, I rather badly *need* to get married. What else am I going to live on?

AGATON: What indeed! Right, then, is this just in the planning stage or have you made any arrangement with the girl?

MICHA: No, I've made no arrangements. Actually, I rather get the impression that she looks at me a bit, sort of, sideways.

AGATON: Well, look at her sideways, then!

MICHA: Of course, if I had succeeded to the property I would have done, but as it is …

SIMKA: Have you . . er . . propositioned her at all?

MICHA: Yes, I'm afraid I have, but I didn't have the slightest idea then that she'd inherit everything. If I'd even suspected it I'd have acted differently. As it is, I think I'm in difficulties with her …

AGATON: Well, that's your problem: it doesn't concern us.

MICHA: I had hoped I might ask for your help.

AGATON: What, me? What could I do?

MICHA: If you were willing, you could win her round.

SIMKA: For goodness' sake, Micha, why should Agaton try to win the girl round? What on earth makes you think that Agaton would be able to do so, anyway?

AGATON: First and foremost, my dear young man, I'm dissociating myself from that girl, as we resolved. I don't want to meet her, let alone talk to her. And, secondly, Micha, what do I know about turning the heads of young women? Whatever gave you the idea that I know anything about that sort of thing?

MICHA: Well, I don't think that exactly, but you *were* the District Administrator, and you were good at dealing with all sorts of situations, and especially at making people see things your way.

AGATON: It's quite another matter making your political opponents see things your way. Yes, it's true, I *was* very good at doing that, but the circumstances were different. Say a man closed his shop at the proper time – I'd still prosecute him for keeping open after hours. Or I'd arrange a Council meeting and write out the notice, but I wouldn't send it to him. Naturally, he wouldn't turn up, so I'd accuse him of dereliction of public duty. Or he'd be heard saying, in a pub: "Oh God Almighty!" – so I'd charge him with swearing in public and blasphemy. Or he'd say: "The times are hard, I can't make ends meet!" – and I'd do him for spreading alarm and despondency. He'd spit on the pavement outside his shop – so I'd prosecute him for depositing litter in a public place. And so on, day after day, until finally he'd get fed up and come whining to me and say he wanted to give in. So I'd give him a piece of paper and, good as gold, he'd write on it: "Until today I belonged to such and such a Party, but from now but from now on . . " – and I'd have him, body and soul! *That's* how I used to get them to see things my way, but I can't do it with this girl. I can't charge her with spitting on the pavement or keeping a shop open after hours.

SIMKA: D'you know what, Micha, I think you ought to speak
to Sarka. She's pretty good at wheedling people round – men
and women.

AGATON: That's very good advice that Simka's given you. Ask
Sarka: nobody's better at this sort of thing than she is. Leave us
out of it: *we* can't talk to the girl now that we've dissociated
ourselves from her. Come along, Simka, let's get our things
together! The sooner we're out of this cursed house the better.
*(**Exeunt** AGATON and SIMKA to their room, leaving Micha still
looking at his piece of paper).*

SCENE 4

Enter DANITSA *(When she sees MICHA she recoils slightly).*

MICHA: Oh, my dear girl! I wanted .. I would like .. only I find it
difficult to know whether I should offer you my condolences as
a relative …

DANITSA: Don't bother! I don't want any sort of offers.

MICHA: Well, we'll pass over that. Life's very strange, isn't it:
so full of surprises.

DANITSA: Yes.

MICHA: Because, of course, as relatives we share your grief but, to
tell you the truth, you and I are not close relatives at all. We're
seven times removed, actually. In fact, we're so distantly related
that we're not really relatives at all.

DANITSA: So much the better!

MICHA: Yes, I agree that in one sense it is better. It means, you
see, that I can speak to you, not as a relative, but as a man who
respects you, who likes you very much, and who is very
worried about your welfare. You have so many troubles and
you must be so lonely!

DANITSA: And I shall stay lonely: I'm quite happy being on my
own, thank you.

MICHA: Well, for a while, obviously. But you can't stay on your
own for ever. Six months, perhaps, until your grief wears off.

DANITSA: Six years, more like!

MICHA: What!

DANITSA: Six years, I said.

MICHA: Six years! Who could wait that long?

DANITSA: Wait for what?

MICHA: For grief to pass.

DANITSA: It won't seem long to me.

MICHA: To you, no .. but .. and while you're grieving for all that time you won't be thinking of getting married, I suppose?

DANITSA: Certainly not. Anyway, what has all this got to do with you?

MICHA: Well, I'm concerned as a relative ...

DANITSA: But you said that we weren't related.

MICHA: We're not, of course. But .. naturally .. may I be frank with you?

DANITSA: If you must.

MICHA: You see, I may have behaved incorrectly towards you earlier, and I'm very anxious to put that right. I may have spoken carelessly, or even out of turn, when I made certain suggestions to you which I had no right to make. I beg you to regard it as a slightly unfortunate misunderstanding on my part, and to overlook it. Please believe that my intentions are serious, very serious indeed.

DANITSA *(astonished)*: Really! Surely you can understand that I'm in no mind to let you go on talking like this?

MICHA: I only wanted ...

DANITSA: If you really want to make up for your rudeness and the unwelcome suggestions that you made to me, the best way you can do it is to pick up your suitcase and get out of this house.

MICHA: Get out?

DANITSA: Yes!

MICHA: Are you ordering me to go?

DANITSA: I'm asking you to go.

MICHA: All right, I will. I was just going to pick up my things anyway. I only ask you one favour – may we continue this conversation later?

DANITSA: In six years' time, perhaps, when I've finished grieving.

MICHA: Does that mean never? *(DANITSA shrugs her shoulders)*
Then... if that's the case... you can strike me off your list of relatives.

DANITSA: I shall do exactly that.

*(**Exit** MICHA up the stairs, leaving DANITSA alone in the room).*

SCENE 5

***Enter** AGATON and SIMKA. Seeing DANITSA they both rush up to her and kiss her.*

AGATON *takes a handkerchief out of his pocket and wipes away a tear from his face.*

AGATON: Oh, my dear, dear girl!

SIMKA: Oh, my sweet child, my darling!

AGATON: Oh Lord! ...*(He sobs)* How wonderful are God's Commandments!

SIMKA: My dear child, I'm lost for words .. I don't know what to say!

AGATON: I said to Simka: "That girl has struck a chord in my heart!"

SIMKA: And mine. As soon as I saw you for the first time my heart turned over. I thought: "In God's truth, she's one of us!"

AGATON: I felt that right from the very start! You remember, don't you, Simka, I said to you: "I'm sure that child is our kith and kin!" – didn't I?

SIMKA: And d'you know what I said to him? I said: "As if she had come from my very own heart."

AGATON: Lord, Lord! How wondrous are Thy works!

DANITSA *(trying to disentangle herself from SIMKA's and AGATON's constant embraces)* Please! Please!

AGATON: So I said to Simka: "We must look after the child, for we're her closest relatives. How's she possibly going to manage on her own?" And I'll tell you what I've already done for you, my dear – I've ordered all those others to leave. You'd have had problems with them, but I know how to deal with them! They started trying to object, saying this and that, but I said to them: "Don't you go thinking that that poor child is defenceless – not while I'm around, she isn't!" Don't you worry – I sent them packing!

DANITSA: And are they going?

AGATON: They didn't want to, but they've got to. They know better than to try it on with me! I got them all together in here and I shouted at them: "Silence!" – and they all stood to attention, and they trembled. I said: "Are you going quietly, or have I got to take stern measures?"

DANITSA: Thank you!

AGATON: There's no need to thank me – I just did my duty. When I visited the dear departed, while he was ill, I felt that there was something he wanted to tell me, but it was difficult for him – should he, shouldn't he …?

DANITSA *(bursting into tears)*: My poor father!

SIMKA: God rest his soul!

AGATON: Such an honourable man! There aren't many like him!

SIMKA: How true!

AGATON: I tell you … he hesitated, but I could see it in his eyes … he *wanted* to say to me: "Agaton, there's no one closer to me than you: I leave this child to you in trust!" He didn't actually say it, but it was as clear as daylight that that's what he wanted to say to me. And, of course, I am in honour bound to obey him and to fulfil his wishes. How could I do otherwise?

DANITSA: But …

AGATON: Simka said to me: "Agaton!" she said, "You did well to order all those others to get out of the house, and to do it so firmly. But hadn't we better leave too?" "Of course not," I said, "How can we leave that poor child on her own? You'll say she has her aunt, but what's an aunt compared with *me*? An aunt can't deal with the Authorities, or cope with all the financial complications, or keep the tenants in order, or fight off the family. An aunt can't do all that, so we'll have to stay here. Danitsa can have the run of the big house, and we'll make do in

that cottage in the grounds – the one she's living in at the
moment – just so that we can be beside her, close at hand, to
look after her!"

DANITSA: I don't know about that: I'll have to ask the lawyer.

AGATON: The lawyer! You don't need to bother with him! On the
contrary, now that he's handed the property over to us, he's no
longer our lawyer.

DANITSA: Maybe, but he has been so good to us and has been so
friendly that I don't want to do anything without consulting
him.

AGATON *(looking hard at* DANITSA*)*: But he … are you thinking
of taking his advice for the rest of your life?

SIMKA: Why not, Agaton? To tell the truth, it's not such a bad
idea. He's young, honest, serious.

DANITSA *(astonished)*: But what do you mean – what on earth do
you mean?

AGATON: *(to* DANITSA*)* The fact is, it's not a bad idea to have a
lawyer about the place. Having a lawyer in the family is like
having a loaded revolver in the house.

DANITSA *(angrily)*: No! No!

AGATON: D'you know, I liked that fellow right from the start.

SIMKA: So did I. They'd make a lovely couple, a really lovely
couple!

DANITSA: Stop it! Stop it! Don't talk like that!

SIMKA: But, my dear …

DANITSA *(putting her hands over her ears)*: I won't listen! I won't
listen!

AGATON: The best thing would be to leave it all to me. I'll arrange
it with him. You don't need to concern yourself: I'll arrange
everything.

DANITSA: Stop! For goodness' sake, stop! Who told you – I never
told you. It's not like that at all! *(**Exit** DANITSA, running)*.

SIMKA: There! Now you've driven her away!

AGATON: She was blushing. There's no harm in her blushing.
You used to blush, once.

SIMKA: It was good of you, Agaton, to make her part of the family.

AGATON: But she *is* part of the family – on the wrong side of the blanket, of course, but what does that matter? D'you think I'd spurn the girl when she's such a rich heiress? I'd rather be related to her than to Proka and Gina!

SIMKA: So would I!

SCENE 6

***Enter Dr* PETROVICH**

PETROVICH: Oh, have we still got visitors?

AGATON: No, I've told them all to go. They're in their rooms, packing their things. I told them firmly: "You came here illegally: don't force me to take steps to eject you – just go home!"

PETROVICH: You acted quite correctly.

AGATON: I know, but I've had to stay to look after our young relative. She's a good, well- brought-up girl, who wouldn't be able to cope with all the problems, and her aunt is old and frail – she couldn't cope, either.

PETROVICH: So?

AGATON: So we've agreed that she should move into the big house here, while Simka and I go into the small cottage, so that we'll be on the spot.

PETROVICH: And you've agreed all this with her, have you?

AGATON: Yes. Actually, she did say she she'd have a word with you, but I don't see what there is to talk about. It's perfectly simple: two women can't stay here alone in such a big house. It'll be different afterwards, when *you* move in.

PETROVICH *(astonished)*: What do you mean – "when I move in?"

AGATON: Later – in due course.

PETROVICH: What on earth are you talking about: why should I move in?

AGATON: I don't mean straightaway, but later, when you get married.

PETROVICH: Get married! Get married to whom?

AGATON: Well, obviously, not to Simka.

SIMKA: Oh Agaton! You are a one!

PETROVICH: Kindly make yourself clear. I wish to know exactly what you are talking about. Who are you talking about: who am I going to marry?

AGATON: I'm talking about that young relative of ours.

PETROVICH: How dare you? This is outrageous! Who put that idea in your head?

AGATON: No one, but it's clear enough. I've got a nose for these things.

PETROVICH: But what possible grounds have you got for even thinking such a thing? It's ridiculous: your imagination's run riot. There's no sensible way you could have come to such a conclusion.

SIMKA: Oh, one can spot these things. Earlier, when we were speaking to her about you, she went as red as a boiled lobster.

PETROVICH *(angrily)*: What! You spoke about this to her?

AGATON: Yes, of course we did.

PETROVICH: And who the devil gave you permission to do that?

AGATON: Why do I need anybody's permission? – it was my duty to speak to her.

PETROVICH: I forbid it. I absolutely forbid you to talk to her about this.

AGATON: But I …

PETROVICH: Not another word!

AGATON: Very well. Simka, take note: not another word! But when the time comes I shall just … *(To* PETROVICH*)* Leave it to me, when the time comes I shall …

PETROVICH: Understand this, sir, once and for all! There's no question of leaving 'it' or anything else to you. You don't come into this at all: it has absolutely nothing whatever to do with you *(He pulls his hair)*. You've had the gall to speak to her about such things – I can understand only too well how that must have distressed and shocked her at the time of her greatest grief. You have got to apologise to her .. no, no …

I shall apologise to her myself, on your behalf.

AGATON: There's no need. I spoke to her very gently, like an uncle.

PETROVICH: No, no, I must apologise to her. I don't want her to think that I …

AGATON: All right, go on then, do! Simka, would you go and call the girl? Ask her to come here, but don't tell her what it's all about: I'll tell her that myself. *(Exit* SIMKA*)*

PETROVICH: Oh, no you won't! I've told you already: not another word about this!

AGATON: No, all right – not while she's still grieving.

PETROVICH: You are driving me to lose patience with you. Understand this! You will *not* speak to her about this, either while she's still grieving, or when her grief has passed, or ever! I have no intention at all of getting married – none at all.

AGATON: I didn't intend to get married, either, but you know how it is! A fellow's just walking quietly along a smooth path; he goes strolling along quite happily when, all of a sudden, when he's least expecting it, he trips over a stone. That's what happened to me: I tripped over my Simka.

PETROVICH *(not listening)*: Yes, yes …

AGATON: No one knows what's going to happen in life.

SCENE 7

Enter SIMKA *with* DANITSA.

AGATON: Come in, child, we need to talk to Dr Petrovich.

PETROVICH: There is nothing to talk about. All I want is to apologise to her.

DANITSA: To me?

AGATON: Yes, because I talked to him about certain things.

PETROVICH: Kindly be silent, sir! Understand, once again: not another word! *(To* DANITSA*)*: This gentleman has taken upon himself the liberty of speaking to you, not about official matters, but about certain other things.

DANITSA: I asked the gentleman to spare me.

PETROVICH: I don't want you to tell me what he said … his

conversation with you has nothing to do with me. I did not ask him to talk to you about .. certain things – absolutely not! It appears that he has completely misunderstood the situation ...

AGATON: Misunderstood! Yes, I suppose I must have done, and I shan't say any more about it. I've only this to say – I did it because she's related to me, she's a young and single girl, and you are a decent young man, and I can see that she's fond of you.

DANITSA *(angrily)*: Who told you that?

AGATON: It's obvious: and he likes you, too.

PETROVICH: I never told you any such thing.

AGATON: No? Well, anyway, I can see that there's no point in talking during this time of mourning. Simka, not another word!

SIMKA: God's honour!

AGATON: Don't be angry with me. I acted with the best of intentions, out of a sense of family duty.

PETROVICH *(to DANITSA, turning his back on AGATON)*: Miss, there are some important details – documents concerning the estate – which I must attend to. I don't expect you'll have them, but your aunt may. It would be better if we changed the subject.

AGATON: Yes, it would be better.

PETROVICH: Would you call your aunt, please, so that I can ask her.

DANITSA: She's not well. Wouldn't it be better if we went to her?

AGATON: All right, let's go and see her.

PETROVICH *(to AGATON)*: Your presence is not required.

AGATON: Very well. But I'm here, and when I'm needed, you can call me.

PETROVICH *(walking off with DANITSA)*: There's no need whatsoever to trouble you.

AGATON *(When PETROVICH and DANITSA have reached the door)*: By the way, there's no need for you to talk to her aunt about *those* things: leave it all to me.

PETROVICH *(turning in the doorway, annoyed)*: For the last time, sir, will you shut up!

AGATON: Very well, but don't talk to her about it.

*(*PETROVICH *gestures dismissively, and he and* DANITSA **exeunt***).

SCENE 8

AGATON: Do you see, Simka, how well I've fixed everything! As they say, you've got to know how to do things. Brains are no good to you unless you're practical.

SIMKA: It seemed to me that you just got their backs up by talking about it.

AGATON: So they were annoyed – that's how it should be. *You* behaved as if you were annoyed when it was suggested that we got married, though really you were pleased.

SIMKA: Well I hope we haven't ruined everything.

AGATON: Leave it to me. You know me: I don't go about ruining things. I've wrecked elections, admittedly, but that was when they weren't going as the government wanted them to. I've messed up government auctions, certainly, but that was when they weren't going as *I* wanted them to. That's different: that's politics, but this ... leave it to me, and you'll see, everything will go as smoothly as if it was on well-oiled wheels.

SCENE 9

Enter*, from various sides, through various doors, and down the stairs, the remaining members of the* FAMILY. *They are all carrying suitcases and various bulging carrier bags: it is clear that they are taking out rather more than they brought with them.*

AGATON: Are you all ready?

TRIFUN, PROKA, and TANASIYE: What about you?

AGATON: Me? Why do you ask about me? I'm different.

PROKA: How are you different?

AGATON: I'm different. It's true that you are relatives as well –

I'm not saying that you aren't. But you're all 'ninth hole'
relatives, as Sarka put it.

SARKA: And what hole are you, may I ask?

*(They all line up side by side, still burdened with their suitcases
and bags, and* AGATON *paces up and down in front of them).*

AGATON: Whatever I may be, I'm closer than you are .. and,
therefore, I'm staying!

ALL: You're staying?

AGATON: I'm staying. Who else could run a property like this?
From now on you have to call me the head of the family.

TRIFUN: You can call yourself 'head', or whatever you like –
I'm not going to!

SARKA: Nor I – not likely!

AGATON: All right, I won't be your head, or Sarka's. But, as far as
this entire estate is concerned, I am now running it, and from
this moment onwards what I say in this house goes.

ALL: Oooh!

AGATON: You've been, you've seen the house, you've looked all
round it, you've stayed a day and a night, and that's it! You
arrived with empty suitcases, and you're leaving with full ones
– plus a lot of carrier bags.

SARKA: You'll have a bag too, Agaton.

AGATON: Maybe, but that's nothing to do with you. You and I are
in different positions. You are all temporary.

TRIFUN: And you're permanent?

AGATON: Permanent I certainly am. You are only here as visitors:
I'm at home in my own house!

ALL: Ooooh!

AGATON: Why do you all sound so surprised?

PROKA: We're not just surprised – we are all completely and
utterly flabbergsted! Who do you think you are, to say such
things?

AGATON: You know who I am: why do you ask?

PROKA: I'm asking because I want to know this: how can you say
that your right to stay in this house is any greater than mine, or

his, or his? On what basis do you say that you are any different from us, and what gives you the right to puff yourself up and strut about in front of us like this?

TRIFUN: Yes, tell us!

AGATON: I would have thought it was obvious to you.

ALL: No! Tell us! Tell us!

PROKA: If you don't come clean we're not moving. If you've got the right to stay, so have we!

ALL: That's right! We're staying put! *(They put down their suitcases and bags).*

AGATON: What the devil have I got to explain?

PROKA: You've got to explain to us on what basis you make yourself out to be the proprietor here.

AGATON: Do you think that it's a simple matter for me to explain?

PROKA: No, I'm damned sure it isn't! That's why we're not agreeing to leave.

AGATON: Well, will you leave if I do explain?

ALL: Explain! Explain first!

AGATON: Well, it's like this. You know, don't you, that that illegitimate girl has inherited the estate?

ALL: We know!

AGATON: Well, doesn't that make it clear?

PROKA: What are you talking about – clear? She's illegitimate, you're not. She's inherited the estate, you haven't.

AGATON: All of you, wait until I finish! I've bestowed what you might call a blessing on the girl.

SARKA: Pah! How could you bestow a blessing on anyone!

AGATON: Because, thanks to me, she's engaged to be married!

ALL: Aaaah!

MICHA: That's impossible – she can't be!

AGATON: Why? Do we have to ask your permission?

PROKA: But none of this explains what we want to know. Very well, Agaton, supposing she is engaged to be married – it's not you that she's engaged to, and it's not you that she's going to marry. So what on earth has it got to do with you?

AGATON: Don't you want to know who she's going to marry?

ALL THE WOMEN: Who is it?

AGATON: The lawyer, that young lawyer of hers.

ALL: What??

MICHA: But that's outrageous!

AGATON: Yes, him. Now perhaps you can understand why I'm here, and why, in the name of both of them, I now say: "Off you go, and leave quietly!" You've done your stint of mourning as 'The Bereaved Family', just as you wanted to, and you'll be compensated for it.

GINA: How shall we be compensated?

AGATON: You'll get everything that's due to you under the Will, and you don't have to come to the Memorial service.

ALL: Don't worry – we won't!

AGATON: No, you won't, and you shouldn't, because, when all's said and done, you can't be expected to mourn the dear departed for ever. We who remain in the house will, of course, continue to mourn, keep all the proper observances, light candles to him … *(Remembers something)* Yes, I've just remembered that when you all moved in the candle was put out. Simka, please go and light the candle in the room where he died: it's disgraceful that it's not still lit!

SIMKA: You're quite right, I'll do it now! *(**Exit** SIMKA upstairs)*.

PROKA: Look, all of you! See how this fellow's twisting and turning to try and avoid answering our question! First it's something about a 'blessing', then it's 'the girl's engaged', then it's 'the lawyer's the bridegroom', then it's 'the deceased's candle' – he'll do anything except come to the point. Now, you just tell us, Agaton, simply and clearly, who you think you are, what you think you are, and what right you have to strut about here like a rooster!

AGATON: All right, I'll tell you, but first pick up your things *(They all pick up their suitcases and bags)*. Now, this is the point. I'm her next of kin, and she asked me to stay.

GINA: What! You're an illegitimate girl's next of kin?

TRIFUN: But what about the resolution we all agreed to?

PROKA: How *can* you be her next of kin?

TRIFUN: I'm much more closely related than you are.

MICHA: What about me?

AGATON: I don't know what you are, but I'm her closest relative in accordance with natural law.

TRIFUN: Here we go again – he's dragged in 'natural law'!

AGATON: Yes, by natural law, because following natural law he asked me to stay, too.

TANASIYE: He? Who's he?

AGATON: The bridegroom – the lawyer.

PROKA *(to the others)*: You just can't get hold of him by the head or by the tail! I suggest that we all go back to our rooms and, when the lawyer comes with the police to eject us, we demand that the first one to be thrown out is Agaton.

ALL: Yes! Yes!

AGATON: But that's not right.

PROKA: Well, what is right, then?

AGATON: I can't tell you.

PROKA: No, you certainly can't, can you?

AGATON: Because I dare not tell you.

TRIFUN: Oho! It's some sort of secret, is it?

AGATON *(He has only just thought of it)*: Yes, that's it! It's a secret.

SARKA: A secret, indeed!

AGATON: Yes, a secret. Why, what were you thinking?

PROKA: Look at him! Look how he tries to deceive us and manipulate us as if we were children! Well, I'm not having him lording it over us any more. *(To the others)* Don't you see? – all he's trying to do is get rid of us so that he can stay. It's obvious – he's only just dreamed up this so-called 'secret' …

ALL: That's right! We're not going!

AGATON *(Even he is confused)*: No, I haven't just thought of it, only it's a great secret. I can't tell you: I daren't.

ALL: Out with it! Tell us!

AGATON: I couldn't possibly betray a confidence but … but … oh,

good people .. *(They all gather round him, full of curiosity)* ..
you're making it very hard for me! I'm staying here because…
just give me a moment, please .. *(he wipes his face with a
handkerchief. At this point* SIMKA *appears at the top of the stairs,
and starts to descend).* I am staying here because, you see …
because that young lawyer, the one who is engaged to be married
to that illegitimate girl, he is .. he is .. my illegitimate son!
*They all drop their suitcases and bags. There are loud shouts of
disbelief and astonishment from all of them, but the loudest noise
by far is* SIMKA'S *shriek. She has just reached the bottom of the
stairs and, on hearing* AGATON'S *last words, she screams and
promptly faints.*
The scene remains frozen for a few seconds.
AGATON *(rather scared by the effect his lie has had, he edges
nervously away, glancing alternately at* SIMKA *and at the
others. Finally, in a resigned tone, he says)*: Well, I've certainly
fixed everything now!

Curtain

"Dr"

A Comedy in four Acts

CAST

Zhivota Tsviyovich

Mara *his wife*

Milorad *their son*

Slavka *their daughter*

Uncle Blagoye *Mara's brother*

Mrs Spasoyevich ⎫ *Governors of Nursery*
Mrs Protich ⎬ *School Number Nine*

Mrs Draga

Velimir Pavlovich

Dr Reisser

Nikolich *a clerk in Tsviyovich's firm*

Soyka

Soyka's Husband

Klara

Maritsa

Pikolo

Translator's note: *The author set the original play in the Belgrade of the 1930's, but the theme and characters are universal.*

Act One

ZHIVOTA TSVIYOVICH's *private office [a large room in a house which has the main business premises downstairs]. A table, a large safe, two telephones, one internal and one for general calls, besides easy chairs, a sofa, and other furniture. [Entrance door from the corridor, rear, and doors into other rooms left and right]. On the wall over the safe, a Doctor of Philosophy's Diploma in an ornate frame from which there hangs, on a ribbon outside the frame, a large seal in a round case. Zhivota and Pikolo are already present when the curtain rises.*

ZHIVOTA *(he takes some money out of the safe, the door of which is open, and, looking through a bill which is lying on the table, he sorts out several banknotes and some small change)*: Here you are. And tell the manager that I will not accept any more bills from him.

PIKOLO *(taking the money)*: Yes sir!

ZHIVOTA: Tell him: "My master says that in future he will not accept any bills at all, not even for five paras, and that he will not pay them."

PIKOLO: Yes, sir! At your service, sir. *(Exit)*

SCENE 2

ZHIVOTA: *(goes to the door, **Left**, holding the bill in his hand and muttering irritably to himself. He calls out)* : Maritsa! Maritsa!

MARITSA *(**Enters** after a short pause)*: Yes, sir?

ZHIVOTA: Is Milorad in?

MARITSA: Mr Milorad is still asleep.

ZHIVOTA: Still asleep! *(He looks at his watch)* It's a quarter to eleven!

MARITSA: Mr Milorad got home very late last night.

ZHIVOTA: Is that so? Well, Maritsa, go and wake the young gentleman and tell him that I, his father, wish to see him.

MARITSA: Oh sir, I daren't. When I wake him up, he always throws things at me – shoes, candlesticks, ashtrays, slippers, and anything else that comes to hand.

ZHIVOTA: Does he, indeed? What charming habits! Very well, please ask my wife to come.

MARITSA: Yes, sir. *(Exit)*

SCENE 3

(ZHIVOTA paces about, agitated and grumbling until MARA enters)

MARA: The maid said you wanted to see me.

ZHIVOTA: Yes. Is the young gentleman still asleep?

MARA: Children do sleep, you know.

ZHIVOTA: Oh yes, children sleep, but father pays the bills.

MARA: What bills?

ZHIVOTA: What bills? Listen, and I'll tell you! *(He waves the bill at her)* Three thousand four hundred and twenty-three dinars! And do you know what it's for? Listen to this *(reads)*: "To three dinners in chambre-séparée." Do you even know what that is – have you ever had dinner in a chambre-séparée?

MARA *(shrugs)*: No, I haven't.

ZHIVOTA: No, quite! And just listen to what this dinner included: champagne, liqueurs, cocktails. "To champagne, three hundred dinars, liqueurs twelve, cocktails thirty dinars." You've never tasted a cocktail – you don't even know whether you eat it or drink it.

MARA: No, I don't know.

ZHIVOTA: Anyway, if that wasn't bad enough, listen to this: "To replacing the mirror which was broken by the chanteuse, seven hundred and sixty dinars."

MARA: Oh!

ZHIVOTA: What does he want with a chanteuse anyway, I ask myself, but if he must have a chanteuse, why the devil can't he choose one that doesn't smash mirrors? What's the point of breaking mirrors?

MARA *(sighs)*: It's just his youth.

ZHIVOTA: Youth! What sort of 'youth', for God's sake? Did you ever go round smashing mirrors? Of course you didn't, and neither did I, and you and I were both young once. What are you dreaming of when you say 'youth'? He stays in bed until mid-day – 'youth'! He doesn't do a stroke of work – 'youth'! He breaks mirrors – 'youth'! He runs up bills – 'youth'! It would be one thing if this latest affair was just an odd example of 'youth', but it's not! Only three days ago I paid *this* bill *(he takes another bill out of the safe)* for one thousand seven hundred dinars, and it's less than a fortnight since I paid one for nine hundred and sixty dinars for some more 'youth'. And how much more is still to come? What's he going to do next, eh?

MARA: What indeed? Anyway, it's your concern, not mine. You're his father.

ZHIVOTA: Father! Father! I hope he doesn't think that 'father' only exists to pay his debts! And look at this! I ask you – he even signs these bills as if he was a book-keeper in the Accounts Department! He certifies them for payment! This can't go on! It's got to stop!

MARA: Well then, just stop paying the bills, and there you are!

ZHIVOTA: Do you think I've been paying these bills because I *like* it? I do it because I *must* – I do it for the sake of his reputation, and not only his personal reputation, but that of this diploma, too. He's a Doctor of Philosophy! Just imagine the scandal – a Doctor of Philosophy being thrown out of a restaurant for not paying the bill and being chased by bailiffs!

MARA: I don't know, I really don't, why on earth you made such a song and dance about getting him to become a Doctor of

Philosophy in the first place.

ZHIVOTA: Why did I concern myself? I concerned myself for his own good. You wouldn't have said that if you understood how much a qualification means in life. I'm not saying that "philosophy" itself is actually worth anything at all. Personally, I wouldn't give you five paras for it, because it would be daft to pay out good money for ... for Scotch mist. I couldn't have cared less whether became a philosopher or not, *but* I was determined that he should be able to put the title "Doctor" before his name.

MARA: I don't see what use that is to him.

ZHIVOTA: What use it is? Do you think that a peacock would be a peacock if it hadn't got a tail? Nobody would give it a second glance. Leaving peacocks aside, let's take me, for example. I've been fortunate, I'm well off, I want for nothing. And people respect me, there's no doubt about that, *but* if I'd had "Doctor" in front of my name, the sky would have been the limit. Zhivota Tsviyovich, that's one thing – anybody could be called Zhivota Tsviyovich – but if I had been "Doctor Zhivota Tsviyovich" .....

MARA: But you didn't really need it.

ZHIVOTA: No, I didn't need it, but Milorad most certainly does. He wasn't gifted at school – he couldn't stand school. He ground his way through class after class like a mule-cart through mud. He grew up, and then what? Without a "Doctor" in front of his name he'd have been nothing and nobody. "Doctor of Philosophy" is a title, Mara, and these days it's a title that opens doors, not brains.

MARA: Well yes, you may be right. But he complains that he's not a philosopher.

ZHIVOTA: Not a philosopher? I don't see why on earth not. You don't imagine, do you, that Doctors of Philosophy are all philosophers?

MARA: But he says: "How can I be a Doctor of Philosophy when I don't know anything?"

ZHIVOTA: Why does he need to know anything to be a
philosopher? When I'm thinking, *I'm* a philosopher. When it's
a case of having to make a big payment, and especially when
it's one due to the government, I get down to *thinking* in a
philosophical way. To pay up? That's not a philosophical
thing to do – any fool can do that! The philosophical answer
is to get out of paying. Anyway, it's not only me that's a
philosopher – you are too, when you keep quiet and don't
chatter for a week or so. A philosopher is someone who stays
silent and thinks.

MARA: Yes, true, but what you're talking about is – how shall I
put it? – a private philosopher. Our Doctor of Philosophy is
something different.

ZHIVOTA: It's me that's the Doctor of Philosophy, not him.
He has a university degree, certainly, but it wasn't what was in
his head that got him through his exams, it was what was in
this safe!

SCENE 4

NIKOLICH *(Enters)*: Excuse me, sir, a telegram.

ZHIVOTA: Where from?

NIKOLICH: From abroad.

ZHIVOTA: What's it about?

NIKOLICH: I haven't opened it. It's not addressed to the firm,
it's addressed to your son, sir.

ZHIVOTA: To my son? *(To MARA)* It'll be a bill, you'll see!
(To NIKOLICH) Open it, even if it is addressed to him.

MARA: Won't that upset the boy?

ZHIVOTA: What do I care if it upsets him, seeing that it's me
that's going to have to pay! *(To NIKOLICH)* Open it, please.

NIKOLICH *(Opens the telegram and glances at it)*: It's from
Fribourg, in Switzerland.

ZHIVOTA: Who's it from?

NIKOLICH: From a Professor Reisser.

ZHIVOTA: God knows who he is. What does he say?

NIKOLICH *(Reads it to himself, and then aloud)*: "Passing
   through Belgrade on way to Athens. Have pleasure in
   accepting your invitation to stay for a few days and see
   the city."

ZHIVOTA: What's the boy doing, writing to this fellow, and why
   has he invited him here? *(To MARA)* My dear, go and wake him
   up, please, and tell him to come here. *(**Exit** MARA)*

SCENE 5

ZHIVOTA: Has someone been to the Stock Exchange?

NIKOLICH: Mister Deutsch.

ZHIVOTA: Good! Remind 'Ador and company' that payment is
   due the day after tomorrow.

NIKOLICH: I have already done so.

ZHIVOTA: There's something else … Never mind, I'll be coming
   downstairs later.

NIKOLICH: May I go now?

ZHIVOTA: Yes, all right. *(**Exit** NIKOLICH)*

SCENE 6

*(**Enter** MARA and MILORAD. MILORAD is dressed in light silk
pyjamas. He is unshaven and still half asleep).*

ZHIVOTA: Have you woken up yet?

MILORAD: Just about.

ZHIVOTA: A telegram's arrived.

MILORAD: Did you wake me up just to tell me that?

ZHIVOTA: For all I know it might be important. It's for you, from
   a Professor Reisser.

MILORAD: Never heard of him.

ZHIVOTA: In that case, how is it that he has sent you this telegram
   saying that he is pleased to accept your invitation and that, on
   his way to Athens, he will be delighted to stay here for a day or
   two looking round the city?

MILORAD: What d'you mean 'my invitation'? Is that telegram
   from Fribourg?

ZHIVOTA: Yes.

MILORAD: Well what are you getting all steamed up about? That telegram's not for me, even if it has got my address on it. Send for your Velimir – that's obviously who it's for.

ZHIVOTA *(remembers)*: Oh yes, of course, you're right.

MARA: There, you've upset him for nothing.

ZHIVOTA: Don't worry. It'll do him no harm. *(He picks up the internal telephone)* Wait a minute, while I send for him. *(Speaks on the telephone)* Is that you, Nikolich? Will you please send the lad round to Nyegosheva Street, number 37, second floor. He knows it: he's been there before. It's where that young man Velimir Pavlovich lives – you know him, he's visited me here a number of times. Tell the lad to find Mr Pavlovich and ask him to come and see me straightaway. Yes! At once! *(puts down the telephone)*.

MILORAD *(making to leave)*: You've got me up for nothing. I could have stayed in bed.

ZHIVOTA: Just a moment! There's something else I want to speak to you about. Very well, let us say, for the moment, that this telegram is not your concern. This bill, on the other hand, is very much your concern. *(He hands it to* MILORAD, *who glances at it).* Three thousand seven hundred dinars, for God's sake! It looks as if you'd not just been smashing mirrors, but that you spent the whole night *eating* mirrors, for it to have come to that much! Well?

MILORAD: How do I know?

ZHIVOTA: How do you know? You signed it, didn't you?

MILORAD: Oh yes, that's my signature.

ZHIVOTA: And the way you signed it was: "Dr Milorad Tsviyovich." Do you think I made you into a Doctor of Philosophy just so that you could sign huge restaurant bills?

MILORAD: Well, how the hell am I supposed to sign them?

ZHIVOTA: Do you seriously think that it's proper for a Doctor, and a Doctor of Philosophy at that, to go round signing restaurant bills?

MILORAD: Maybe not, but what can I do? I don't know why the devil you had to string that stupid title round my neck – what use is it to me?

ZHIVOTA: You don't know? – well, I do! I didn't go to all the trouble of getting that diploma for you just because I happened to have an empty picture-frame to put it in!

MILORAD: It's caused me nothing but trouble.

MARA: He's right – the child's right.

ZHIVOTA *(to* MARA*)*: Well, kiss him better then! Child, you say? Some child – swallowing three thousand seven hundred dinars-worth of mirrors! *[To* MILORAD*]* And how, pray, does the qualification do you any harm?

MILORAD: Well, for instance, a few weeks ago you paid that fellow Velimir to write and publish an article, in my name and over my signature, entitled "The Dynamic Mechanism of the Unconscious Mind". I happened to meet Professor Radosavlyevich a few days ago and he said: "Excellent! Excellent! But haven't you perhaps inclined a little too much towards Freud-Adler!" I had to agree, didn't I? I hadn't the faintest idea what he was talking about. So what use is that damned diploma, when people ask you questions like that?

ZHIVOTA: What use is it? The use is that I have plans for you, my son! Every man must have some plans for his life, to achieve his aims and desires. You, now …

MILORAD: I have no particular desires.

ZHIVOTA: What! *(To* MARA*)* Listen to him! *(To* MILORAD*)* D'you mean to say that you have no aim in life?

MILORAD: Well, yes, I have, actually.

ZHIVOTA: What is it?

MILORAD: To inherit your business.

ZHIVOTA: Good God Almighty! *(To* MARA*)* Do you hear what he thinks his aim in life is? *(To* MILORAD*)* But, of course, you don't give a damn for any of my worries! Well, my son, I have other plans for you, and they are even broader than the frame round that diploma.

MILORAD: Go on, then, I'm listening.

ZHIVOTA: You'd better listen, because you're going to have to adapt your behaviour to fit in with my plans.

MILORAD: How?

ZHIVOTA: Within one year from today you're going to become an assistant professor at the university.

MARA *(pleasantly surprised)*: Oh, good!

MILORAD: That's ridiculous! How can I be an assistant professor when I don't know anything?

ZHIVOTA: You've got your qualification, and that's enough.

MILORAD: It's nothing like enough! I'd have to give lectures.

ZHIVOTA: It's not my intention that you should become an assistant professor just so that you can give lectures. You're going to be an assistant professor at the university so that you can get married to the Prime Minister's daughter.

MARA *(excited and delighted)*: Oh, marvellous!

(MILORAD bursts out laughing).

ZHIVOTA: What are you laughing about?

MILORAD: The Prime Minister hasn't got a daughter.

ZHIVOTA: What of it? Over the next year or two there'll be at least three different Prime Ministers, and one of them's bound to have a daughter.

MILORAD: Father, I think you had better alter your plans so far as they concern me. How can I be an assistant university professor? You know very well that I am no Doctor of Philosophy, and that there is not the slightest chance that I could ever become one.

ZHIVOTA: Why not?

MILORAD: Why not? Because I simply wasn't born to it, and that's that.

ZHIVOTA: Not born to it! What d'you mean 'not born to it'? Do you imagine that peoples' occupations are determined by their birth? Do you think that some men are born to be Generals, some to be Bishops, and some to be Government Ministers? Is that what you think? You are wrong, my boy. In real life it is completely the opposite. One man's born to be an guitar player and he becomes a professor. Another's born to be a butcher and he becomes an artist. Another's born to be a ballet dancer and he becomes a bishop. And another's born to be a robber and *he* becomes a government minister! That's what happens in real life.

MILORAD: That may well be so. However, so far as your plans for me are concerned, you can drop them altogether.

ZHIVOTA: Understand this, my lad! – if I have to drop *my* plans for you, you can forget all about *your* 'aim in life'.

SCENE 7

MARITSA *(Enters)*: Two ladies are here.

ZHIVOTA *(to* MARA*)*: Probably to see you.

MARA: I don't know.

MARITSA *(to* ZHIVOTA*)*: They have come to see you, sir.

ZHIVOTA: They can't want me – perhaps they want to see my son?

MILORAD: I'm not expecting anybody.

ZHIVOTA: They're probably people who go in for swallowing mirrors.

MILORAD: It's not me they're after. *(Exit)*

MARA *(reproachfully)*: Zhivota, you're much too hard on the boy.

ZHIVOTA: Really! Well, if he's upset you can go and console him.
(Exit MARA. *To Maritsa)*: Ask the ladies to come in.

(Exit MARITSA *and immediately afterwards* **enter** MRS PROTICH *and* MRS SPASOYEVICH*)*

SCENE 8

PROTICH & SPASOYEVICH *(speaking in unison)*: We, dear Sir, are members of the Governing Body of the Nursery School Number Nine. This Nursery School …

ZHIVOTA: I beg your pardon, ladies, please sit down.

PROTICH & SPASOYEVICH *(sitting down and once again speaking in unison)* We, dear Sir, are members of the

Governing body of the Nursery School Number Nine. This
Nursery School, which is an establishment of such great social
importance, has no resources of its own but is wholly
dependent upon charitable donations.

ZHIVOTA: I would ask you, please, to explain just what this is all
about; I have not clearly understood you so far.

PROTICH: Mrs Spasoyevich, kindly allow me to explain it to the
gentleman.

SPASOYEVICH: Very well, please continue.

PROTICH: We, dear Sir, are members of the Governing Body of
the Nursery School Number Nine ...

SPASOYEVICH *(continuing)*: ... This Nursery School, which is
an establishment of such great social importance ...

PROTICH *(continuing)*: ... has no resources of its own ...

SPASOYEVICH *(continuing)*: ... but is wholly dependent upon
charitable donations.

PROTICH: Yes, wholly dependent upon charitable donations.

ZHIVOTA: Well then, this is about charitable donations.

PROTICH: You are a gentleman of generous nature ...

SPASOYEVICH: ... who would understand the importance of
such an establishment.

ZHIVOTA: Oh yes, I understand but, you know, it's difficult to
cope with all these requests for charitable donations. Some
want donations for day-nurseries, others for overnight refuges.
Some want donations for fallen women and others for women
who haven't fallen yet. One really doesn't know how to decide
between them.

PROTICH and SPASOYEVICH *(in unison)*: Yes indeed, but in this
case we are concerned with an establishment which has, in its
many years of existence, produced such excellent results. It has
taken care of poor children, given comfort to worried parents,
relieved the strain on so many mothers ...

ZHIVOTA: Yes, yes. I quite understand. I'm not defending myself:
I will do what I can. Don't expect too much, but I'll go as far
as I am able. Only, to tell the truth, I think that this business

of collecting charitable donations may not be enough for you. There are ways of obtaining somewhat more substantial benefits. Wouldn't it be a good idea, for instance, if you were to ask one of our distinguished philosophers to give a public lecture?

PROTICH: Why certainly! That would be marvellous!

SPASOYEVICH: But it would be very difficult to find anyone who would be willing.

ZHIVOTA I know it would be difficult, but in such a worthy cause … It just so happens that my son is a Doctor of Philosophy. Look at that framed diploma on the wall – it's his diploma. You can see how important it is: it's written in Latin. I'm not saying it just because he's my son, but the fact is he's a first-rate philosopher. He hardly sleeps at night for philosophising. I don't know if you've read his recent article on Dynamics? That article caused a sensation. Dr Radosavlyevich, the eminent University Professor, could hardly contain his excitement over it. And it's not only him who is amazed – everyone else is, too. Scholars, scientists, universities, faculties, deans of colleges, rectors – all are astonished by its brilliance!

PROTICH and SPASOYEVICH *(in unison)*: Oh, do you think he might consent?

ZHIVOTA: I think he will. Why not, for such a worthy cause? But it goes without saying that, if you approach him, you must be sure not to mention that I gave you the idea.

PROTICH: Of course, of course.

SPASOYEVICH: Is the young gentleman in?

ZHIVOTA: Yes, he is.

PROTICH: Well, couldn't we speak to him now?

ZHIVOTA: I'm afraid not. He's completely exhausted. He so exhausted himself by working all last night that he hasn't raised his head yet. He's writing a huge new work – again, something to do with Dynamics – and when he's working nobody dares to disturb him. If you were to disturb him now he'd be likely to throw things at you – shoes, candlesticks, ashtrays, slippers, or anything else that came to hand. Well, that's philosophers for you – odd characters!

PROTICH: Very well. But how to you suggest that we should approach him?

ZHIVOTA: Write a letter to him, on behalf of your estblishment, asking him to give a public lecture.

PROTICH and SPASOYEVICH *(in unison)*: Oh yes, certainly!

ZHIVOTA: And so far as I am concerned *(he reaches into the safe)* please accept, for now, this donation of a hundred dinars. Perhaps when times are better…

PROTICH and SPASOYEVICH: Bless you! We are very grateful.

ZHIVOTA: There's no need to thank me. I give you that from the heart and I seek no thanks. You might just put a small mention of it in the newspapers – not for my sake, you understand, but as an example to others.

PROTICH and SPASOYEVICH: Of course! *(they both stand up)*.

PROTICH: Well then, you advise us to write to your son?

ZHIVOTA: Yes, and as soon as possible.

SPASOYEVICH: We shall do it today.

ZHIVOTA: Yes – today!

PROTICH and SPASOYEVICH: Bless you, Sir! We are most grateful. Good bye! *(Exeunt)*.

ZHIVOTA *(accompanying them to the door)*: Good bye, ladies. This lecture will be a real sensation, you'll see. Good bye!

SCENE 9

ZHIVOTA *(returns, rubbing his hands like a man who is pleased with what he has done. He picks up the internal telephone)*: Hullo! Is that Nikolich? What? What? Well, has Deutsch got back from the Exchange yet? What? It's not possible? We're heavily overdrawn there? Yes, that could be the case but … Right! What does Deutsch say about such a sudden fall in government stocks? Yes, yes, all right, I'll come downstairs directly. *(He puts down the telephone and goes to the door, left)* Slavka! Oh, Slavka dear! *(To someone outside the door)* I'm not calling for you. Where's Slavka? Ask her to come here straightaway, please. *(He returns to his desk, closes the safe door, and locks it).*

SCENE 10

(Enter SLAVKA)

SLAVKA: Did you call me, father?

ZHIVOTA: Yes, my dear, I did. I'm sorry, I'm tied to this telephone. I'm waiting for some information from my agent in Budapest. I told him to contact me on my private telephone because I don't want the staff downstairs to hear what he says. At the same time, I've got to go downstairs to sort something out. Be an angel - wait here by the telephone and call me when they ring from Budapest, would you? Is that all right?

SLAVKA: Yes, all right, but I'd like to get a book to read.

ZHIVOTA: Go and get it, then. *(He kisses her)* You are quite my favourite secretary. *(Exit).*

SCENE 11

(SLAVKA goes out of the door, left, and at the same time VELIMIR enters, standing in the doorway)

SLAVKA *(Enters with a book in her hand. She is startled to see VELIMIR)*: Oh!

VELIMIR: Good morning!

SLAVKA: What are you doing here?

VELIMIR: Your father sent for me.

SLAVKA: I thought he must have. Otherwise, it seems as if you'd given up visiting us – you're almost a stranger.

VELIMIR: I accept the rebuke. I admit, I have no excuse.

SLAVKA: How can you excuse such indifference and neglect?

VELIMIR: Not that!

SLAVKA: Once, when you were my brother's schoolfriend, you were always coming round to our house and you and I had a lot of good times together. I'd have thought that such happy memories would have encouraged you come and see us again.

VELIMIR: Believe me, they were the happiest of memories.

SLAVKA: Do you know, I've still got one of your love-letters – one which you wrote to me when I was in the third form, and you were in the sixth?

VELIMIR: Oh, you haven't kept it, have you? Throw it away! – I was always ashamed of it.

SLAVKA: What! Oh, now I understand your indifference. You're ashamed of being in love with me!

VELIMIR: No! That's not fair! I'm just ashamed of all the grammatical mistakes I made in it.

SLAVKA: Love takes no notice of grammatical mistakes. On the contrary – the greater the love, the more the mistakes in grammar! Anyway, if that's all you're bothered about, I can give you the letter back so that you can correct the mistakes.

VELIMIR: All right!

SYVIA: On the other hand, I would have no objection if you wished to correct the feelings which you expressed in that letter.

VELIMIR: Why should I?

SLAVKA: Because you have in fact already corrected them. You have so distanced yourself from us, you have shown yourself to be so indifferent to us all …

VELIMIR: Oh no! No! That's not true, however it may seem to you.

SLAVKA: You've stopped seeing my brother.

VELIMIR: It's just that he's found himself some new friends who don't approve of me.

SLAVKA: And you've stopped seeing me.

VELIMIR: If only you knew how much I've longed to renew our friendship!

SLAVKA: Well, what's been holding you back?

VELIMIR: Life. Circumstances. You can't always have what you want in life.

SLAVKA: I don't understand.

VELIMIR: I admit I don't seem to be making much sense, but

I don't know how to make it more clear.

SLAVKA: The way I see it, you don't want to be honest with me.

VELIMIR: Surely you don't doubt my sincerity?

SLAVKA: I do, and I have reason to. Something's been going on in this house that's been kept from me, but I can feel that there's something which is not right. There's been whispering behind closed doors and odd conversations which seem to concern you. And my father often invites you here, doesn't he.

VELIMIR: Yes, but there's nothing secret about that. Your father often gets letters in German or French which he doesn't want to pass to the staff downstairs until he knows what's in them.

SLAVKA: And you translate them for him?

VELIMIR: He's done a lot for me, as you know, and I feel under an obligation to him.

SLAVKA *(unconvinced)*: That's as maybe, but I still don't think you're being honest with me.

SCENE 12

ZHIVOTA *(Enters)*: Ah, you're here.

VELIMIR: You sent for me.

ZHIVOTA: Yes, that's right. *(To SLAVKA)* Any telephone calls?

SLAVKA: No.

ZHIVOTA *(kisses her)*: Have you been reading?

SLAVKA: No. Mr Pavlovich has been entertaining me, though he's been rather dull today.

ZHIVOTA: Good, good. And now, my dear, would you please leave us? I've got some confidential matters to discuss with Velimir.

SLAVKA: Oh, yes, of course you have. Good bye, then. *(Exit)*.

SCENE 13

ZHIVOTA *(once Slavka has gone)*: Now, what's all this about?

VELIMIR: What?

ZHIVOTA: This. *(He hands VELIMIR the telegram)*.

VELIMIR *(glances at it)*: Oh, it's from Professor Reisser.

ZHIVOTA: And who the devil's he?

VELIMIR: Professor Reisser? He's a very eminent professor at the University of Fribourg. A great orientalist: he knows all the eastern languages, Hebrew, Arabic, Coptic, and Ancient Greek. Of the Slavonic languages he speaks ours and Czech. People come from universities all over the world to hear his lectures. He's a member of many scientific institutions and the author of some monumental academic works. I wasn't personally one of his students, but I went to a lot of his lectures and, as he was at that time studying Slavonic languages, I became friendly with him.

ZHIVOTA: Stop, for God's sake! I wasn't asking you about all that. What I want to know is – why has he sent this telegram to my son?

VELIMIR *(glances at the address)*: Well, how else could he have got in touch with me?

ZHIVOTA: What d'you mean? If you got so friendly with him, why couldn't he have sent a telegram to you?

VELIMIR: But Mr Zhivota, sir, why are you so surprised? You know perfectly well that I was using your son's name while I was studying in Fribourg, so Professor Reisser could only know me by that name.

ZHIVOTA *(sees the point)*: Yes, of course, you're right! I'd completely overlooked that. Very well: so be it! The problem is, your 'monumental' professor says that he wants to come here.

VELIMIR: Yes, he often mentioned to me that if he ever went to Athens he would drop in on us for a day or two on the way.

ZHIVOTA: What d'you mean 'on us'? What's it got to do with 'us'? You, perhaps, not 'us'.

VELIMIR: Yes, of course, he's coming to see me, but he'll expect to see you, too.

ZHIVOTA: Why me?

VELIMIR: Because he thinks I'm your son. I'll simply have to go on pretending that I am.

ZHIVOTA: Right then – when he comes you simply look after him yourself.

VELIMIR: I'm quite prepared to, but what's going to happen if he wants to visit my home and meet my family? I used to tell him a lot about you, and how much you loved me.

ZHIVOTA: Why the devil did you tell him stories like that?

VELIMIR: I had to. He was very kind to me. He often invited me to his house and gave me lunch or dinner.

ZHIVOTA: D'you mean to say that I've got to invite him back, for God's sake!

VELIMIR: That would be very nice.

ZHIVOTA: Then I'd have to pretend to be your father! Oh Lord, that's all I needed! Now, my lad, see what a fine mess you've got me into!

VELIMIR: Yes, I quite see that I've put you in an awkward situation, and I wish it hadn't happened, believe me. After all, one only gives these invitations for form's sake.

ZHIVOTA: Well, since you issued the invitation 'for form's sake', you can receive him yourself 'for form's sake'.

VELIMIR: I can understand why you're angry but, I do assure you, this only happened in the course of ordinary conversation. He told me how much he was looking forward to going to Athens and I simply said, to make conversation, that if that meant passing through Belgrade he should drop in and see us. I had to say something like that, out of politeness.

ZHIVOTA: Yes, yes! And now he's going to drop in on us, out of politeness.

VELIMIR: There's more, I'm afraid. It's obvious, out of politeness and out of consideration for you, that he will particularly ask to see you.

ZHIVOTA: Keep him away, for God's sake. I shan't reproach him for being inconsiderate.

VELIMIR: Apart from that, he knows that I'm the son of a wealthy father.

ZHIVOTA: Who's the son of a wealthy father?

VELIMIR: I am.

ZHIVOTA: You! Your father's the caretaker of a village primary school!

VELIMIR: Yes, but I don't mean my real father, I mean you.

ZHIVOTA: How does that affect me?

VELIMIR: Well, I'll have to spend some money on him. I'll probably have to take him out for ride in a car and give him lunch.

ZHIVOTA: Here we go again – more expense! I hope this professor of yours isn't in the habit of smashing mirrors?

VELIMIR: I'm very sorry to be putting you to trouble and expense, but what else can I do?

ZHIVOTA: You're very sorry to be putting me to expense, and I'm very sorry to be having to pay. I just can see what's going to happen. You invite him 'for form's sake' and I pay 'for form's sake'. But, my lad, suppose, on the other hand, I were to give you the opportunity to earn some money, then you could meet the expense of his visit yourself, couldn't you.

VELIMIR: Certainly! I'm willing.

ZHIVOTA: It just so happens that I've got to give a public lecture: you can write it for me.

VELIMIR: *You've* got to give one?

ZHIVOTA: Well, Milorad's got to. Some extremely well-connected ladies have asked him to give one.

VELIMIR: But why on earth did he agree?

ZHIVOTA: He didn't agree: I did. It goes without saying, I'm relying on you.

VELIMIR: Do you want it soon?

ZHIVOTA: I want it immediately.

VELIMIR: But I'm doing something else at the moment.

ZHIVOTA: Just finish it.

VELIMIR: Yes, I'll have to finish it because Reisser's coming tomorrow.

ZHIVOTA: We'll talk some more about it; we've got a bit of time. Just write that lecture.

VELIMIR: I will. Do you want anything else?

ZHIVOTA: No, that's all.

VELIMIR: Very well. Good morning, sir.

ZHIVOTA: Good morning to you. *(Exit* VELIMIR*)*.

SCENE 14

(Enter BLAGOYE, *passing* VELIMIR *in the doorway)*.

ZHIVOTA: Where the devil have you been? I've been waiting …

BLAGOYE: I can't help that. What's so important now? You're always loading me down with things to do – 'Uncle Blagoye, do this' and 'Uncle Blagoye, do that', and then, when I do them, you shout at me: "Where've you been?"

ZHIVOTA: Never mind all that – have you been?

BLAGOYE: Yes.

ZHIVOTA: Did you see him?

BLAGOYE: Yes, and I talked to him man-to-man, just as we're doing now.

ZHIVOTA: And?

BLAGOYE: Hold on. Let me tell you about it in proper order. He welcomed me at the University and sat me down in an easy chair in his office and, I must say, I felt quite at home in the academic environment …

ZHIVOTA: Never mind how you felt. What did you say?

BLAGOYE: Just what you asked me to. I started by saying: "My dear Professor, my relative, Zhivota Tsviyevich, is a wealthy man. God has blessed him with good fortune, but he is the sort of man who greatly respects both science and its representatives …"

ZHIVOTA: Exactly!

BLAGOYE: "… and for that reason he wishes to make some contribution to science. He has not yet decided who to give it to or how much it will be, but he has asked me to seek your advice, my dear Professor, since he has heard that you are always at the forefront of any new movement, and that you … "

ZHIVOTA: You're droning on as if you were giving an academic lecture. Get to the point. You didn't give him any promises, did you?

BLAGOYE: No, I didn't. He tried to draw me out, but I carefully held back. He said: "We have a students' dining hall in the University. Your relative might consider making a contribution towards the running of the dining hall."

ZHIVOTA: Just so!

BLAGOYE: And this is how I answered him, in scholarly fashion, you understand: "My dear Professor, a dining hall does not constitute a lasting memorial. If, for instance, my relative were to make a contribution to the purchase of crockery, crockery gets broken, and if it were used to buy groceries, the students would eat them. My relative does not wish his permanent memorial to be eaten."

ZHIVOTA: Quite right! Well said!

BLAGOYE: So after that we got round to talking generally about dining halls and the cost of groceries at the market.

ZHIVOTA: Oh, fine! I didn't send you there to discuss the price of groceries.

BLAGOYE: Wait! Hold on! I could see that this conversation was getting away from the point, so I turned it skilfully. The Professor was getting very heated about the price of tomatoes, and that gave me a brilliant idea. You see, I realised that tomatoes could be a useful lead-in to what I wanted to say. So I said to him: "Yes," I said, "I have to admit that the price of tomatoes is very high, but so also is the price of building-bricks. I happened to notice, my dear Professor, that you are building a house, and that the walls are up to roof-level, but that now you've stopped building." "Yes," he said, "I'm a bit short of money." "My goodness!" I said, "You're a Professor, and you're short of money? But there must be lots of people who appreciate you." "Maybe," he said, "But appreciation is one thing, money is another. Generally speaking, the more the appreciation, the less the money. So, with the appreciation included, I've only managed to build up to roof-level. Now I need a trivial ten or fifteen thousand-odd dinars to be able to continue."

ZHIVOTA: He said that, did he?

BLAGOYE: "Goodness me!" I said, "I'm sure that my relative, Mr Tsviyevich, would be able to accommodate you."

ZHIVOTA: Aha! And what did he say?

BLAGOYE: Wait! I went on: "My relative, Mr Tsviyevich, would probably be prepared to advance you such a sum as an interest-free loan."

ZHIVOTA: And he said?

BLAGOYE: He was astonished. He could hardly believe it. He said: "Why? How? I don't understand. I've never met Mr Tsviyevich: I don't know him. Why should he do that for me?" Well, now that things had got to this stage I saw that the time had come for me to put my cards on the table without more ado. I said: "My dear Professor, there are, in the Philosophical Faculty, two vacancies for assistant professors. Mr Tsviyevich has a son who is a Doctor of Philosophy, and so ...

ZHIVOTA: *(curiously)* What did he say?

BLAGOYE: Nothing. We didn't talk about it any more.

ZHIVOTA: What d'you mean, you didn't talk about it any more? Why not, for God's sake?

BLAGOYE: Because he threw me out of his office.

ZHIVOTA: He threw you out?

BLAGOYE: Yes. He said: "Sir, I am a University Professor, and I am not for sale."

ZHIVOTA: The idiot! But then, of course, if he wasn't an idiot he wouldn't have been a University Professor – he'd have followed some more intelligent occupation.

BLAGOYE: I must say, Zhivota, as I was coming down the steps of the university I thought to myself. I thought: "We have overreached ourselves this time, we have definitely gone too far." I tell you, that article is not for sale.

ZHIVOTA: Rubbish! Your brain must have gone as woolly as a professor's, just from sitting in that chair in the university for

a few minutes. What d'you mean – "he's not for sale"?
Tell me any article these days that is not for sale!

BLAGOYE: I don't know, but …

ZHIVOTA: No, you don't know: you certainly don't! Don't you
realise that nowadays everything and everybody can be
bought? Here, look! *(He reaches into the safe and brings out a
sheaf of papers)*. Look at this! *(He passes one sheet to* BLAGOYE*)*
D'you see what it is?

BLAGOYE: It's a receipt for ten thousand dinarss.

ZHIVOTA: That's right. I paid that sum for a conscience.

BLAGOYE: A conscience?

ZHIVOTA: Yes. Do you think I paid too much?

BLAGOYE: I don't know, I've never bought one.

ZHIVOTA: Well, I did pay too much! A conscience, my dear
brother, is not an article to be traded and which follows market
prices. On the market things have a value which can be
ascertained. Nobody seeks to have a conscience these days and
it therefore has no market value.

BLAGOYE: Well, when one looks at it like that …

ZHIVOTA *(shows him another sheet)*: Now look at this one – six
thousand dinars for some purchased integrity.

BLAGOYE: That's worth something, surely.

ZHIVOTA: Is it? And you, a man who possesses vast integrity,
think you know how much it's worth. I'll tell you – it's
valueless, my friend, it's worth nothing at all. Do you know
what integrity is? It's goods in a shop which are remaindered
because they're no longer fashionable, and are sold off below
cost price just to get rid of them.

BLAGOYE: No more!

ZHIVOTA: And look at this. *(shows him another sheet)* A woman's
honour – three thousand seven hundred dinars, including the
lawyer's fee.

BLAGOYE: My word! What have you been up to, then, at your age?

ZHIVOTA: Not me, you fool! That Doctor of Philosophy son
of mine.

BLAGOYE: Then I suppose one could say that you hadn't paid too much?

ZHIVOTA: Well, it was rather expensive in terms of today's prices. Nowadays, a woman's honour is worth about as much as goods that are sold off in the sales and in second-hand shops for whatever anyone will pay for them.

BLAGOYE: Are all those receipts for the same sort of thing?

ZHIVOTA: Yes, all of them – the lot. The fact is, my dear brother, that these days everything is for sale and everything is bought and sold. Everything! – honour, virtue, integrity, love, friendship, reputation, respect – everything! And that ass in the University has got it into his head that he can't be bought! Doesn't he realise that these days *that (he points at the safe)* is the University, not his ancient pile of bricks?

BLAGOYE: You're probably right.

ZHIVOTA: I can deal with him easily enough and, anyway, he's not the only professor in the university. Enough of that! What about that other matter? Have you found out anything?

BLAGOYE: Yes, I have.

ZHIVOTA *(interested)*: Well?

BLAGOYE: The Minister of Transport has a marriageable daughter.

ZHIVOTA *(disgusted)*: The Minister of Transport? What use is he to me?

BLAGOYE: What do you mean, 'what use'? You know that there is a project to build a Trans-Balkan Railway.

ZHIVOTA: What's that?

BLAGOYE: Don't you know? It's a new railway. You've probably heard of the Trans-Siberian railway, and you've heard of Trans-Atlantic traffic, and you've probably heard of Transylvania and the Transvaal. Whenever you hear the word 'Trans' you can be sure there's money to be made!

ZHIVOTA: And is this particular 'Trans' a big job?

BLAGOYE: Very big.

ZHIVOTA: And the Minister of Transport has a daughter, you say?

BLAGOYE: Yes, he has. I happen to know a Mrs Draga – she's a distant relative of my late wife – and this Mrs Draga visits the Minister's house, and …

ZHIVOTA: Have you spoken to her?

BLAGOYE: Yes, I have, but sort of obliquely, you know. I asked her to go there and scout out the situation. I told her all about Milorad, and painted a very rosy picture of him. By the way, Zhivota, it would be a good thing if Milorad's name were to be publicised a bit, so that more people had heard of him.

ZHIVOTA: Certainly. I know that, and I'm not sitting here twiddling my thumbs. Write down what I'm going to say and see to it that it comes out as a Notice in all the newspapers. If you can persuade them to include a picture of him, so much the better. I'll pay their charges. *(BLAGOYE picks up a pencil and notepad from the desk and ZHIVOTA dictates to him)* : "At the invitation of some of the most distinguished ladies in the City, members of a prestigious Organisation, the young scientist Dr Milorad Tsviyevich will shortly be delivering a Public Lecture concerning .. " .. er .. er. Well, come on! Concerning what?

BLAGOYE: … concerning General Philosophy?

ZHIVOTA: Fine! Write: " concerning General Philosophy." Hold on, that's not enough. *(Dictates)* : "Out of consideration for his young former pupil, the eminent world-renowned scientist Professor Reisser will be coming specially from Fribourg to attend the lecture." *(He hands the telegram to BLAGOYE)* Look, have you spelled his name right?

BLAGOYE: Yes, that's right – Professor Reisser.

ZHIVOTA: Good for you! – at least you can read and write German.

BLAGOYE: I remember it from school.

ZHIVOTA: If you'd got it just from school you wouldn't have been able to string two words together! Let's be thankful that before the War you spent that time as a waiter in an Austrian restaurant and learned German from reading the menus.

BLAGOYE: Well, anyway, I can speak German, however I learned it.

SCENE 15

(Enter Maritsa, *carrying two letters, one of which she gives to* Zhivota*)*.

Zhivota *(opening the letter)*: Who's the other one for?

Maritsa: For Mr Milorad.

Zhivota: Very well, take it to him.

Maritsa: Oh, sir! If Mr Milorad's asleep I daren't.

Zhivota: All right, leave it here and I'll give it to him.

Maritsa: Thank you, sir! *(She leaves the letter on the desk and Exit)*

SCENE 16

Zhivota *(after he has read his letter)*: Good! The ladies tell me that they have written to my son asking him to give the lecture. That other letter must be the one. *(He picks up the other letter and looks at the envelope)* No, it's not. The handwriting's foreign, and so's the stamp. It must be from abroad.

Blagoye: It's probably from that Professor Reisser.

Zhivota: Yes, probably. Can you make out the postmark, so that we can see where it's from?

Blagoye *(examines it closely)*: Fer . . Far . . Fri . . Fribourg!

Zhivota: That's it, then. We can open it *(he opens the letter)*.

Blagoye: What about Milorad?

Zhivota: This has nothing to do with him. *(He passes the letter to* Blagoye*)*. Right then, now let's see how much German you know.

Blagoye *(reading)*: "Mein lieber Milorad … " *(To* Zhivota*)* That means …

Zhivota: Get on with it! I know that much German myself. What does he say?

*(*Blagoye *reads the letter through and then turns his head away)*

Zhivota: What's the matter?

Blagoye: This letter is not from the Professor. It finishes: "Ewig deine Klara".

Zhivota: You must have got it wrong. Read it more carefully. It's probably 'Karl' or something, and you've read it as 'Klara'.

BLAGOYE *(looks closely at the signature)*: No, it's 'Klara', all right. It's clearly written 'Klara'.

ZHIVOTA: Klara, Klara? But that's a woman's name.

BLAGOYE: I'd say so.

ZHIVOTA: Couldn't it be Mrs Reisser?

BLAGOYE: What d'you mean?

ZHIVOTA: Professor Reisser's wife. It must be from her. Go on, what does she say?

(BLAGOYE reads the letter with a look of amazement, and again turns his head away).

ZHIVOTA: What's up now?

BLAGOYE: I just don't know how to put it.

ZHIVOTA: For goodness' sake, get on with it! Tell me what the letter says.

BLAGOYE: This letter is from his wife.

ZHIVOTA: Whose wife?

BLAGOYE: Your son's wife.

ZHIVOTA: Have you gone mad? Are you drunk? What d'you mean 'my son's wife'? Do you know what you're saying?

BLAGOYE: It's not what I say, it's what the letter says.

ZHIVOTA: You must have got it wrong. Are you sure you understand German that well?

BLAGOYE: Certainly I understand it. She writes perfectly clearly *(reads)*: "Mein lieber Milorad, I have to give you the sad news that my dear mother has passed away and that I and the child are left alone."

ZHIVOTA: What! How does a child come into it?

BLAGOYE: Her child, presumably.

ZHIVOTA: Her child, eh? So why's she dragging my son into it!

BLAGOYE *(looks at the envelope)*: Yes, her child – and she's addressed the letter to your son.

ZHIVOTA: Why him? *(He remembers something and suddenly starts)* Yes, of course! Of course! Now I see it all – it's that Velimir who's been messing around. It's him, by God! What else does she say?

BLAGOYE *(reads)*: " … so I have decided to come to you …"

ZHIVOTA: Who's decided to come?

BLAGOYE: Why, this Klara, of course.

ZHIVOTA: Klara?

BLAGOYE: Yes.

ZHIVOTA: Well who is she? "I have decided to come to you" – those aren't the words of a married woman – they're what you'd expect from someone who's had a child by mistake.

BLAGOYE: But she is married.

ZHIVOTA: Who says so?

BLAGOYE: She does. She says *(reads)* : "Since I am married to you I have become a Yugoslav citizen. The Yugoslav Consulate in Berlin has confirmed this and has issued me with all the necessary travel documents. I've sold all the furniture, so I have enough for the fare."

ZHIVOTA: My God! To think he'd be capable of such recklessness! The fellow's a pauper – he couldn't afford to keep a dog! I only sent him to Fribourg so that he could attend college – at my expense, mind! – and he goes and gets married and fathers a child! And if one asks how the devil he's going to maintain a wife and child when they turn up on his doorstep, what's the answer? – there isn't one!

BLAGOYE: Who are you talking about?

ZHIVOTA: Him, of course – that Velimir.

BLAGOYE: But she's not Velimir's wife.

ZHIVOTA: Well, whose wife is she?

BLAGOYE: She's your son's wife.

ZHIVOTA: Don't be ridiculous! Brother, have you got so senile that you don't know what you're saying?

BLAGOYE: I am saying it as it is.

ZHIVOTA: How on earth can anyone understand you when you've got everything upside-down and back-to-front? It was *Velimir* who went to Fribourg. *He* stayed there for four years, *he* got married, *he* fathered a child, so how can you say that this woman is my son's wife.

BLAGOYE: Yes, I know it was Velimir who did all those things, but he went to Fribourg under your son's name, he studied at the University under your son's name, he graduated under your son's name and, evidently, he got married under your son's name – he couldn't have done it any other way.

ZHIVOTA: How d'you know?

BLAGOYE: Because it's his wife who calls him 'Liebe Milorad', and it's his wife who's sent this letter to him by name …

ZHIVOTA: But wait a minute – that can't be right. Do you mean to say that any Tom, Dick, or Harry could take my name, get married, father a child, and then one day turn up here and say to me: "Excuse me, Mr Tsviyevich, this is your wife and this is your child!" Such a thing couldn't happen, could it?

BLAGOYE: It could, if you had allowed him to go under your name, if you had lent him your passport, and if you had given him money to live on.

ZHIVOTA: *You* wheedled me into this: it's all your fault! It was *you* who said: "My dear brother-in-law, why should your son go to all the trouble of trying to get a qualification when he hasn't a hope in hell of passing the exams. Instead, why don't you send that clever friend of his to the University, the one without a penny to his name. He can use your son's name," you said, "and he can get the degree in your son's name."

BLAGOYE: Yes, I admit that it was my idea. But it was your wish that your son should somehow get the title of 'Doctor' in front of his name – and now he's got it. I concede that I thought of it, because when I was in the Police Force …

ZHIVOTA: That was totally different. In the Police Force you could arrange for people to vote in the elections under a false name, but you certainly couldn't arrange for them to get married under a false name. Voting under a false name is one thing – it's no more than a mere trifle – but this is a child, not a trifle. You're not saying that a child is a trifling thing, are you?

BLAGOYE: No, you're right. But the main point now is that this Clara is certainly your son's wife.

ZHIVOTA *(agitated)*: And the child?

BLAGOYE: He also has your son's surname.

ZHIVOTA *(confused)*: But how? ... Wait a minute ... But that means ... Oh, no! That's impossible! If what you say is right it means that my son is actually married.

BLAGOYE: Yes, of course he is!

ZHIVOTA: And the child is his?

BLAGOYE: It's not anybody else's.

ZHIVOTA: You're either drunk or crazy! You're talking complete gibberish! How can it possibly be my son's child, when he's never in his life met its mother or even set eyes on her? It was that other young idiot, and I sent him to get a *degree*, not a wife and child.

BLAGOYE: Maybe, but that's what's happened.

ZHIVOTA: If it's happened, its happened to *him*. I won't listen to another word, d'you hear? Not another word!

BLAGOYE: It would be better like that, I agree, but I'm afraid it won't do.

ZHIVOTA: I shall prosecute him! I shall get him sent to prison! How could he have dared to get married in my son's name?

BLAGOYE: You can prosecute him if you want to but I can assure you that the Court will send both of them to prison.

ZHIVOTA: What, him and his wife? That's fine!

BLAGOYE: Not him and his wife – him and your son.

ZHIVOTA *(leaps to his feet and bangs the table with his fist)*: Not another word! Shut up! – or I'll smack your head!

BLAGOYE: All right, I'll shut up.

ZHIVOTA *(thoroughly upset, he paces up and down and suddenly stops)*: Well, what have you got to say?

BLAGOYE: Nothing. You told me to shut up.

ZHIVOTA: I told you to stop talking drivel. You can talk if you've got something sensible to say. *(He paces up and down again, and stops)* Right, then! What d'you mean – why would they send my son to prison?

BLAGOYE: Because, my dear brother-in-law, he was an

accomplice in the crime of falsely obtaining that degree: that's what that bogus Doctorate does for him. Think about it. If you prosecute Velimir he'll certainly tell the Court exactly why he went and lived under your son's name and why he got married under that false name.

ZHIVOTA: You mean ... he can fill my house up with spare children, and I can't do anything about it?

BLAGOYE: I'm afraid your hands are tied.

ZHIVOTA: God Almighty! Oh, good God Almighty! *(In despair, he sits down and buries his face in his hands on the table. Then he looks up at the diploma on the wall. He sighs deeply)* Very well. What now?

BLAGOYE: I think the best thing is for us to go over what we know, so that we can think about it rationally.

ZHIVOTA: Right! Go on!

BLAGOYE: This Klara is in fact Velimir's wife, isn't she?

ZHIVOTA: Yes.

BLAGOYE: And she is also your son's wife, isn't she?

ZHIVOTA: There you go again! First she's Velimir's wife, then she's Milorad's wife. Whose wife is she, for God's sake?

BLAGOYE: Well, legally she your son's wife.

ZHIVOTA: I refuse to accept that.

BLAGOYE: That's up to you.

ZHIVOTA: That safe is mightier than the law!

BLAGOYE: You're probably right. The problem is, who are you going to pay? Who can you bribe? The woman? – what's money to her, when she's your daughter-in-law, the wife of your son and heir? And if you pay off Velimir, what would he do? He'd either abandon her – and if he did, it could be even worse for you – or he'd stay with her. But how could he live with her, when she's legally married to your son? He can't live with somebody else's wife. And if you were to give money to your son ...

ZHIVOTA: No chance – I'm not completely mad! He'd simply take it and spend the lot.

BLAGOYE *(thinks)*: How would it be if she were to pretend to be your son's wife in the eyes of the world, but actually be Velimir's in secret?

ZHIVOTA: I thought you were an intelligent man. D'you think that my son would for one moment agree to that? He'd want it the other way round!

BLAGOYE: Yes, I suppose so.

ZHIVOTA: And even if he did agree to such an arrangement, I would not. I've no intention of letting my son even appear to be married – I won't have it! Besides, if that happened I'd be a grandfather. I'm nobody's grandfather, I can assure you!

BLAGOYE: I'm afraid you are. She says so in the letter. Here – *(reads from the letter)* : "Pepika can hardly wait to kiss Grandpa and Grandma."

ZHIVOTA: Who does he want to kiss?

BLAGOYE: You – you're 'Grandpa'.

ZHIVOTA *(hysterically)*: What!

BLAGOYE: You're 'Grandpa', and Mara's 'Grandma'.

ZHIVOTA: What's the brat called?

BLAGOYE: Pepika.

ZHIVOTA *(shouting)*: Pepika! Pepika! For God's sake, what sort of a name is 'Pepika'? *(He rushes about the room, as if out of his mind; he overturns his chair; he picks up things and throws them about; he bangs his fist on the table and rolls his eyes)* Whatever you want, I won't give it to you! I won't! I'm going to kill you! I'm going to kill you all, every one of you!

BLAGOYE: Zhivota! For God's sake, calm yourself!

ZHIVOTA *(Picks up the chair and makes to hit Blagoye with it)* Damn you! I hate you! It's all your fault. I'm going to kill you first!

BLAGOYE *(Runs to the door, left, and shouts for help)* Mara! Children! Mara! Children! Come quickly! Come quickly!

SCENE 17

(Enter, running, MARA, SLAVKA, MILORAD, and MARITSA)

ALL: What is it?

MARA: What's the matter?

BLAGOYE: He's gone mad!

(ZHIVOTA drops the chair and looks, resignedly, at the family)

SLAVKA: What's wrong?

MARA: Zhivota!

ZHIVOTA: I'm not Zhivota, I'm 'Grandpa!'

MARA *(looks, bewildered, at the others)*: What are you talking about?

ZHIVOTA: That's what I said. And you're 'Grandma!'

SLAVKA *(looking fearfully at MILORAD)*: Milorad, father's not well!

MILORAD: Father, pull yourself together!

ZHIVOTA *(to MILORAD)*: 'Pull myself together,' you say! What about Pepika?

MILORAD *(astonished, as are all the others)*: Pepika? Who's Pepika?

ZHIVOTA: You ask me that? *Your* Pepika! Your Pepika, who's swallowed up the whole Trans-Balkan Railway!

MARA *(quietly, to BLAGOYE)*: Hadn't we better send for the doctor?

BLAGOYE: No need. *(To ZHIVOTA)* Calm down, for goodness' sake!

ZHIVOTA: Me – calm down? What about the university, and the daughter of the Minister of Transport, and the Transvaal, and all the rest of my plans! And who's brought them all to ruin? – this damned Pepika! Oh! Oh!

MARA *(frightened, she leads ZHIVOTA to a chair)*: There, there! Calm yourself, my dear. You'll be all right soon.

ZHIVOTA *(collapses on the chair, sighing deeply and pulling his hair)*: Pepika! Wretched, wretched Pepika! *(Concerned, they all gather round him)*.

Curtain

Act Two

A living room in Tsviyovich's house. [Doors left, right, and rear].

SCENE 1

SLAVKA *is writing a letter at a small table.*

VELIMIR: *(**Enters** and stops when he sees* SLAVKA*)* I'm sorry! Am I disturbing you?

SLAVKA *(gathering up her writing materials)*: No, not at all.

VELIMIR: I interrupted what you were doing.

SLAVKA: Actually, I was just writing to you.

VELIMIR: To me?

SLAVKA: Yes, to you. I haven't been able to see you for three days now, even though you've been to the house several times. I very much want to hear from you whatever it is that nobody else will tell me.

VELIMIR: What?

SLAVKA: For the last three days the house has been in a state of complete turmoil. You've been sent for at least twice a day, and everyone's talking in whispers behind closed doors. They're hiding something from me and I want to know what it is.

VELIMIR: But why do you want to get yourself involved?

SLAVKA: Because I've got to know! Three days ago my father got into such a furious rage that I became seriously worried for him. He spent the whole day tramping about the house, roaring and shouting the same word – "Pepika!" – over and over again. Mother said that he was repeating it all night, in his sleep. What does "Pepika" mean? Is it someone's name? Why does it upset my father so much?

VELIMIR *(embarrassed)*: I . . I don't know.

SLAVKA: You must know. You're all tied in with this somehow: it's got something to do with you. Tell me, for God's sake! I can't go on like this. *(*VELIMIR hangs his head, *but says nothing).* On the other hand if, in all these goings-on, you've been doing something that I would think shameful – something that would make me think badly of you – then perhaps it would be better if you didn't tell me. I'd rather not know.

VELIMIR: Do you care enough to want to think well of me?

SLAVKA: Yes, actually, I do.

VELIMIR: Oh, that's wonderful! The trouble is, though, it puts me in a very difficult position. If you're to think well of me I'll just have to tell you what's going on, even though I solemnly promised your father, on my word of honour, that I'd never tell anyone.

SLAVKA: Well, if you're bound by your word of honour …

VELIMIR: I'm anxious to keep my word, but at the same time I treasure your regard for me and because of that I'm just as anxious that you shouldn't think badly of me. Listen, then, and I'll tell you what it's all about.

SLAVKA: Go on.

VELIMIR: You know that I lived abroad for nearly five years, studying at university, and that your father supported me all that time?

SLAVKA: Yes, I know.

VELIMIR: But what you don't know is that all the time I was there, at Fribourg in Switzerland, I was living and attending the university under your brother's name.

SLAVKA *(astonished)*: But why?

VELIMIR: Your father was determined that his son should, by hook or by crook, get the degree of Doctor of Philosophy.

SLAVKA *(amazed)*: Then … that diploma … ?

VELIMIR: That diploma has your brother's name on it, but the fact is he's never been anywhere near Fribourg.

SLAVKA: But … where was he all that time?

VELIMIR: Him? He spent the time living it up all over the
Continent. As long as he stayed abroad, it didn't really matter
where he was.

SLAVKA: So it was you who passed all the exams – not him.

VELIMIR: Yes, that's right.

SLAVKA: My God! My God! That's shocking, shocking! So that's
why everyone was talking in whispers – that's what they were
keeping from me. But why did you agree to do it?

VELIMIR *(shrugs his shoulders)*: I'm ashamed of it now. I see now
that it was a stupid and dishonest thing to do, but at the time
I could only see one side of the arrangement. I longed,
desperately, to learn and study at a foreign university – to sit at
the feet of world-famous professors – but it was an impossible
dream, because I was so poor. So when I was offered the
chance of making my dream come true I couldn't resist it.
I accepted rashly, without thinking twice.

SLAVKA: Without thinking twice, certainly. After all, what was the
use of all that studying when, at the end of it, you were left with
no degree, no diploma, nothing?

VELIMIR: That's the least of my problems. I never had the
slightest interest in getting one of those scraps of paper. Plenty
of ignorant fools have got diplomas – a truly educated man
doesn't need one.

SLAVKA: That's all very well, but you can't get on in life
without one.

VELIMIR: It may prevent me from getting a good job, but nothing
can prevent me from pursuing the path of learning.

SLAVKA: That may be some consolation, but it's no excuse for the
mess you've got yourself into.

VELIMIR: If that were all, I could happily bear your rebuke, but
I'm afraid that, rashly, I went even further.

SLAVKA: Even further? Don't tell me – I don't think I want to hear.

VELIMIR: My dear Slavka, at the moment I feel that I just have to
confess all. *(Pause)* In Fribourg I lived with a family that let out
rooms for single students. My landlady was the widow of some

low-paid official in the Post Office, and she had a daughter who was also a student at the university.

SLAVKA *(a little anxiously)*: Was she pretty?

VELIMIR: In the circumstances, that's rather beside the point. We often went to and from the university together; we were often in each other's company – we'd go together to museums and libraries, or just on outings. Simply out of curiosity she started to learn our language, and she got on very well with it. Within two or three years she was quite able to hold an ordinary conversation, and she continued to improve.

SLAVKA *(with increasing anxiety)*: So, she was studying for …

VELIMIR: I think it might be best if I didn't tell you the rest.

SLAVKA: Tell me! Tell me everything!

VELIMIR *(turning aside in confusion)*: At one of our meetings, in a moment of utter madness ..

SLAVKA *(tensely)*: Go on! Go on!

VELIMIR: I can't say it. Afterwards, repentance was no use: I felt like a criminal. I couldn't bear the thought of having acted dishonourably, and so that day I proposed to her.

SLAVKA *(stunned)*: You … you …

VELIMIR: And we got married.

(SLAVKA, overcome, bursts into tears, covering her face with her hands)

VELIMIR *(startled and concerned)*: But Slavka, my dear, I don't understand …

SLAVKA *(She pulls herself together and tries to conceal her distress, but does not have the courage to look Velimir in the face)*: I beg your pardon. It was just a turn, a slight turn. I get them sometimes. It's nothing. Let's go on talking.

VELIMIR: That's all that I had to tell you.

SLAVKA *(confused)*: Yes, of course, but … I suppose I'd better not ask …

VELIMIR: Please do ask.

SLAVKA *(even more confused)*: So this was a marriage for love, and you …

VELIMIR: She is pretty, yes. And, more than that, she is a very nice young woman. If it hadn't been for my disenchantment, I could very well have fallen in love with her.

SLAVKA: What disenchantment?

VELIMIR: It didn't take me very long to realise that what had seemed to me to be a natural flow of events was in fact a premeditated plot by her and her mother. Perhaps it is unfair to blame the girl herself, but it's clear that her mother, as soon as she realised that my father was a rich man, set about throwing me and her daughter constantly together – it was a calculated plan. It's possible that how it actually turned out was not exactly as she planned it, but she had arranged things to go in that direction all along.

SLAVKA: I don't know whether to feel sorry for you, but ...

VELIMIR: And, yes, we had a child.

SLAVKA: That's Pepika, I suppose?

VELIMIR: Yes, that is Pepika.

SLAVKA: Even so, I don't see why all this should have upset my father so much.

VELIMIR: Don't you? Well, my wife, whose name is Klara, wrote a letter saying that she and the child were coming here.

SLAVKA: And so?

VELIMIR: But she is not in fact my wife.

SLAVKA: What d'you mean?

VELIMIR: Legally, she's your brother's wife.

SLAVKA: How on earth can that be?

VELIMIR: When I married her I had to do it under the name that I was using while I was there.

SLAVKA: Of course! Of course! Now I see it all!

VELIMIR: And that's what has put your father into such a rage.

SLAVKA: I'm not surprised! He had very different plans for my brother.

VELIMIR: As you can imagine, he is absolutely furious with me – and I owe him so much.

SLAVKA: Yes, it's obviously a dreadful situation. Well, anyway, have you thought how things could be put right?

VELIMIR: That's what we've all been racking our brains about for three days.

SLAVKA: Oh, my word! Now I can understand just how worried my father must be.

VELIMIR: Yes, and I sympathise with him. I'm completely ready and willing to do anything I can, however unpleasant, to put things right. That's why I'm here. I met him and Uncle Blagoye on their way to a conference with a lawyer, and he told me to wait here.

SLAVKA: If I could only … but what can I do?

SCENE 2

*(**Enter** ZHIVOTA and BLAGOYE)*

ZHIVOTA *(to VELIMIR)*: So, you're here, are you?

VELIMIR: Yes, I waited for you, as you said.

ZHIVOTA *(to SLAVKA)*: Slavka, my dear, we've got some business to talk about.

SLAVKA: All right, I'm going. *(She goes to the door and pauses)* Father dear, do calm yourself. We'll find a way, we're all behind you and we're all willing to help. I don't think you should blame Velimir too much for what's happened.

ZHIVOTA: No, I blame myself! But please go now, my dear.

SLAVKA: I'm going. *(**Exit**)*

SCENE 3

ZHIVOTA *(to VELIMIR)*: You've told her, then?

VELIMIR: I had to. I couldn't bear her thinking badly of me.

ZHIVOTA: And the fact that I think badly of you doesn't matter, eh?

VELIMIR: I'm very, very sorry about that, but what can I do?

ZHIVOTA: I made a serious mistake in your case, a very serious mistake. I sent you there, to the university, to produce examination results, and what do you produce? – a child!

VELIMIR: But I did produce a diploma.

ZHIVOTA: Yes, you did. But you're not going to stand there and tell me that it's the custom in Switzerland for a child to be awarded along with the diploma, and I hope you don't think that I'd have sent you there at all, if that had been the case. If I'd wanted that, I'd have said to you: "Velimir, my lad, why don't you just trot along to Switzerland and supply me with a few spare children!" But, damn it, that's not what I said to you, and still less did I say that you were to start filling my whole house up with foreign children!

VELIMIR: He's not foreign, he's my child.

ZHIVOTA: Oh, he's yours, all right! The question is, who's his father?

VELIMIR: The question doesn't arise.

ZHIVOTA: The devil it doesn't! What about my son?

VELIMIR: Well he's only formally the child's father.

ZHIVOTA: Only 'formally'! He's 'formally' married, he 'formally' has a child, and I'm 'formally' banging my head against the wall! Well, my lad, you've 'formally' got us into such a mess that it'll take divine intervention to sort it out.

BLAGOYE: My boy, have you thought about what to do?

VELIMIR: I just don't know what to do.

ZHIVOTA: You don't know what to do! No, you don't know what to do now, but when you were in Switzerland you knew what to do all right!

BLAGOYE: We've talked to the lawyer, but he doesn't know what to advise. Of course, it doesn't help that we didn't dare to tell him exactly how the whole problem arose.

ZHIVOTA *(to* VELIMIR*)*: Well, anyway, tell me, what sort of a woman is your wife?

VELIMIR: She's very decent ...

ZHIVOTA: I don't mean that! What I want to know is if, for instance, I were to offer her ten, or perhaps twenty thousand dinars, would she be willing to clear off back to where she came from?

VELIMIR: I don't know.

ZHIVOTA: Twenty thousand dinars – that's not a sum to be sniffed at, you know. At today's prices I could buy five women for that, without any children.

VELIMIR: It's not so much the amount: I rather think that it wouldn't work.

ZHIVOTA: What d'you mean, it wouldn't work? I've simply got to get rid of her. She's a confounded nuisance – she's wrecking all my plans. *You've* looked after yourself, you've got married. Well *I'm* damned well going to look after my son. I've got plans for him, but how can I get on with them when you've tied my hands like this? Obviously, I want to get rid of her.

VELIMIR: I understand you, but I don't see how that would help. Even if she did agree to take the money and go back to Switzerland, she'd still be your son's legal wife and her child would be your descendant, and your heir.

ZHIVOTA *(recoils)*: My God! Now you're dragging inheritance into it! Aha, now I can see what you've got your eye on!

VELIMIR: We're not talking about me …

ZHIVOTA: But about Pepika?

VELIMIR: Yes, him.

ZHIVOTA: I'm surprised you haven't nominated him my 'formal' heir.

VELIMIR: Well, that could be right.

ZHIVOTA: Listen! I've had that Pepika up to *here!* He's cast a shadow over me – over my whole life. I'll settle accounts with his mother in a civilised manner, but just let me get my hands on him!

VELIMIR: He's only a little child.

ZHIVOTA: Little be damned! It's the little children who cause the worst problems in life, not the big ones! *(He paces about angrily, and then stops)* Yes. You're right. The marriage would remain valid.

BLAGOYE: So it would!

ZHIVOTA *(decisively)*: Right, then! You, my lad, can start divorce proceedings today.

BLAGOYE: I agree. That would be the best thing.

VELIMIR: But how can I divorce a woman who isn't my wife?

ZHIVOTA: There you go again! You don't think I can divorce her, do you?

VELIMIR: But I'm not married to her.

ZHIVOTA: What the hell are you talking about?

VELIMIR: Yes, I did marry her, but I did it in your son's name.

ZHIVOTA: Hah! I was just waiting for you to say that. Don't you realise, my lad, that that's a criminal offence, and that we have laws in this country?

VELIMIR: I do realise how much trouble I've brought upon you, and how badly I've behaved. I'm quite prepared to do anything to put things right.

ZHIVOTA: By doing what?

VELIMIR: I'll go straightaway, if you want me to, to the Public Prosecutor's office and there swear out a confession that in Fribourg I unlawfully took your son's name and got married in that false name. I shall admit that marriage, and shall state that that the woman whom I married is not the wife of Doctor Milorad Tsviyevich, who is still a bachelor, but that she is my wife. I shall accept full responsibility for any criminal acts which I may have committed.

ZHIVOTA (pleased): That's all right then! I must say, that's decent of you.

VELIMIR: If you agree, I could do it today.

ZHIVOTA: You won't just do it today, you'll do it this *minute!*

BLAGOYE: Hold on! Wait a moment! Let's think about this. It's not a bad idea but, you know, when you start telling all this to the police they're going to ask you why you did it. They're going to want to know why you married under a false name.

VELIMIR (shrugs his shoulders): Well ...

ZHIVOTA: He can say that it was a joke. He can say that he and Milorad had been friends since boyhood, and that he did it as a practical joke.

BLAGOYE: I rather doubt, you know, whether such practical jokes are allowed in Switzerland – I'm pretty sure they aren't here. After all, you may say that marriage is a joke but you can't say that a child is a joke. In any case, when you get married you have to produce some documents – proofs of identity and so on. The police will certainly ask him whether he had the proper documents.

ZHIVOTA: But he did have the documents.

BLAGOYE: I know he had them, but that's the problem. The police are going to ask him: "Well now, laddie, how did you come by these false documents? Have you been using them for any other purposes, eh? And what were you doing abroad all that time?"

VELIMIR: I shall say that I was studying at the university and that I passed all my exams.

ZHIVOTA (starts): You can't say that!

VELIMIR: I'll have to tell the truth.

ZHIVOTA: Tell the truth! Whoever gave you the idea that you have to tell the truth to the police? If everyone told the truth to the police half the population would be in prison!

VELIMIR: Well, what am I to do, then? I'll agree to anything. Just tell me what to do.

ZHIVOTA: Just do nothing. Leave it to me: I'll do what I has to be done. You've already thrown everything into chaos – now just keep out of it.

VELIMIR: Whatever you want.

ZHIVOTA: Anyway, have you written that lecture for Milorad?

VELIMIR: Oh, yes. Sorry, I'd forgotten. Here! (He hands some sheets of manuscript paper to ZHIVOTA).

ZHIVOTA (glances at them): What's it about?

VELIMIR: Anticipatory dynamics.

ZHIVOTA (ironically): Couldn't you have done something a bit more interesting? Blagoye here wouldn't even be able to pronounce it. He's never seen anything like it (He passes the papers to BLAGOYE) There! You can't even read it, can you? (To VELIMIR) Where's that fellow of yours, by the way?

VELIMIR: What fellow?

ZHIVOTA: That fellow Reisser. What have you done with him?

VELIMIR: I met him last night, took him to his hotel, and had dinner with him. This morning we looked round the town and after that I took him to the university. He's still there, talking to some of the other professors. That's how it is that I've got some spare time.

ZHIVOTA *(taking the manuscript from* BLAGOYE *and putting it in his pocket)(To* BLAGOYE*)*: Good! You remembered. *(To* VELIMIR*)*: It was a good idea to dump him at the university.

VELIMIR: Yes, but I must warn you that he's very anxious to come here: he insisted on seeing you.

ZHIVOTA: What the devil does he want to see *me* for? I'm not a university. Put him off, for goodness' sake. Haven't you done enough dropping Pepika in my lap, without producing this Reisser as well?

VELIMIR: I don't know if I can. He thinks that you'd be offended if he didn't call on you. I can't think how I could put it to him.

BLAGOYE *(to* ZHIVOTA*)*: It's no good. You'll have to see him.

ZHIVOTA: Now you've dropped me in it too! Very well, then – *you* receive him.

BLAGOYE: What, me? How can I?

ZHIVOTA: Listen, that would be by far the best way of doing it. Yes! *You* can be Velimir's father, and there we are – no problem! You can speak German. You just tell him that the house is being redecorated, or something, so you can't invite him here. Take him out to lunch instead. That's the best way of getting rid of him.

VELIMIR: Are you seriously suggesting that Uncle Blagoye should pass himself off as my father?

ZHIVOTA: Yes, I am. If he's so anxious to meet your father, there he is – let him meet him!

VELIMIR: It's not possible!

ZHIVOTA: Rubbish! Of course it's possible! – you managed to impersonate my son all right! *(He takes some money out of his*

wallet and gives it to BLAGOYE) There! That should be enough
for a lunch, provided that you don't break any mirrors.

BLAGOYE: D'you really mean this seriously?

ZHIVOTA: I certainly do. Don't you see? This boy's intent on
dragging the whole of Switzerland into my house – first
Pepika, then Klara, now Reisser. *(To* VELIMIR) It's quite a
surprise that you didn't invite the President of the Swiss
Republic as well, to make up the numbers – why not? Now,
instead of moaning, you and Blagoye here can make yourselves
useful by keeping them all away from here.

BLAGOYE: I'm not moaning.

ZHIVOTA: In that case, you can go off with him and be his father
for the day. Just keep that damned professor out of my house.

BLAGOYE: Well, all right, but …

ZHIVOTA: It'll be quite easy for you to play the part. You ought to
thank me for giving you the opportunity of paying for someone
else's drinks for once in your life, but you …

BLAGOYE: All right! All right! I think it's … Anyway, what you
say goes. Come on, Velimir! (***Exeunt***).

SCENE 4

(Immediately after going out, BLAGOYE **re-enters** *by himself,
staying by the doorway)*

ZHIVOTA: What is it – have you forgotten something?

BLAGOYE: No, but I forgot to tell you: that lady Mrs Draga, my
late wife's sister-in-law – I told you about her – she's the one
who's well in with the wife of the Minister of Transport …

ZHIVOTA: Yes, yes! Well?

BLAGOYE: She told me the day before yesterday that she was
going to see how the land lay.

ZHIVOTA: Has she done it?

BLAGOYE: She must have: she's here.

ZHIVOTA: Where?

BLAGOYE: Here. She's waiting in the other room.

ZHIVOTA *(going to the door)*: She shouldn't have been kept

waiting. *(Speaking through the doorway)* Come in, madam, come in!

BLAGOYE *(still by the doorway)*: Please come in!

ZHIVOTA: Yes, come in, please. *(To* BLAGOYE*)* You can go and do what's needed. *(**Exit** BLAGOYE, getting somewhat in the way of* MRS DRAGA *as she **enters**)*.

SCENE 5

ZHIVOTA: Welcome, madam. I'm so sorry that you've been kept waiting.

DRAGA: The maid suggested that I should come in, but I preferred not to. You had those other gentlemen with you, and the matter I wish to speak to you about is strictly between ourselves, you know.

ZHIVOTA: I quite understand, but if I'd known you were here I could have put them off. Anyway, please take a seat.

DRAGA *(sitting down)*: I expect you can guess why I've come?

ZHIVOTA: Yes, Blagoye mentioned it.

DRAGA: I hadn't expected things to move so fast, you know. I had intended simply to drop by and pay a call in the next day or two, unexpected, like. But yesterday it came out in the newspapers that your son was giving a philosophical lecture and that an eminent professor from abroad was going to turn up for it. "Right!" I said to myself, I said, "That's a good opportunity to strike up a conversation." So I rolled up the paper, stuck in my handbag, and off I went.

ZHIVOTA *(rubbing his hands)*: And?

DRAGA: Isn't your lady wife here? Shouldn't she hear about this?

ZHIVOTA: No, she's not interested.

DRAGA: What? His mother – not interested?

ZHIVOTA: Well, yes, but only as a mother. Please go on, tell me what happened.

DRAGA: All right, then. But it only seems right and proper, you know …

ZHIVOTA: Yes, yes, I understand, I'll call her. *(He goes to the door)*

Mara! Mara! *(To* MRS DRAGA*)* But at least tell me, before she comes, how do things stand, generally speaking?

DRAGA: I am hopeful, very hopeful.

SCENE 6

(Enter MARA. DRAGA *rises)*

ZHIVOTA: My dear, this is Mrs Draga, Blagoye's sister-in-law.

MARA *(shakes hands with* DRAGA*)*: But we know each other, don't we?

DRAGA: Of course we know each other – we're family.

MARA *(sitting down)*: It's just that we haven't met. Well, how are you?

DRAGA *(sitting down)*: Mustn't grumble.

ZHIVOTA *(to* MARA*)*: Mrs Draga, you know, is a friend of the wife of the Minister of Transport. I hadn't mentioned it to you before, but it just so happens that the Minister of Transport has an unmarried daughter, and …

MARA *(She lights up)*: You mean – for our Milorad?

ZHIVOTA: Well, not for me, obviously. Yes, for our Milorad.

DRAGA: Yes, of course.

ZHIVOTA: Blagoye talked to Mrs Draga and she thought she would pay a visit to the minister's residence in the next few days but, as the notice about Milorad's lecture came out in the papers yesterday, she said to herself that this gave her an excellent opportunity for striking up a conversation, so she rolled up the paper in her handbag and off she went.

MARA: And?

ZHIVOTA: 'And?' is precisely the point we had got to to when I called you. Now, Mrs Draga, please go on.

DRAGA: So off I went to their house, and when I got there – "Good morning, how are you?"

ZHIVOTA: I'm quite well, thank you. How are you?

DRAGA: No, I mean, that's what I said. I know it's conventional, but you can't just plunge in like a bull at a gate.

ZHIVOTA: No, of course not.

DRAGA: After that, as you might expect, we started to talk about how nice the weather was, and what the latest gossip in town was, and so on and so on, until eventually I was able to steer the conversation round to the lecture.

ZHIVOTA: Ah, yes!

DRAGA: I said: "I wonder if you'll both be going to the lecture which that nice young philosopher Dr Tsviyovich is giving tomorrow?"

ZHIVOTA: What did they say?

DRAGA: The mother, Mrs Yelka, said: "I'm not sure that we want to go." But I said: "Oh, you really should go!" And I said, openly: "You really should go, not just for the lecture but so that you can meet that young philosopher. He is a wonderful scholar, you know, with a brilliant future in front of him."

ZHIVOTA: That's right. Very well said.

DRAGA: Well, I don't know if it's true, but I'm something of a match-maker, you know.

ZHIVOTA: Yes, certainly!

DRAGA: I said: "He's a young man who hardly raises his head from his books by day or night."

ZHIVOTA: That describes him perfectly – ask Mara. *(MARA, surprised, hesitates to say anything)* How many times have I said to him: "Son, do not sacrifice your youth to those books! 'Go out with your friends and enjoy yourself a bit!" And do you know what he says to me? He says: "Father, do not disturb me. Learning is for me a holy thing!" There! That's the sort of man he is!

DRAGA: And I said: "That young man is absolutely reliable and sober. He doesn't even know what the inside of a public house looks like."

ZHIVOTA *(emphatically)*: He has no idea!

DRAGA: I said: "He doesn't drink and he doesn't smoke." Mind you – I've no idea if that's true, but what sort of a match-maker would I be if I'd said anything different?

ZHIVOTA: And what did they say?

DRAGA: Hang on until I've told you everything that I said to them. I said: "He's a well-educated young man, he's rich, and he's very good-looking." By the way, I don't know – is he good-looking in fact?

MARA: He certainly is!

DRAGA: And he's well-educated, I suppose.

ZHIVOTA: Obviously. Look at that diploma.

DRAGA: Good! Then I got everything right.

ZHIVOTA: Yes, you did. But what did they say?

DRAGA: Well, how shall I put it? – up to now they hadn't said anything much, they'd been endlessly asking questions about your family, its general standing, and goodness knows what else. But then they said: "But we don't know the young man." So I said: "Well here's your opportunity. He's giving this lecture tomorrow – if you go along and listen to it you'll be able to see him." And do you know what she said? – the daughter, I mean – she said: "Oh, Mama, do let's go!"

ZHIVOTA: D'you think they'll come, then?

DRAGA: I'm sure they will. They want to see him.

ZHIVOTA *(to* MARA*)*: D'you hear? It looks as if there could be an introduction!

MARA: Let's hope so.

DRAGA: And when I was leaving, her mother, Mrs Yelka, said to me: "Do come again, Mrs Draga, come again often."

MARA: Is that all?

ZHIVOTA: What more do you want? They're coming to the lecture, *and* she said to her: "Do come again, Mrs Draga." Posh folk like them don't usually go as far as saying that, like we do – they usually say something meaningless.

DRAGA: That's true. Apart from that, this isn't the first time I've done some match-making: I know what lies behind "Come again, Mrs Draga, come again often".

ZHIVOTA: But … how can I put it? … you know, I'm not short of a few bob, so I'm not particularly concerned about the dowry, but at the same time I'd be interested, purely out of curiosity, you understand, to know what you think it might amount to. How many kilometres d'you think her father would give her as a dowry?

DRAGA: Kilometres! I don't see how you can measure a dowry in 'kilometres'.

ZHIVOTA: Don't you? Well, for instance, you don't ask a baker how much money he draws out of his oven every day, do you? You ask him how many loaves – they're his currency. It's the same with a Minister of Transport – kilometres, they are his currency.

DRAGA: I still don't understand.

ZHIVOTA: Listen, and I'll explain. The contracts for the construction of the Trans-Balkan Railway are in his hands – that means thousands and thousands of kilometres. I'm not suggesting that he's going to give his daughter the whole railway as a dowry, that's not on, but the odd four or five hundred kilometres wouldn't come amiss.

DRAGA: Ah, yes, I understand now. After all, he's bound to look after his own child, isn't he! And .. er .. perhaps there might be a few kilometres for the match-maker?

ZHIVOTA: That goes without saying, Mrs Draga. I can't promise you a viaduct or a tunnel, but a few kilometres – certainly!

MARA: I beg your pardon – there was one other thing.

DRAGA: Yes, Mara dear?

MARA: What's the girl like? Is she pretty?

DRAGA: Pretty! Of course she's pretty – she's a Minister's daughter, isn't she?

MARA: Is she a delicate sort? Is she modest?

DRAGA: Modest? Of course she is! How could she have got to twenty-seven without being married, if she wasn't modest?

MARA: You're right, of course.

DRAGA: I'll tell you my idea of how we should proceed now. Tomorrow they will see each other at the lecture – that is to say, they'll see him. Right! The next day I'll go and see them and I'll ask them straightaway: "What did you think of him?"

ZHIVOTA: Yes! Good!

DRAGA *(rising)*: I'll do that, and then I'll come here and tell you all about it.

ZHIVOTA: Better still!

DRAGA: Right, then! That's all we have to talk about today, but I'll be back if I'm needed. Good bye for now. *(She shakes hands with* MARA *and* ZHIVOTA *and moves to the door).*

MARA *(accompanying her to the door)*: Good bye, and thank you.

ZHIVOTA *(also going to the door)*: Thank you very much. Do come again!

*(**Exit** DRAGA).*

SCENE 7

ZHIVOTA *(returning)*: Did you hear what the woman said?

MARA: Yes, I heard. How marvellous!

ZHIVOTA: Daughter of a government minister, eh? How about that!

MARA: I'm so glad, Zhivota, and it should be wonderful but … how shall I put it? – it doesn't seem quite right. We're marrying off a married man.

ZHIVOTA: Oh, you don't have to take that seriously.

MARA: But I *do* take it seriously. I'm worried. You yourself told me that he was legally married.

ZHIVOTA: My dear, *he's* not married, it's only his *name* that's married. And we're going to deal with that.

MARA: I can't sleep. I toss and turn all night for worrying.

ZHIVOTA: Why, what's troubling you?

MARA: Obviously I'm troubled. When I think of how I used to look forward to the happiness of seeing our son married, and how it's turned out – a daughter-in-law that we don't know, and that her husband doesn't know either – and now, a grandchild! Dear God preserve us!

ZHIVOTA: It's all going to be sorted out, don't worry.

MARA: I imagined a daughter-in-law that I could take into my home like my own child, that I'd be proud of as she went about the house, and a dear little grandchild that would coo at me and that you and I could hold in our arms, and could kiss. And I wanted a grandchild with a normal name, like Miroslav, or Dobroslav, or Radovan, or Milovan – not … *Pepika!* Oh, Zhivota, where on earth did they find a name like that? I've never heard of it and I can't even pronounce it properly – it sticks in my mouth like glue. I tell you, I shall be a laughing-stock. Other women will nudge each other and sneer at me. They'll say, sniggering: "Oh, hullo, Mara dear, and how's 'Pepika'?"

ZHIVOTA: And what d'you think's going to happen when he goes to school and at roll-call they call out "Pepika Tsviyovich"? All the Radovans and Milovans will fall about laughing, and they'll humiliate him.

MARA: Yes, they will!

ZHIVOTA: Well it won't happen. I'm going to put a stop to it.

MARA: Is it possible?

ZHIVOTA: The lawyer says it's possible.

MARA: I hope he's right. I don't know much about these sort of things, but I'd have thought it shouldn't be too difficult. All Milorad has to do is to go to the authorities and say: "Some other person married her in my name; I don't recognise her as my wife." And that's that.

ZHIVOTA: That's the very thing he *can't* say, because the authorities would immediately say to him: "Then you must bring this other person before us to tell us why he used your name and why he lived for four years under that false name."

MARA: Well, let Velimir tell them, then.

ZHIVOTA: He could tell them, but he'd say a lot more. He'd have to explain himself, and then the whole story would come out.

MARA: Well, let it.

ZHIVOTA: Good God! – that's all we need! No, we've got to think up something else. The lawyer suggests that it would be better to come to a mutual arrangement. For instance, the moment Klara comes in through the door, and before she's had time to say "Good morning", Milorad must hit her.

MARA: What sort of a mutual arrangement is that?

ZHIVOTA: It'd be a mutual arrangement because you and I and Milorad would have agreed it was to happen.

MARA: But, for the love of God, why should he hit her?

ZHIVOTA: As proof of cruelty. Cruelty is good grounds for divorce.

MARA: Milorad wouldn't agree to do that.

ZHIVOTA: Then let's arrange that the woman hits him. Same thing – cruelty!

MARA: For goodness' sake, Zhivota, there must be something more sensible than coming to blows! Only this morning I was talking to Blagoye and he said the best thing would be for her to be caught committing an act of infidelity in front of witnesses.

ZHIVOTA: Damned fool! No woman's going to commit an act of infidelity in front of witnesses.

MARA: I tell you plainly, I don't want to get involved: I don't know much about things like that. I'm just telling you what Blagoye said. He said: "Infidelity could be arranged."

ZHIVOTA: How could it be arranged?

MARA: Blagoye said: "Milorad may not agree to hit the woman, but he would probably agree to kiss her."

ZHIVOTA *(emphatically)*: Yes – I'm damned sure he would! I know him only too well!

MARA: Well then, Blagoye said that it could be arranged for Milorad and her to be alone in a room. Milorad would kiss her and at that moment witnesses would burst in from the next room, and there you are – off to the Divorce Court straightaway!

ZHIVOTA: To do what?

MARA: Why, to accuse her of infidelity.

ZHIVOTA: It's easy to see that you're Blagoye's sister: you're almost as stupid as he is.

MARA: What d'you mean?

ZHIVOTA: How the devil can you accuse a woman of infidelity on the grounds that she let her *husband* kiss her? Can't you get it into your head that he's a married man? How can you and Blagoye be so daft as to imagine that anyone could seriously say to the judge: "I ask for a divorce on the grounds that I and my lawful wedded wife kissed each other"?

MARA *(crushed)*: Oh dear! It is a bit silly, isn't it. But what can I think, when I'm so confused by the whole thing that I don't know whether I'm coming or going.

ZHIVOTA: Well, don't think, then! The most important thing at the moment is to talk Milorad into giving this lecture, and you've got to help me. You know what he's like – he'll refuse. He won't listen to me – you'll have to persuade him, because you can see for yourself what a crying shame it would be to miss such a marvellous opportunity. *(He leads her to the door)* Go on, my dear, you talk him round! Don't let him get out of it!

MARA: All right, I'll try. *(**Exit**, left)*

SCENE 8

*(ZHIVOTA, alone, takes the manuscript which Velimir had given him out of his pocket and reads through it. He raises his head as MARA and MILORAD **enter** together, left. MILORAD is holding a newspaper in his hand).*

ZHIVOTA: So there you are! I've got something important to say to you.

MILORAD: And so have I. *(He points to the newspaper)*. What's this, father? What on earth are you playing at?

ZHIVOTA: What d'you mean?

MILORAD: This! – it says in this paper that I'm giving a lecture, that Professor Reisser has come specially to hear it, and that ...

ZHIVOTA: Oh, yes, that's true, obviously. If it says it in the newspapers it must be true.

MILORAD: What's true?

ZHIVOTA: Well, it's true, for instance, that Professor Reisser has come.

MILORAD: But it's not true that I'm giving a lecture.

ZHIVOTA *(to* MARA*)* There you are, you see what he's like – I told you! *(To* MILORAD*)* Now you just listen to me, my lad! As you can see, it's all there, in the newspaper, and it's going to happen. We're going to have to give that lecture.

MILORAD: What lecture, for God's sake? What are you talking about, father?

ZHIVOTA *(to* MARA*)*: You see – there he goes again! I told you! *(To* MILORAD*)* I know perfectly well that you're not really up to giving a lecture, but sometimes a man's got to do his duty, whether he likes it or not. A lot of very important people are coming to your lecture tomorrow. For instance, there's the wife of the Minister of Transport and her daughter, and plenty of other eminent people – with their daughters. We can't possibly say to people like that: "We regret that the lecturer is unable appear."

MILORAD: Oh, yes we can, because I never said to anyone that I was going to do it!

ZHIVOTA: You didn't, but I did.

MILORAD: Well, if you said it, you do it. You give the lecture!

ZHIVOTA: Don't worry, I would, if I was a Doctor of Philosophy!

MILORAD: Who's a Doctor of Philosophy?

ZHIVOTA: You are!

MILORAD: Oh, don't be ridiculous! For the love of God let's put an end to this charade once and for all! I'm no Doctor of Philosophy, as you well know, and I'm not competent to give any sort of lecture.

ZHIVOTA: As far as competence goes, don't you worry about that – that's my concern. And as to the lecture – here, take this! *(He hands the manuscript to* MILORAD*)*.

MILORAD: You keep it: I don't want it.

ZHIVOTA: Listen, your whole future is at stake. *(To* MARA*)* Well, say something, can't you!

MARA: What can I say? The boy's intelligent enough; he'll do what you say.

ZHIVOTA: It's not only a matter of your future, it's a matter of honour – don't you understand?

MILORAD: Whose honour?

ZHIVOTA: Yours.

MILORAD: Leave my honour out of it! What's my honour got to do with it?

ZHIVOTA: All right, never mind your honour, but what about mine? *My* honour is in question.

MILORAD: Oh, I see. When your honour's at stake I have to help you, but when my honour's at stake you don't care. *(To* MARA*)* Mother, yesterday I begged and prayed him to let me have ten thousand dinars to settle a matter of honour affecting me, but he wouldn't listen.

ZHIVOTA: I should think not! Ten thousand dinars! What sort of honour is it that costs ten thousand dinars?

MILORAD: But ...

ZHIVOTA: Ten thousand dinars? I deal with 'honour' in my business, and I'm well acquainted with the price of *that* article. Ten thousand dinars – poppycock!

MILORAD: Well, maybe, but don't expect me to save your honour, then.

ZHIVOTA: Very well. Suppose I were to give you the ten thousand dinars, would you give the lecture then?

MILORAD: Well ... perhaps ... I suppose I'd have to.

ZHIVOTA: Come down a bit. Ten thousand dinars is a lot of money.

MILORAD: That's the amount I owe, and I gave my word of honour that I'd pay within forty-eight hours.

ZHIVOTA: You gave your word of honour! Do you seriously imagine that that's worth anything at all? Go into any bank and ask them to take your 'word of honour' as security for a loan and you'll soon find out how much *that's* worth!

MILORAD: It's worth a lot to me.

ZHIVOTA: And this lecture's worth a lot to me.

MILORAD: What lecture, father? For goodness sake! – the more you go on at me about this the more entangled I get. First you load me down with a diploma, and then a wife, and then a child as well, and now, on top of all that, a lecture!

ZHIVOTA: I'm doing all this for your own good. You just don't appreciate how profitable this lecture's going to be for us. Tell him, Mara! Explain to him that it's all for his own good. Just tell him who's going to be at the lecture.

MARA: Milorad, my dear, the daughter of the Minister of Transport will be there! She's coming specially to see you – the match-maker told us.

MILORAD: But how on earth does a match-maker come into it, when I'm married?

ZHIVOTA: So what? Plenty of married people get divorced. Leave it to me.

MILORAD: But who's the Minister of Transport's daughter? I don't even know her.

ZHIVOTA: You don't know Klara either, and she's your wife!

MILORAD: And I've got you to thank for that, but, make no mistake, I'm going to clear all this up somehow.

SCENE 9

MARITSA *(Enters)*: Two ladies to see you.

ZHIVOTA: Who are they?

MARITSA: The same ones that came a couple of days ago, sir.

ZHIVOTA: Oh, they'll be the ladies from the Day Nursery.

(To MILORAD*)* They'll have come about the lecture.

MILORAD: What's that got to do with me?

ZHIVOTA: You just behave yourself, and don't disgrace us.

(To MARITSA*)* Ask them to come in.

MARITSA: Yes, sir. *(Exit)*.

SCENE 10

ZHIVOTA: Listen, you've got to look after both of us now.

MILORAD: I'm going to look after myself. *(He makes to leave the room)*.

ZHIVOTA *(grabbing hold of* MILORAD'S *coat)* Mara! Stop him! He's trying to escape!

MILORAD: Are you going to give me the ten thousand dinars?

ZHIVOTA: Are you going to give the lecture?

MILORAD: I will if you give me the money.

ZHIVOTA *(He hesitates but, seeing* MRS PROTICH *and* MRS SPASOYEVICH *coming through the doorway, he grudgingly agrees)*: Very well, I'll give it you.

SCENE 11

(Enter MRS SPASOYEVICH *and* MRS PROTICH*)*

SPASOYEVICH and PROTICH *(in unison)*: Good morning, Madam, good morning! *(They shake hands with* MARA*)*. Good morning, sir!

ZHIVOTA: May I introduce my son, Doctor Milorad Tsviyevich.

SPASOYEVICH and PROTICH *(still in unison)*: Ah, our philosopher! A pleasure to meet you! *(They shake hands with* MILORAD*)*.

ZHIVOTA: My son was just saying to me how much he was looking forward to meeting the ladies who had invited him to give this lecture.

SPASOYEVICH and PROTICH: What a great honour!

PROTICH: You flatter us by your condescension!

SPASOYEVICH: We are formally authorised …

PROTICH: … by the Board of Management of Nursery School Number Nine …

SPASOYEVICH: … by the entire Board of Management …

PROTICH: We would formally wish …

SPASOYEVICH: I do beg your pardon, Mrs Protich, would you please allow me …

PROTICH: Please go on, Mrs Spasoyevich.

SPASOYEVICH: You can't imagine how pleased we were to read in the newspapers that the eminent Professor Reisser from Fribourg was also going to attend the lecture.

PROTICH: That is a great honour for us.

SPASOYEVICH: So we have come here especially …

PROTICH: … because we wish to have the great pleasure of meeting Professor Reisser ..

SPASOYEVICH: … and you will no doubt be able to tell us where we may find him.

ZHIVOTA: I would not trouble yourselves looking for him, ladies. He's not very keen on being lectured to.

PROTICH: But how can that be? It says in the papers that he has travelled here specially to hear it.

ZHIVOTA: Yes, for that lecture – that's one thing. I only say that he doesn't like lectures – that's another matter.

SPASOYEVICH *(To* MILORAD*)*: There was one thing we wanted to ask you. Since this is your first public appearance, wouldn't it be best if one of the members of the Board of Management accompanied you to the platform and introduced you to the audience?

MILORAD: It's all the same to me.

PROTICH: Or perhaps you would prefer *two* members of the Board of Management?

ZHIVOTA: Let's have two, provided that only one of them speaks.

SPASOYEVICH: What does the young gentleman prefer?

MILORAD: I have no preference.

ZHIVOTA: It's no good asking him. These philosophers are an odd lot, they can't make up their minds about anything.

SCENE 12

*(****Enter*** BLAGOYE. *He bursts in, panting breathlessly)*

BLAGOYE: He's coming!

ZHIVOTA: Who's coming?

BLAGOYE: Professor Reisser!

SPASOYEVICH & PROTICH: *(they jump up excitedly)*: Oh, that's wonderful!

ZHIVOTA *(confused)*: What d'you mean, Reisser? Are you mad? Why the devil have you brought him here?

BLAGOYE: I tried, but he wouldn't listen. He insisted on meeting

Milorad's mother.

MARA: Goodness! Why does he want to meet me?

ZHIVOTA: Yes, why, for God's sake? He's met Milorad's father –
what does he want to meet his mother for?

SPASOYEVICH: How marvellous! We are so delighted! This is an
ideal opportunity for us to meet and welcome the eminent
professor in person.

ZHIVOTA: Oh yes, ideal! *(To* BLAGOYE*)* Well, you'll have to ask
him in, then.

BLAGOYE: I couldn't help it …

ZHIVOTA: Oh, to hell with both of you!

*(**Exit** BLAGOYE, confused).*

SCENE 13

ZHIVOTA: My God, what am I going to do now? *(To* MILORAD,
who is laughing) What the devil are you laughing about?

MILORAD: I'm laughing at Uncle Blagoye.

BLAGOYE: Oh yes, he's a joke, all right. Anyway, what are we
going to do?

PROTICH: In the name of the Board of Management of the
Nursery School Number Nine, we shall formally welcome him
and sincerely thank him for coming all the way from Fribourg
to attend the lecture of his former pupil.

ZHIVOTA *(totally confused)*: Yes, do. Only, be brave … that is, not
you, ladies. Milorad, be brave!

MILORAD: I'm not worried.

ZHIVOTA *(ever more worried)*: No, no. Well then, Mara, be brave!

MARA: Why me?

ZHIVOTA: Why you? Somebody's got to be brave. Very well, it'll
have to be me, if no one else will. Oh, I've just thought – Mara,
why don't you and I and Milorad stand to one side and let
these good ladies make their welcoming speech? – we'd only
be in the way.

SPASOYEVICH: Oh, that would never do!

PROTICH: He's come to see you.

ZHIVOTA: Yes, I suppose so. I just wanted to help. *(The door opens)* Here he is!

SCENE 14

*(**Enter** BLAGOYE, DR REISSER, and VELIMIR. BLAGOYE, trembling with confusion, leads the way)*

BLAGOYE: This way! Please come in! *(When they are both in the room)* I have the honour to present ... Mr Zhivota Tsviyovich, Milorad's father.

ZHIVOTA: What d'you mean? – I'm not his father.

BLAGOYE *(even more confused)*: No, no ... that is ... er ... I'm his father, aren't I? No – this gentleman is his mother.

SPASOYEVICH: & PROTICH: Oh! *(*MARA *crosses herself, and* MILORAD *bursts out laughing)*.

VELIMIR *(to BLAGOYE. Getting angry, but trying to save the situation)*: No, no, 'father'! For God's sake! – this is mother. *(indicates MARA)*.

BLAGOYE: Oh yes, of course. *(He introduces REISSER to MARA)* I have the honour to introduce Milorad's mother.

REISSER *(He speaks slowly in a strong German accent, with gaps between his words, like someone who has only learned the language from books)*: My respects, Madam. I your son greatly esteem.

MARA: Much obliged, I'm sure.

REISSER: He is a young man most excellent.

SPASOYEVICH and PROTICH *(to ZHIVOTA)*: Please introduce him to us, also!

ZHIVOTA *(to BLAGOYE)*: You do it.

BLAGOYE: But I don't even know them.

SPASOYEVICH and PROTICH: *(approaching Reisser, and speaking in unison)*: We are, honoured sir, members of the Board of Management of the Nursery School Number Nine. This Nursery School, which is an establishment of such great social importance ...

REISSER *(to VELIMIR)*: Please, translate what are saying these ladies.

SPASOYEVICH *(to* PROTICH*)*: There! You see! The gentleman will not be able to understand unless you allow me to speak to him by myself.

PROTICH: Very well. Please continue.

SPASOYEVICH: We are, my dear Professor, members of the Board of Management of the Nursery School Number Nine …

PROTICH: This Nursery School, which is an establishment of such great social importance ..

SPASOYEVICH: … is holding a public lecture.

ZHIVOTA *(aside, to* BLAGOYE*)*: Now the sparks are going to fly!

PROTICH: The lecture is to be given by your excellent pupil *(indicating* MILORAD*)*, Doctor Milorad Tsviyovich.

REISSER *(confused)*: I beg your pardon …

SPASOYEVICH: His distinguished father, *(indicating* ZHIVOTA*)* Mr Zhivota Tsviyovich …

ZHIVOTA: Here we go!

PROTICH: … has been so very kind as to make his son available to us.

SPASOYEVICH: We are especially delighted and honoured that you, dear Professor, should have journeyed all the way from Fribourg to attend the lecture.

REISSER *(to* VELIMIR*)*: I do not understand. What lecture shall you give?

SPASOYEVICH: No, *he's* not giving it. It's *this* gentleman, Doctor Milorad Tsviyovich, who's giving the lecture *(indicating* MILORAD*)*.

REISSER Yes. *This* gentleman's son. *(indicating* BLAGOYE*)*.

PROTICH: Oh no. *This* gentleman's son *(indicating* ZHIVOTA*)*.

ZHIVOTA *(to* PROTICH*)*: Leave me out of it.

REISSER *(to* ZHIVOTA*)*: But whose father are you?

ZHIVOTA: I don't know.

MARA: Zhivota! How could you!

REISSER *(to* BLAGOYE*)*: Then whose father are you?

BLAGOYE: I don't know.

PROTICH *(to* ZHIVOTA*)*: But, my dear sir, isn't it your son, Doctor

Milorad Tsviyovich, who's giving the lecture?

REISSER I beg your pardon, Madam, Doctor Milorad Tsviyovich
is the son of *this* gentleman. *(indicating* BLAGOYE*).*

BLAGOYE: That's right.

SPASOYEVICH and PROTICH: Oh!

ZHIVOTA: There! It's all quite clear, as you can see. There's no
need to talk about it any more.

SPASOYEVICH: But we don't know …

PROTICH: … to whom to address ourselves?

SPASOYEVICH *(to* MARA*)*: Please, Madam, be so good as to tell
us, who is the father of your son?

MARA: Now *I* don't know.

SPASOYEVICH and PROTICH: Oh!

MILORAD: Mother, what are you saying?

MARA: I just don't know what I'm saying. I'm utterly confused.

SPASOYEVICH and PROTICH: I beg your pardon. It is all so
difficult …

ZHIVOTA *(He has restrained himself so far, but now he bursts out)*:
Just shut up, the lot of you! How dare you intrude in my family
affairs? What's your Nursery School Number Nine doing
meddling in my private business? Pepika's more than enough
for me to have to deal with, without having the whole damned
Nursery School Number Nine on top of everything!

SPASOYEVICH and PROTICH: Sir!

REISSER *(trying to calm him down)*: But these ladies are right.
They are wishing only …

ZHIVOTA *(infuriated)*: Don't you start! What sort of a devil are
you, anyway, coming here and driving me mad? Why've you
dragged yourself all the way here from Fribourg to interfere in
my family affairs? Why didn't you stay in your ivory tower and
leave me and my family alone, instead of dumping the whole of
Fribourg on my head? It's too much! *(He shouts)* I can't stand
any more!

(General chaos ensues. VELIMIR *tries to pacify the offended*
REISSER. SPASOYEVICH *and* PROTICH *argue vociferously with*

BLAGOYE *and* MARA. MILORAD *stands to one side, laughing)*
ZHIVOTA *(sadly, to himself)*: Pepika, oh wretched Pepika!
See what you've done to me!

Curtain

Act Three

The same room as in Act Two.

SCENE 1

MILORAD *is lounging on a sofa, smoking nervously, with his feet up on a coffee table.* ***Enter*** MARITSA, *centre.*

MARITSA: Sir!

MILORAD: *(starts, and leaps to his feet)* What is it? I said nobody was to disturb me!

MARITSA: I wanted ...

MILORAD *(picks up a cushion and throws it at her)*: Out! Get out! *(**Exit** MARITSA, in haste, left).*

SCENE 2

*(*MILORAD *lies down again on the sofa and continues to smoke.* ***Enter*** SLAVKA, *from the other room, left, with* MARITSA *hiding behind her).*

MILORAD *(starts, and leaps to his feet, as before. He picks up another cushion)*: Didn't I say ..

SLAVKA *(going up to him)*: Calm down, for goodness' sake! *(At this point* MARITSA *seizes the opportunity to escape and **exit**, centre)* What's the matter with you today?

MILORAD: What's the matter? You calmly ask me 'what's the matter?' – and I'm in such a state that I'm surprised that I haven't actually bitten anyone yet! Watch out! I'm likely to!

SLAVKA: Why on earth ... ?

MILORAD: Why! Didn't you see with your own eyes the shame

that Father brought on me by making me do that damned lecture?

SLAVKA: Yes, I'm afraid you did get rather badly muddled, didn't you. It was awful for all of us when the whole audience burst out laughing. I wanted to run out of the hall.

MILORAD: Well, of course I got muddled, when Father'd got that egg-headed genius Velimir to write out what I was to say, and he … Here! Just listen to this *(He takes the manuscript out of his pocket and reads from it)*: "In the contemplative essential-instinctive presentation of fluctuating logocentric and biocentric problems, one comes into conflict with derivative profanations of the climacteric culture … " Good God Almighty! It's gobbledeygook – just try even pronouncing it! I tell you, when I saw those words I felt as though I was in an impenetrable jungle full of howling wild animals. I was on the verge of howling myself. Was it any wonder that I got muddled?

SLAVKA: Well, for goodness' sake, why did you agree to give the wretched lecture?

MILORAD: Why? Because I had no choice. Father caught me at a bad moment, just when I needed ten thousand dinars.

SLAVKA: Was some bank after you?

MILORAD: Not a bank, a woman.

SLAVKA: Oh, Milorad!

MILORAD: She was a very pretty woman.

SLAVKA: Was that all she was?

MILORAD: All! It's more than enough! No bank's as dangerous as a pretty woman. A bank will give you notice, then dun you, then it'll sue you, and the court will make the decision one way or the other. With a woman it's one long reproachful promissory note and she always wins.

SLAVKA: Perhaps you'd better give up these theories of yours.

MILORAD: And take up philosophy?

SLAVKA: I didn't say that, but …

SCENE 3

MARITSA *(poking her head round the rear door, not daring to enter)* Sir, there's a lady who wishes ...

MILORAD *(shouting)*: What lady?

MARITSA: A lady with a child.

MILORAD: It's her! *(He picks up a cushion and some other things)* I'm going to make her pay for all this!

SLAVKA: Milorad! Don't!

MILORAD: Go away! It's that wretched woman from the Day Nursery. She told me yesterday that she was going to come here with some children from the Nursery, to thank me.

SLAVKA: Well, for goodness' sake be polite to her.

MILORAD: I'll probably throw a chair at her! That damned Day Nursery's got on my nerves. *(To MARITSA)* Ask her to come in.

SLAVKA: I'm going: I don't want anything to do with this. *(At the door of her room)* Milorad, do behave yourself! *(Exit)*

SCENE 4

*(MARITSA withdraws her head from the door, **enter** KLARA. She has PEPIKA, a four-year-old boy, with her. MILORAD raises the cushion as if to throw it at her).*

KLARA *(startled)*: Excuse me! *(MILORAD, seeing that it is not one of the ladies from the Day Nursery, but a young and attractive woman, slowly lowers his hand and the cushion)* Excuse me, please. I'm looking for Mr Milorad Tsviyovich..

MILORAD: That's me.

KLARA: I mean, Doctor Milorad Tsviyovich..

MILORAD: That's me.

KLARA: No, I'm sorry, I'm looking for my husband.

MILORAD: That's me, too.

KLARA: I'm afraid I don't find this very amusing, sir!

MILORAD: Madam, believe me, that's who I am.

KLARA: But I know perfectly well who my husband is.

MILORAD: Yes. I am.

KLARA: Oh dear! Perhaps it's the language. Have I not spoken your language correctly?

MILORAD: My dear lady, you speak it extremely well – I'm surprised at how well you speak it. I wonder if Pepika understands? Come here, Pepika, come to me!

KLARA: You know his name?

MILORAD: Of course I know his name. Come, little boy! Don't be afraid! Extraordinary, isn't it – he doesn't look a bit like me.

KLARA: But sir, who am I talking to … ?

MILORAD: I've already introduced myself.

KLARA: Since you know my name and my child's name as well, it's clear that I haven't come to the wrong address. But it seems very odd that you should have the same name as my husband.

MILORAD: It's not odd at all. I have your husband's name because I am your husband.

KLARA: Please explain. I don't understand any of this.

MILORAD: It's a bit difficult to explain if you won't accept that I am Doctor Milorad Tsviyovich.

KLARA: I'm prepared to accept that, but …

MILORAD: But you still don't believe it. I'll prove it to you. Will you accept that the mother who bore me will know who I am?

KLARA: Is she in?

MILORAD: Yes. I'll call her now. *(He rings a bell)*

KLARA: Please do. Perhaps she can make sense of this.

SCENE 5

MARITSA *(Enters)*: You rang, sir?

MILORAD: Please ask my mother to join us. Tell her that Klara has arrived with Pepika.

MARITSA Yes, sir. *(Exit left)*

SCENE 6

KLARA: Is your mother expecting me, then?

MILORAD: Yes, of course. You wrote, didn't you?

KLARA: Yes, but I wrote to him – my husband.

MILORAD: And sent your greetings to Grandpa and Grandma?

KLARA: Yes, but ... I simply can't understand this ... transformation. Nobody could possibly have changed so much. You don't look anything like my husband.

MILORAD: I haven't the slightest desire to look like him, but I give you my word of honour that I look exactly like Doctor Milorad Tsviyevich..

KLARA: That's as may be, but ...

MILORAD: Anyway, here comes Mother.

SCENE 7

(Enter MARA)

KLARA *(She runs to MARA and kisses her hand)*: Oh, mother dear, I'm so glad to see you!

MARA *(confused)*: But ...

KLARA *(to the little boy)*: Pepi, Liebchen! Küsse die Grossmutter! Dass ist deine Grossmutti!

MARA *(still more confused)*: Is this Pepika? Oh, I am so confused! What should I do now, Milorad?

MILORAD: Why don't you kiss your grandson?

MARA: Yes, of course. The child's not to blame. *(She kisses PEPIKA, then speaks to KLARA)* So, you're here at last. When did you arrive?

KLARA: About half an hour ago.

MARA: All alone? Didn't your husband meet you?

KLARA: No, he didn't.

MILORAD: That was rather rude of him.

KLARA: I wasn't sure which train I was coming on, or what time it arrived. *(She kisses MARA)*: Mother, you do look well! Milorad always spoke very fondly of you and told me how much you loved him. He said you were the best mother in the whole world.

MARA *(kissing and fondling MILORAD)*: All mothers are. And didn't you tell her that you were my one and only dearest son?

KLARA: No, not him!

MARA: What d'you mean?

KLARA: It wasn't him, it was my husband who told me all about you.

MARA: Your husband? I'm afraid I don't know your husband's mother.

MILORAD: No, I don't, either.

KLARA *(astonished)*: But ... but .. Madam, please tell me what's going on. I am here as a foreigner in a strange country. I don't know about your customs and habits. I don't know what's supposed to be a joke and what isn't. I'm totally confused: please explain.

MARA: Frankly, I wish someone would explain it to me too! I'm completely confused myself, and don't quite know how to manage all this.

KLARA *(indicating MILORAD)*: This gentleman says he is my husband.

MARA *(to MILORAD)*: Why on earth did you tell her that? Your father'll be very angry. *(To KLARA)* Actually, he is your husband, but for goodness' sake don't tell anyone else.

KLARA: But, Madam, really! Oh, this is awful! What on earth's going on? *(She breaks down in tears)*

MARA *(coming to comfort her)*: There, there! Don't cry! It'll soon be over: we're doing everything that needs to be done to get you divorced.

KLARA *(raising her head)*: Divorced? Why?

MARA: Well, you can't possibly remain his wife.

CLARA: Why not?

MARA: Why not? Oh, I don't know. Milorad, dear, tell her!

MILORAD: It'd be better if Father explained. *(To KLARA)* Grandpa will explain.

KLARA: Well, where is he?

MILORAD: He's out at the moment, but he'll be back soon.

KLARA *(impatiently)*: Oh! So now I've got to wait for him, I suppose!

MILORAD: Mother, she's been travelling: she's tired. I expect Pepika's hungry, too.

MARA: Oh, of course, of course! I'm so sorry, Klara. Come into the other room and we can wait for him together.

MILORAD: Please make yourself at home.

KLARA: Thank you.

MARA: This way *(She shows* KLARA *to the door, left, and follows her.* **Exit** KLARA *with* PEPIKA*)*.

MILORAD *(taking* MARA's *arm to detain her)*: I say, mother, this wife of mine's a good-looker, isn't she! *(*MARA *gestures to him to be quiet as she follows* KLARA *out.* **Exit** MARA*)*. Who'd have thought I'd have married such a pretty woman! *(**Exit** MILORAD, also left)*

SCENE 8

*(After a short pause, **enter** ZHIVOTA and BLAGOYE, arguing).*

ZHIVOTA: You did me out of at least eighty seats!

BLAGOYE: I tell you I didn't.

ZHIVOTA: I gave you the money to buy a hundred tickets and give them out to people on condition that they'd applaud enthusiastically, but in fact barely ten of them clapped at all. So, you cost me the price of at least eighty useless tickets.

BLAGOYE: But there was *some* applause.

ZHIVOTA: What applause? A few of them clapped – pretty unwillingly – but when Milorad got in a muddle and stumbled a bit over his words, all hundred of them burst out laughing as though they'd been given free tickets especially to jeer at him.

BLAGOYE: The ones who laughed were the ones who *had* paid for their tickets and you couldn't do anything about that – they laughed at their own expense.

ZHIVOTA: Idiots! And do you know what it was that made them laugh? It was all those long words – they were too stupid to realise that philosophy isn't philosophy unless there's a lot of long words. Here, you just tell me what 'Anticipatory Dynamics' means! I've learned those words by heart and I still haven't the faintest idea what they mean. You tell me!

BLAGOYE: I don't know.

ZHIVOTA: No, you don't, do you! And that proves that it's real philosophy. Philosophy is when you don't understand what I'm saying and I don't understand what you're saying.

BLAGOYE: I expect you're right.

ZHIVOTA: That's philosophical, that is. What's *not* philosphical is me giving you the money for a hundred tickets and you only buying twenty!

BLAGOYE: There you go again!

SCENE 9

(Enter MARA, leading PEPIKA)

ZHIVOTA *(stiffening with shock as he sees them)*: MARA: … it's not …

MARA: It is!

ZHIVOTA: Pepika?

MARA: Yes.

ZHIVOTA: Is it really him?

MARA: Yes, I assure you, it is.

ZHIVOTA: Pepika! Pepika! Oh, my word! *(He takes out a handkerchief and dabs his eyes)*

BLAGOYE: What are you crying for?

ZHIVOTA: My grandson!

BLAGOYE: What d'you mean, your grandson?

ZHIVOTA *(pulling himself together and looking stern)*: Yes, of course, you're right. It's silly to be sentimental over someone else's child.

MARA: I see that, but …

ZHIVOTA: I forgot myself. But, you know, 'formally' he is my grandson.

MARA: He's a very good little boy. He's quiet and he doesn't cry.

ZHIVOTA: What's he got to cry about? – he was born in Switzerland. If he'd been born in this country he'd have good reason to cry from the cradle to the grave! Anyway, have you told him what he's done to all of us?

MARA: Told who?

ZHIVOTA: Pepika.

MARA: Zhivota, for goodness' sake, he's only a child!

ZHIVOTA: A child he may be, but he's got to know. Someone's got to tell him. *(He bends down to speak to Pepika, talking him to him with great seriousness as though he could understand)* Now you listen to me carefully, my boy, and don't let what I say go in through one ear and out through the other. You were born – fine! That was your own business, and no one has any right to interfere with it. But that doesn't mean that you've got any right to interfere in other people's private business, either. But, my lad, from the moment you drew your first breath you've been interfering with my hopes and plans and you've thrown them into such disorder that it'll need God's help to sort them out. I'll give you one example to convince you that I'm not talking just for the sake of talking. Look at your little tummy. It's so small that you couldn't get half a kilo of cherries down into it, but it's already swallowed up my four hundred and seventy kilometres of Trans-Balkan railway, four viaducts, and seven tunnels. Do you know what that means? Have you ever even heard of the Trans-Balkan railway? You haven't, have you? But at least you should know what a Trans-Balkan railway is, and what translatlantic traffic is, and Transylvania, and … *(to* BLAGOYE*)* what was the other thing?

BLAGOYE: Transvaal.

ZHIVOTA: Yes – Transvaal. That's what you've done to me – eaten the lot!

BLAGOYE *(to Pepika)*: Versteht Du?

ZHIVOTA *(to* BLAGOYE*)*: 'Versteht' or not 'versteht', it's all the same to me so long as he listens to what I have to say. *(To Pepika)* Now, my boy, in time you're going to grow up. Let's say, for instance, that you leave school without any qualifications and then, not knowing how to amuse yourself, you turn into an idle layabout and start forging things – receipts, and cheques, and postal orders, and promissory notes, and suchlike. Very well, that's understandable when you're grown up, but you, my lad, were born a forgery! Was that proper? I ask you – was it proper? You're not a child – you're a forgery! I ask you – yes, you, my lad! – why did you have to choose to sign *my* name on your promissory note? Well, Pepika, my fine boy, you're just going to have to rub it out, yes you are!

MARA: Zhivota, you're talking to him as if he could understand.

ZHIVOTA: I wanted to tell him now, so that he couldn't come back later and say that I'd never told him. Anyway, frankly, it's made me feel better, explaining it all to to his face.

MARA: You should explain it to his father.

ZHIVOTA: I already have. Anyway … but … surely Pepika didn't come alone?

MARA: No, she's here.

ZHIVOTA: Who? Klara?

MARA: Yes.

ZHIVOTA: Well, what does she have to say about it?

MARA: She doesn't say anything: she's completely confused. She doesn't understand anything that's going on, and she's crying. She's in there with Slavka and Milorad.

ZHIVOTA: Make sure you tell Milorad that he's not her husband.

MARA: He knows that.

ZHIVOTA: Of course he knows – just tell him not to forget it! Is Velimir here yet?

MARA: No, but Milorad has sent for him.

ZHIVOTA: Good.

MARA: I thought I'd come in first. You know, she'd like to kiss you.

ZHIVOTA: What does she want to do that for?

MARA: Now don't be silly, dear! You can't get out of it. I'll call her.

ZHIVOTA: Oh, Lord, I don't know what to do. What do you think, Blagoye?

BLAGOYE: Well, a kiss on the cheek's all right. Only, keep your dignity – don't weaken or start crying.

ZHIVOTA: Why the devil should I cry?

BLAGOYE: When you saw Pepika, just now, you cried.

ZHIVOTA: Nonsense! – I just forgot myself for a moment. Would you please go and see her, Mara? I'll be with you in a second, but I just want to have a word with Blagoye.

MARA: Very well. *(To Pepika)* Come along then, Pe … Pe … Oh, Lord, I'll have to learn how to say it somehow. Come along, then. **(Exit**, *with Pepika)*.

SCENE 10

ZHIVOTA: Well now, Blagoye, you see how it is. She's here. She's come. We can't put it off any longer: we've got to decide what to do. We can't chuck her out, obviously. And it's no good offering her money to go away, either – if she took it and went, what then? That would leave Milorad still married to her, and we'd be no better off. We've got to think of a better idea. Come on – say something! You've sat on one of those chairs at the University – produce some high-grade learned advice, then!

BLAGOYE: I told you my idea before, Zhivota, and if you give it a bit of thought you'll see that it really is the best way.

ZHIVOTA: What way?

BLAGOYE: The way I said – we should catch her committing an act of infidelity, and on those grounds your son can apply for a divorce.

ZHIVOTA: But surely he could apply for a divorce without all that palaver?

BLAGOYE: He could, certainly, he could. Yes, he could say that someone else married her in his name – but that 'someone else' would promptly come and say why and how he did it.

ZHIVOTA: Don't mention that again! Leave that for now – what other ideas have you got?

BLAGOYE: Well, he could say that he can't stand her and that they're always quarrelling, but that way he'd be just as likely to get a judgment refusing him a divorce, and then he'd still be married and we'd have got nowhere.

ZHIVOTA: That's all we need!

BLAGOYE: The other way's better – it must be.

ZHIVOTA: All right, then. How are we going to arrange it?

BLAGOYE: Like I told you. Velimir is coming, isn't he?

ZHIVOTA: Yes, I sent for him.

BLAGOYE: Those two are husband and wife, aren't they? – and they haven't seen each other for over a year, have they? When they do they'll fly into each other's arms, and there you are – infidelity, because she's your son's wife! All you need is two witnesses, and the job's done. You know, when I plan something it always goes on oiled wheels.

ZHIVOTA: Oh yes! And when you planned Pepika, he appeared on oiled wheels, didn't he!

BLAGOYE: I only planned for the diploma, and you got it. It was Velimir who planned Pepika.

ZHIVOTA: Well, where are the witnesses you recommended?

BLAGOYE *(glances at his watch)*: I'm surprised they're not here yet. I told them to be here at eleven sharp. Hang on, I'll see. *(He rings the bell)*.

SCENE 11

MARITSA *(Enters)*: Yes, sir?

BLAGOYE: Have a lady and a gentleman arrived to see me?

MARITSA: No, sir.

BLAGOYE: As soon as they arrive show them in here, please.

MARITSA: Yes, sir. *(She goes out, but returns immediately)* A lady and gentlemen have just arrived, sir.

BLAGOYE: That'll be them. Ask them to come in.

(Enter SOYKA and HER HUSBAND. Exit MARITSA after ushering them in).

SCENE 12

BLAGOYE *(to ZHIVOTA)*: This is Mrs Soyka and her husband.

ZHIVOTA: How do you do?

SOYKA: This gentleman asked us to come.

ZHIVOTA: Yes, he said that you were experts in this business.

SOYKA: We certainly are. Mr Sima and I have been operating successfully for several years now.

ZHIVOTA: Who's Mr Sima?

SOYKA: My husband.

ZHIVOTA: But why do you call him 'Mr Sima'?

SOYKA: Well, he is my husband and he isn't. We live together under the same roof, but we were divorced five years ago.

ZHIVOTA: Why? That's strange.

SOYKA: On account of our work, for professional reasons. We found that when we gave evidence as husband and wife it always tended to be less credible, because we were suspected of having collaborated. Now, being divorced, we give evidence as two separate people and we've had no more problems. He's Mr Sima Yechmenich and I'm Miss Soyka Purich. I always call him 'Mr Sima' and he always calls me 'Miss Soyka', so that we get used to it and don't make any slips when we're before the court giving evidence.

ZHIVOTA: So you are, as it were, professional witnesses?

SOYKA: Yes, but only in divorce cases.

ZHIVOTA: Do you have plenty of work?

SOYKA: We're rushed off our feet. The fashionable things these days are politics, football, and divorce – everybody's at it. They get married, they live together for a few months, they get sick of each other, and it's off to the divorce court. And for a divorce you need witnesses.

ZHIVOTA: Do you charge a lot?

SOYKA: It's fairly expensive. Of course, a lot depends on the quality of the evidence. The rate for "We *heard* so-and-so" is one thing; the rate for "We *saw* so-and-so" is different, and so is the rate for "We *surprised them* doing ... "

ZHIVOTA: " ... so-and-so?"

SOYKA: No, not "so-and-so", but "this-and-that".

ZHIVOTA: What, actually ... "this-and-that"?

SOYKA: Yes, of course.

ZHIVOTA: I suppose that's the most expensive?

SOYKA: No, the most expensive is perjury.

ZHIVOTA: You don't do that, surely?

SOYKA: Why not, if it's necessary?

ZHIVOTA: But it's a criminal offence.

SOYKA: It's a criminal offence in every other sort of case, but in divorce cases it isn't. In other cases it's wrong to tell lies on oath. In divorce cases, on the other hand, you are carrying out a blessed duty to enable two people to be free of each other.

ZHIVOTA: You must be making a lot of money, then?

SOYKA: If only we could find a financier to invest some capital in the business we'd be able to expand still more.

ZHIVOTA: Expand? How?

SOYKA: Well, for instance, we would be able to supply plots and intrigues. Say some husband wants to dump his wife, but he hasn't got any grounds. All he has to do is come to us and we'll fix up an intrigue for him.

ZHIVOTA: But I thought that, in our society, plots and intrigues were supplied free.

SOYKA: Oh, yes, that's true, they are. But those sorts of plots and intrigues have to be done on the quiet, whereas in divorce cases they have to be shouted from the rooftops. That costs money.

ZHIVOTA: It's quite obvious that you know your business.

BLAGOYE: Indeed they do. That's why I recommended them.

ZHIVOTA: Well then, what are you proposing to do in this affair of mine?

SOYKA: Whatever you want: we are at your disposal.

ZHIVOTA: Blagoye, tell her your plan.

BLAGOYE: Right, then. We are arranging for Mr Zhivota's daughter-in-law to be unfaithful to her husband.

SOYKA: That's interesting. But just one question – is she inclined that way?

ZHIVOTA: More than likely – she's a woman, isn't she?

SOYKA: It's no good just saying that it's God's will that all women should be unfaithful, and that they can't oppose God's will. We need facts. Does she go out much? Where does she go? Has she women-friends? That sort of thing.

BLAGOYE: Hold on! Let me explain. She's here and she's not going out. But we know that at any moment now a young man is going to arrive here and that, as soon as she sees him, she'll run to him and kiss him.

SOYKA: Are you sure about that?

BLAGOYE: Absolutely.

ZHIVOTA: Yes, we're absolutely sure.

BLAGOYE: All we need is two witnesses who will swear that they saw see them kissing.

SOYKA: Actually *saw* them doing it? H'm – 'seeing' can be tricky. We don't actually *need* to see them, you know – we can give evidence about it anyway.

ZHIVOTA: No, no, I'd rather you actually saw them.

SOYKA: And do you think they'll be prepared to kiss each other in front of us?

ZHIVOTA: Oh, yes, they will!

BLAGOYE: I think that it would be better if you were to conceal yourselves, in that other room, say, and then jump out at them when they're in the middle of kissing.

ZHIVOTA: Yes, that would be better.

SOYKA *(thinks)*: Yes, possibly. Only, how are we going to know when it's the right moment to jump out?

ZHIVOTA: Perhaps you could look through the keyhole?

SOYKA: No, it'd be better if someone gave us a signal.

ZHIVOTA: How about that, Blagoye?

BLAGOYE: What kind of signal?

SOYKA: The simplest thing would be to drop something that makes a noise. *(She looks about)* This tray might do. *(Picking up a large silver tray, she raps it with her knuckles and it makes a loud noise)* Yes, we'd be able to hear that all right.

ZHIVOTA: That seems fine. What d'you say, Blagoye?

BLAGOYE: Yes, all right.

ZHIVOTA: Do you agree, Mr .. er .. Sima?

SOYKA's HUSBAND Excuse me, I can't say anything. My wife has forbidden me to speak when we're with other people.

SOYKA: He's damned right, I have! He never stops talking – I had to put my foot down. He could ruin all my hard work by his chattering. And yet when we're due to give evidence I have to write out everything that he's supposed to say, make him learn it by heart, and then cross-examine him on it before I dare take him to the court-house.

ZHIVOTA: Right, then, that's it! We'll have to hurry, though – he'll arrive any minute.

BLAGOYE: Shall I take them into the other room?

ZHIVOTA: Yes, in there.

BLAGOYE: Come with me, please. *(Exeunt* SOYKA *and her* HUSBAND *into the room, right, with* BLAGOYE *leading them.* BLAGOYE *immediately returns).*

SCENE 13

ZHIVOTA: What an extraordinary woman!

BLAGOYE: It's because of her job.

ZHIVOTA: I forgot to ask her how much she'll charge for this.

BLAGOYE: It'll be according to her price-list. She charges fixed prices.

ZHIVOTA: Anyway, the moment this is over I'm off to the lawyer and he can draw up the application for divorce on the spot.

BLAGOYE: D'you think Milorad will sign it?

ZHIVOTA: He'll sign – but no doubt it'll be according to *his* price-list. *He* charges fixed prices. For giving one public lecture – ten thousand dinars. For signing one divorce application – we'll have to wait and see.

SCENE 14

MARA *(poking her head round the door)*: Are you coming, Zhivota, or do you want her to come out there?

ZHIVOTA: I'm coming! I'm coming! *(*MARA *withdraws.* ZHIVOTA *goes toward the door and stops)* There now . . ! I don't know what I'm to do.

BLAGOYE: Just stay aloof.

ZHIVOTA: All right. And you … just you mind that tray! *(Exit)*.

SCENE 15

*(*BLAGOYE *moves the tray so that it is close to his hand.*
Enter MRS DRAGA).*

DRAGA: Good morning to you!

BLAGOYE: Oh, good morning! How are you?

DRAGA: Well, thank you. Blagoye, I've come to ask you an important question.

BLAGOYE: Yes, what?

DRAGA: What went wrong? Why did the young gentleman so disgrace himself over the lecture?

BLAGOYE: Oh, I wouldn't say he disgraced himself.

DRAGA: How can you say that – the whole audience laughed at him!

BLAGOYE: Pah, the audience! Look, they paid for their tickets and so they had the right to laugh – or to burst into tears, if they wanted. They're of no importance. On the other hand, I've talked to the experts, university professors – you know, I'm very intimate with some of the professors at the University – and they all admitted that the lecture was academically remarkable. Believe me, I've spoken to a lot of them, and they were amazed.

DRAGA: That's all very well – that's philosophy: I don't know anything about it and I've no wish to insult it. I just want to know why he got so confused and muddled that he started to pronounce his words back-to-front.

BLAGOYE: Well, that was our fault, not his.

DRAGA: How could it have been our fault? – he was doing the talking.

BLAGOYE: It certainly was our fault, though. We'd told him that the daughter of the Minister of Transport would be coming to the lecture. That wouldn't have mattered in itself, because it was a public lecture, after all, and all the daughters of all the ministers in the entire government could attend if they wanted to – they'd only have been part of the audience like everyone else. But just before he started we told him where she was sitting, with her mother, the Minister's wife, in the front row on the left. And he – he told me himself afterwards – started speaking perfectly well until, suddenly, he saw her sitting there. Their eyes met, he said, and he immediately felt something … something – I don't know how to say it …

DRAGA: Well, something, anyway.

BLAGOYE: Yes, something. He felt something – his heart turned over and a mist came before his eyes.

DRAGA: He was struck on her, was he?

BLAGOYE: He was indeed! He was bowled over. And that's why he got so confused. The letters danced before his eyes like snowflakes. 'S' looked like 'F', 'F' like 'C', 'C' like 'R', 'R' like 'S', and 'S' like 'A' – he said. Everything was all over the place, and so he couldn't read anything properly. Her beauty so fascinated him that he got all the letters mixed up, and that's a fact! In the circumstances, even the Rector of the University himself would have been confused.

DRAGA: Well, that may be so, but there's something else that's much more serious.

BLAGOYE: What?

DRAGA: I must ask you, dear Blagoye, to be frank. We must avoid scandal.

BLAGOYE: So far as frankness is concerned, you can rely on me. What is this other thing?

DRAGA: I can hardly believe it, it's all a matter of whispered rumours – and you know what it's like when people whisper …

BLAGOYE: What are they whispering about?

DRAGA: The rumour is that young Doctor Tsviyovich is married.

BLAGOYE: Oh my God!

DRAGA: As I say, that's the rumour.

BLAGOYE: But if it was true they wouldn't be whispering, they'd be shouting out loud.

DRAGA: But where could this idea have come from?

BLAGOYE: It's a rotten plot – an intrigue – it can't be anything else.

DRAGA: Just imagine what a scandal it would be! The Government Ministers' wives would look down on me as nothing more than a cheat and swindler, and they'd all close their doors to me, and I'd be .. Oh! oh! I can't bear to think of it.

BLAGOYE: But it's ridiculous! Why would we be seeking a bride for a married man?

DRAGA: Well, who could have started such a rumour?

BLAGOYE: I'll tell you. He's a good-looking lad, isn't he, well-educated, a fine philosopher, with a diploma in a big frame on the wall – in other words, a young man with a glittering career in front of him. On top of that, he's the only son and heir of a very rich man. Who wouldn't want to marry their daughter off to a catch like him? So, obviously, you see, lots of would-be match-makers have been swarming all over Zhivota – swarming all over him like flies round a sugar-bowl. He just brushes them off, but it's no good – they keep at him. Quite recently one of them, a Mrs Vida … do you know her, by the way?

DRAGA: No, I don't.

BLAGOYE: I don't know her either. But this Mrs Vida came round to talk about a rich girl with an enormous dowry – a house, two houses, three houses, a vineyard, two vineyards, three vineyards, and money too – plenty of cash in the bank. She came trying to press this girl's attractions on Zhivota, but do you know what he said? He said: "Madam, I accept that this is a very attractive proposition, but my son has certain obligations."

DRAGA: What obligations?

BLAGOYE: Surely you understand? – Zhivota considered himself to be under an unbreakable obligation, since he had approved you as match-maker, and had said: "The daughter of the Minister of Transport – none other!" Believe me, if anyone had offered him the daughter of the Minister of Social Security or anyone else you like, even the daughter of the Minister of Internal Affairs, he would have said: "No! Either the daughter of the Minister of Transport or no one!"

DRAGA: No, of course, those others don't have any kilometres.

BLAGOYE: Exactly! Don't you see? – when he said to Mrs Vida: "My son has certain obligations," she probably jumped to the conclusion that if he turned down such a marvellous opportunity simply because of 'obligations', that could only mean that he must be married already. That's how the rumour started – it must have been like that.

DRAGA: Maybe. But will you give me your word that the rumour is untrue?

BLAGOYE: I'll swear it on the Bible if necessary!

SCENE 16

VELIMIR *(Enters)*: Good morning!

BLAGOYE: Ah, there you are! Where've you been?

VELIMIR: Is it true that Klara's here?

BLAGOYE: Yes.

VELIMIR: And the boy?

BLAGOYE: Yes.

VELIMIR *(going towards the left-hand door)*: Where is she, then? Is she in here?

BLAGOYE: Steady on – she's not in there! She asked me to call her as soon as you arrived. *(He starts to go, but suddenly stops, confused. He turns to* MRS DRAGA*)* But you're still here ... oh, er, don't you think you ought to be going?

DRAGA: What, without having a word with Mr Zhivota?

BLAGOYE: Yes, I thought you might want to talk to him too, but there's no need. I promise you that I will tell him everything you said, word for word ...

DRAGA: But that's not the same as talking to someone directly.

BLAGOYE: No, I suppose not.

VELIMIR *(impatiently)*: Uncle Blagoye, please ...

BLAGOYE *(remembers)*: Oh yes, very well! *(Exit)*.

SCENE 17

DRAGA: You seem rather impatient, young man?

VELIMIR: Yes, I'm afraid I am, rather. But he was going on and on … *(At this moment he sees* BLAGOYE *and* KLARA *in the doorway as they **enter**)* Klara!

KLARA: Milorad! *(They rush together, embrace, and kiss passionately.* BLAGOYE *hurries over and grabs the tray, which he bangs and rattles energetically).*

SCENE 18

*(**Enter** SOYKA, bursting out of the other room like a jack-in-the-box, with* HER HUSBAND *behind her).*

SOYKA: Oh! oh! oh! oh!

SOYKA'S HUSBAND: Well! well! well! well!

SOYKA: Shamelessly kissing another man's wife!

SOYKA'S HUSBAND: Scandalous!

VELIMIR *(turning his head)*: And, pray, who are you?

SOYKA: We shall introduce ourselves in a moment.

VELIMIR: Uncle Blagoye, do you know who they are?

BLAGOYE: I've no idea.

VELIMIR *(to* MRS DRAGA*)*: Do you know, Madam?

DRAGA: I've never seen them before.

VELIMIR: Well, who are you, then?

SOYKA: We are witnesses to the fact that you have been kissing another man's wife – and in public, too! *(To* MRS DRAGA*)* You saw it, didn't you!

DRAGA: I certainly did.

SOYKA *(to* BLAGOYE*)*: And you saw it too?

BLAGOYE: Of course, nobody could have failed to see it.

SOYKA: Four witnesses, then. That's quite enough – too many, in fact.

VELIMIR *(angrily)*: Madam, whoever you are, you are impudent!

SOYKA: Good! Write that down, Mr Sima.

VELIMIR *(now furious)*: Yes! And write this down too: "Barging in to someone else's house without introducing yourselves to anyone, and thrusting yourselves into a family matter which is none of your business – that is the very height of impertinence!" Uncle Blagoye, with your permission I shall now throw these two people out of the house.

SOYKA: Oho!

SOYKA'S HUSBAND: Oho!

BLAGOYE *(embarrassed)*: Well, you know, I'm not the master here.

VELIMIR: Then let's get him in here! *(He goes to the door and shouts)* Mister Zhivota! Mister Zhivota! *(He returns)* Now we'll see!

SCENE 19

(Enter ZHIVOTA, MARA, MILORAD, and SLAVKA, who is leading Pepika)

ALL OF THE ABOVE *(variously)*: What is it? What's happening?

ZHIVOTA: Who called me?

SOYKA: This gentleman wishes to throw us out of your house.

(Meanwhile VELIMIR, seeing Pepika, runs to him, picks him up, and kisses him. KLARA goes to SLAVKA and starts to speak quietly to her).

ZHIVOTA: What are you talking about? Why should he throw you out?

SOYKA: As you know, Mr Zhivota, we simply came here to discuss the letting of your apartment in Molerova Street. We were asked to wait in that room because we were told that you were for the moment engaged in family matters. We waited there, and when we opened the door to see if you were in here we were presented with a most scandalous sight. *(She points to KLARA)* This young woman is your daughter-in-law, isn't she?

ZHIVOTA *(embarrassed)*: Well, er … in a manner of speaking … Yes! She is!

DRAGA *(who has hitherto been in the background, unnoticed by ZHIVOTA, now bridles and says, in an ominous voice)*: What did I hear? *(She starts to come forward).*

SOYKA: Well, we have just surprised her in the very act of kissing this young man.

ZHIVOTA: Why, that's terrible! That's brazen infidelity! I cannot allow that sort of thing to happen in my house – my honour, my reputation are at stake! It is disgraceful! Will you please be witnesses?

SOYKA: Gladly!

VELIMIR *(shocked, to* MARA *and the others)*: What on earth is going on?

DRAGA *(confronting* ZHIVOTA*)*: I also was present. I shall be a witness too.

ZHIVOTA *(shocked at unexpectedly seeing her)*: You! What are you doing here?

DRAGA: I came here to enquire into an unheard-of scandal. So, your son *is* married, then?

ZHIVOTA *(embarrassed)*: No, he's not!

DRAGA *(to* BLAGOYE*)*: And you, dear Blagoye, a few moments ago you were prepared to swear on the Bible, weren't you?

BLAGOYE: Well, I …

DRAGA: Mr Zhivota, what is the meaning of this?

ZHIVOTA: It doesn't mean anything..

DRAGA: I have been deceived! It is disgraceful! So much for your honour and your reputation!

ZHIVOTA *(in despair)* But wait … please!

DRAGA: You have brought humiliation upon me – you and this so-called friend of mine Blagoye! And not only that, don't you think that you're going to get off lightly with also bringing into disrepute the reputation and honour of the highly respectable family of a government minister!

ZHIVOTA: But please, wait a minute! Blagoye! – explain it to her!

VELIMIR: Madam, I can explain …

ZHIVOTA: You shut up! It's your behaviour that has brought disgrace on us and wrecked a happy marriage!

MARA: But, Zhivota …

ZHIVOTA: And you shut up, too!

DRAGA: And I am most surprised that your son, the wronged husband, can stay so calm.

MILORAD *(laughs and shrugs his shoulders)*: What's it got to do with me?

ZHIVOTA: It may not have anything to do with you, but it has a lot to do with me! *(To* SOYKA*)* Very well, I count on you to act as witnesses. *(To* MRS DRAGA*)* And in the end you'll find that my son is not married.

SOYKA: What d'you mean – he's not married?

ZHIVOTA: Well, maybe he is – don't confuse me! As far as you're concerned, he's married. As far as this lady is concerned, he isn't.

DRAGA: What? Oh no, that won't do at all!

KLARA *(to* SLAVKA, *despairingly)* What on earth is going on?

SLAVKA: We'll see. Don't worry.

DRAGA: I would be much obliged to you, sir, if before I leave you would kindly tell me what I am to say to the Minister's wife.

VELIMIR: And I would be very grateful for an explanation of what's happening.

SOYKA: And I would like …

ZHIVOTA *(in such a tangle that he does know which way to turn)*: Now wait a minute, all of you! You're all coming at me at once – you're all asking questions. Keep calm, all of you – I can explain everything. Right! This is the situation. *(To* BLAGOYE*)* What the devil are you looking at me like that for? – you haven't the guts to explain it yourself.

BLAGOYE: But I don't know …

ZHIVOTA: No, you don't! And since you don't know, why are you interfering? Let me explain – don't interrupt! Right! Where was I? … oh yes. *(To* SOYKA*)* You came here to see me about that apartment in Molerova Street, didn't you? Well, it's a very desirable property, with a hall, three rooms with parquet floors and good heating arrangements, a nursery room, a pantry, a kitchen, a scullery, and all modern conveniences. The apartment is not damp, I can assure you, and it occupies a sunny location. Believe me ...

VELIMIR: That's nothing to do with it. That's not what I want to
know.

ZHIVOTA: What d'you mean – 'what you want to know'? You've
ruined everything, and now you have the impertinence to
question me!

DRAGA: What about the answer to *my* question?

ZHIVOTA: But of course, I'll answer your question. When you
next visit the Minister, please give him my compliments and
say that I have the greatest respect and admiration for him.

DRAGA: That's not what I asked. What am I going to tell him?

ZHIVOTA: Tell him ... er ... tell him ... Blagoye, what should she
tell him?

SCENE 20

(Enter MRS SPASOYEVICH *and* MRS PROTICH. *They bring in
four young children from the Nursery School, two boys and two
girls. One of them is the* GIRL *with a* BOUQUET*)*

ZHIVOTA: *(pulls his hair)* Oh good God Almighty! The 'Nursery
School Number Nine' – that's all we needed!

SPASOYEVICH and PROTICH: *(in unison)* We have come with
some children from our Nursery School to thank Doctor
Tsviyovich, in the name of the Board and on behalf of all the
neglected children, for giving his lecture for the benefit of our
establishment.

ZHIVOTA: Thank you! Thank you!

MILORAD: *(He picks up a cushion, but* SLAVKA *seizes his arm)*
Let me go! I want to chuck it at them!

SLAVKA: Milorad! Stop it!

GIRL with the BOUQUET *(Curtseys, and starts to recite)*: "Your
most gracious Excellency!"

ZHIVOTA: Who can that be? Does she mean you, Blagoye?

MILORAD *(still struggling with* SLAVKA*)*: Let me go, I say!

SPASOYEVICH: I'm sorry. I'm afraid the child got confused with
the greeting we gave the Bishop when he consecrated our

school. *(To the girl)* Start again, dear!

GIRL with the BOUQUET:

"Dear Doctor of Philosophy, we're glad
That you could come and lecture us. We had
A lovely time. Now please accept these flowers
With all the thanks of this dear school of ours."

SPASOYEVICH: It was Mrs Protich who composed that poem.

PROTICH: Yes, that's right.

MILORAD: An exceptionally beautiful poem!

SPASOYEVICH *(to the girl with the bouquet, urging her towards* MILORAD*)*: Go on – give the bouquet to the gentleman, dear!

DRAGA: No, she'd better give it to this lady *(indicating* KLARA*)*. She's his wife.

SPASOYEVICH and PROTICH: What? His wife! He's married?

DRAGA: He most certainly is! – isn't he, Mr Zhivota?

ZHIVOTA: Don't interfere – it's got nothing to do with him being married!

DRAGA: As I said, he's married. *(To* SOYKA*)* That's right, isn't it?

SOYKA: Of course he's married.

SPASOYEVICH: Oh dear! We sold over a hundred tickets by specially telling people that the lecturer was unmarried.

PROTICH: Oh, Mr Tsviyovich, why didn't you tell us before?

ZHIVOTA: What are you interfering for? What's the Nursery School Number Nine doing, getting mixed up in my affairs? For God's sake leave me in peace!

MILORAD *(to* SLAVKA*)*: I can't hold back any longer! I've got to do it! *(*SLAVKA *keeps hold of him)*.

SPASOYEVICH and PROTICH: We are not interfering. We are simply drawing attention to the difficulty that you have got us into.

DRAGA: Your difficulties – pshaw! What about mine!

KLARA: And mine!

VELIMIR: And mine!

ZHIVOTA *(looking at each of them)*: What about mine?

DRAGA: What do they matter to us?

ZHIVOTA: And what do yours matter to me?

DRAGA: So! It's time we heard the truth. At least everything's out in the open now!

SPASOYEVICH and PROTICH: Yes, it's better out the open.

ZHIVOTA: Oh, shut up, you stupid women!

SPASOYEVICH and PROTICH: Sir! We are ladies!

ZHIVOTA: All right, you're ladies – now shut up!

DRAGA *(to* ZHIVOTA*)*: The gentleman is so polite!

SPASOYEVICH and PROTICH: So we see!

ZHIVOTA: *(tearing his hair)*: God Almighty! – this place has become a madhouse! *(To his family)* Don't just stand there, looking! Put me in a straitjacket! I think I'm going crazy. My head's going round in circles. I can't think straight any more – do you hear? I just can't think straight any more!

SCENE 21

(Enter MARITSA *and* DR REISSER*)*

REISSER *(as Maritsa shows him in)*: Good morning!

ZHIVOTA: Good God! – not him too! What the devil does he want?

REISSER *(approaching* BLAGOYE*)*: I have come, sir, to inform you …

ZHIVOTA *(to* REISSER*)*: For God's sake, man, why are you still hanging about here? Why the devil haven't you gone off to Athens by now?

REISSER *(offended)*: I beg your pardon!

VELIMIR *(to* ZHIVOTA*)*: Sir, you can't adopt that tone with the Professor.

ZHIVOTA: Really? Well, I don't know what the Swiss tone is.

SPASOYEVICH and PROTICH *(to* REISSER*)*: Dear Professor, we are deeply sorry that you were unable to honour us with your presence at the lecture which your protegé gave last night.

ZHIVOTA *(shouting)*: Just shut up, you Nursery School lot!

SPASOYEVICH and PROTICH *(deeply offended)*: Oh! Did you hear that? This is too much!

(MILORAD *wrenches himself free of* SLAVKA'S *grasp and hurls the cushion, which hits one of the Nursery School ladies on the head. The scene becomes one of compete uproar.* VELIMIR *heatedly argues with* DR REISSER, BLAGOYE *with* SPASOYEVICH *and* PROTICH, MILORAD *with* MARA, *while* SLAVKA *comforts* KLARA).

ZHIVOTA: Pepika! Poor, wretched little Pepika! Now you can see with your own eyes what you have turned my house into!

Curtain

Act Four

Zhivota's office, as in Act One.

SCENE 1

*(**Enter** MARITSA, left, carrying a tray on which is an emptied glass of milk and one or two other things). A moment later **enter** VELIMIR from the door at rear)*

VELIMIR: Oh, Maritsa, I'm glad I ran into you. Have you just come out of that room?

MARITSA: Yes, I took in some milk for the little boy.

VELIMIR: Is my wife in there?

MARITSA: Do you mean Mr Milorad's wife?

VELIMIR: Whichever – is she in there?

MARITSA: Yes, she's in there with Miss Slavka. Oh sir, I do beg your pardon for saying such a thing, but I'm afraid I'm in a complete muddle about whose wife she is.

VELIMIR: Don't worry, that's not your concern, Maritsa. Would you please go in there and ask Miss Slavka if she would come out and see me.

MARITSA: Only her?

VELIMIR: Yes, only her. Don't tell her it's me – just say ; "There's a gentleman to see you."

MARITSA: Very well. *(She puts the tray down on a table and goes into the room, left).*

SCENE 2

MARITSA *(coming back after a few moments. She picks up the tray):* She's coming now.

VELIMIR: Thank you, Maritsa. *(**Exit** MARITSA, by rear door).*

SLAVKA *(**Enters**, left, and is surprised to see Velimir):* Oh, it's you?

VELIMIR: I do sincerely beg your pardon for disturbing you.

SLAVKA: Not at all! – but why all this excusing yourself? Won't you come in and see Klara and the little boy?

VELIMIR: No, I'd rather not see them for the moment. I wanted to have a word with you.

SLAVKA: What? Are you trying to avoid them?

VELIMIR: Yes, I'm afraid I am. After all that's happened I feel I owe Klara an explanation. From the moment she came into this house she's had nothing but trouble and confusion. She hasn't the slightest idea what's going on. She's completely bewildered: she goes round asking everybody what's happening and nobody answers her.

SLAVKA: Well you're certainly the one who should tell her.

VELIMIR: I know, but I'm afraid I don't quite know how to go about it. I'd have to make myself out a criminal.

SLAVKA: And haven't you got the courage to do it?

VELIMIR: I have, yes, but I'd much rather you helped me.

SLAVKA: I don't see how I can help.

VELIMIR: You tell her – tell her everything, absolutely everything, please! And don't spare me – tell her the very worst about me, as I'd have to do myself.

SLAVKA: And why can't you do it yourself?

VELIMIR: It's very hard for a fellow to confess to wrongdoing – it makes him feel small. It's not so bad when someone else makes the accusation.

SLAVKA: Well, tell me, what am I to accuse you of?

VELIMIR: Anything you like – don't try to spare me.

SLAVKA: If I do, aren't you afraid that Klara will be disappointed in you?

VELIMIR: She's going to be disappointed anyway – it can't be avoided.

SLAVKA: I don't like it a bit, but I will do it. I am prepared to do it for you, but mainly out of consideration for that poor girl. She's poured out her heart to me and asked for comfort and, above all, for an explanation – but I didn't like to explain everything to her unless you agreed.

VELIMIR: I'm very, very grateful to you, Slavka. If you don't mind, I'll make myself scarce.

SLAVKA: All right. But afterwards, as soon as this is over, you'd better come back so that it won't look as though you were running away from everything.

VELIMIR: No, I wouldn't want that to happen. I'll be back later. Thank you very much, again. *(Exit)*.

SCENE 3

SLAVKA *(going to the doorway, left)*: Klara! Klara! May I have a word? *(Enter KLARA)*

KLARA: Did you call me?

SLAVKA: Yes. I want to talk to you. Mother's in there with Pepika and the others, isn't she? We can be alone here, then. Let's sit down! *(They sit on the sofa, side by side)* You've been asking me since yesterday to explain everything to you.

KLARA: I'd be very grateful..

SLAVKA: I realise that I'll have to do it. It has been very cruel, keeping you in suspense like this.

KLARA *(embraces her)*: Oh, you are so understanding!

SLAVKA: I must ask you to forgive me for not explaining everything straightaway, but there were some problems and, anyway, I thought someone else was going to do it.

KLARA: Yes, I expected my husband to tell me what was going on, but he seems to have been avoiding me since yesterday.

SLAVKA: I don't think he's been deliberately avoiding you, but the fact is, he's in a rather difficult position.

KLARA: Why?

SLAVKA: Listen, and I'll explain everything. *(Pauses)* My brother,
Milorad Tsviyovich – and I tell you, truthfully, that he's the
only person in this house with that name – is a decent and
good-hearted man, but nobody could pretend that he was
much good at school work and academic studies. On the other
hand, my father was desperately anxious that his son should
go to university, obtain a degree, and be able take the title of
'Doctor'. That simply wasn't possible – there was no way that
Milorad could fulfill his father's ambition, and so they resorted
to a rather peculiar plan. Milorad had a schoolfriend, an
extremely clever boy called Velimir Pavlovich, who was too
poor to be able to afford to go to university, so my father
arranged for him to take Milorad's place, using his name and
pretending to be him. Father provided him with all the
necessary documents, school certificates, and so on, all in my
brother's name, and sent him abroad to the University of
Fribourg, to be a full-time student there, pass the exams, and
gain a Doctor of Philosophy degree.

KLARA *(She has been listening attentively to what* SLAVKA *is
saying, and now suddenly realises its implications. She sits
upright, initially too shocked to speak, but then she looks* SLAVKA
steadily in the eye and says quietly): Then that means …

SLAVKA: Try not to get too upset, you should hear the rest.

KLARA *(bursts out)*: The rest! D'you mean to say there's more
yet? My husband married me under a false name, so legally
I'm not his wife. Is that what you're going to tell me? Have you
got to spell it out – that I have been tricked, deceived, and
disgraced! *(She chokes and lies back on the sofa, sobbing. Then
she raises her head)* So that's why he didn't have the courage to
tell me himself! So that's why he's been avoiding me!

SLAVKA: You must try to be calm.

KLARA: I am the wretched victim of a disgraceful deception.

SLAVKA: It wasn't a deception, really.

KLARA: I don't know what happens here, but where I come from,
and in the rest of the world, this would be regarded as a

disgraceful deception, and the man – what was his name? …

KLARA: Velimir.

KLARA: … Yes him, Velimir – he's an out-and-out deceiver.

SLAVKA: I don't think it's fair to call him a deceiver.

KLARA: What is he, then?

SLAVKA *(stubbornly)*: He's not really a deceiver.

KLARA: Well, what's the right word in your language for a man who marries a woman fraudulently, under a false name?

SLAVKA: We'd call him the same as you do. But, even so, Velimir didn't deceive you. A man who, in a reckless moment, brings a woman's good name into question but who then takes the risk of marrying her, even under a false name, just so as to save her reputation, who doesn't let her pay in humiliation and pain the consequences of her rash behaviour – a man who does that is not a deceiver.

KLARA: You appear to know the whole story. Are you his representative, then?

SLAVKA: I have been a friend of his since childhood.

KLARA: That doesn't explain why you should be defending him so fiercely. Don't forget that he didn't just stop at one deception – he held himself out as coming from a wealthy family!

SLAVKA: What difference did it make whether he came from a rich or a poor family?

KLARA *(astonished)*: But I thought I was marrying a rich man's son!

SLAVKA: But I thought that it was love that drove you to take that step.

KLARA: Well … love, of course, but we people in the west understand love rather differently to you southerners. With us, love is a practical thing: to you it is simply romantic. We don't think of the passing delirium of cooing and kissing as love: with us, love is the bond which ties two creatures into a single entity for life.

SLAVKA: But Klara, love can't be defined – it's just the same here as it is with you, whether at the North Pole or the South Pole.

KLARA: Nowhere between the North and the South Poles can the union of two paupers bring happiness. So, obviously, the matter of how rich he was a serious consideration – and he didn't dare to tell the truth about it. And because of that I can't regard him as anything other than a deceiver.

SLAVKA: But really!

KLARA: It's no use trying to persuade me – I'm not convinced. From this moment onward I shall regard him as nothing more than a common cheat and my only feeling towards him is one of contempt.

SLAVKA: Oh!

KLARA: So far as I am concerned, he no longer exists.

SLAVKA: Oh, don't let your disappointment drive you that far! He is a poor man, yes – a poor man now, as he was all along – but he has borne his poverty bravely. He's a man with the intelligence, energy, and the courage to overcome all life's difficulties. He doesn't deserve your rebuke. You should think kindly of him, because he is a decent and honest man who has not allowed himself to be corrupted by circumstances.

KLARA (*her eyes widening as she realises the truth*): Are you … in love with him?

SLAVKA (*starting like a thief caught in the act*): Of course not! That's ridiulous!

KLARA (*drawing out the words*): You are in love with him! (*SLAVKA says nothing. She lowers her head and makes a gesture of denial*). You *are* in love with him, and that's why you've started blurting it all out. It could all have been explained to me before. I see now that the gulf between us is even deeper than I had originally thought. I am a hindrance to your father and to his ambitions; I am a hindrance to your brother and to his future; I am a hindrance to you and to your happiness.

SLAVKA (*crying*): I never said it! Never! Never! (*She curls up in a corner of the sofa and buries her face in a cushion, sobbing bitterly*)

KLARA: And what about my little boy? My little boy! *(She curls up in the other corner of the sofa, also burying her face in a cushion, and weeps)*.

SCENE 4

(Enter ZHIVOTA*)*

ZHIVOTA *(nonplussed at finding them in this state, stares at them for a moment)*: Well now, have you two been having a nice talk? *(*KLARA *and* SLAVKA *do not raise their heads)*. Slavka, my dear, why don't you go and have a cry in the next room – I want to have a word with Klara. *(*SLAVKA *gets up and, holding a handkerchief to her face, exit)*.

SCENE 5

ZHIVOTA: Klara, I need to talk to you.

KLARA *(sitting up and composing herself)*: Very well!

ZHIVOTA: Klara, there are certain things that I have to tell you. For a start, you need to know whose wife you are. For instance, you think that you are your husband's wife, but in fact you're not …

KLARA: I know all about it.

ZHIVOTA: What, everything?

KLARA: Yes, everything.

ZHIVOTA: Right! That saves me from having to explain. And now that you know everything you can see for yourself why I had to accuse you of infidelity.

KLARA: Oh yes, I quite understand. I'll not stand in your way. I'm quite prepared to help.

ZHIVOTA: Excellent! I'm very grateful to you. In what way could you help, then?

KLARA: You can accuse me of anything you like – the more sensational the better. You can say, for instance, that while I was there, in Fribourg, I used to entertain a lover whenever my husband was away.

ZHIVOTA: Oho! That's marvellous! What was his name?

KLARA: Whose name?

ZHIVOTA: Your lover's.

KLARA: How should I know? – I never had a lover. But you're welcome to say that I did.

ZHIVOTA: But who shall we say he was?

KLARA: Oh … put down … Johann Wolfgang Goethe!

ZHIVOTA *(busily writing)*: Fine! And it's good that he's got three names – you can always remember one of them even if you forget the others. Is there anything else you can admit to – anything as serious as that?

KLARA: Not really, but if it's any help to you you can say that I travelled here with a rich Romanian gentleman who paid my train fare.

ZHIVOTA *(excitedly)*: Excellent! What was his name?

KLARA: I don't know. I've never met any Romanians in my life.

ZHIVOTA: Let's call him Titulescu. If he was a Romanian he was probably called that. *(Writes it down)* Look – you're not going to take any of this back later, are you?

KLARA: No, I'll admit it all!

ZHIVOTA: I don't really understand why you're prepared to do this.

KLARA: I just want to get it all over, so that I can get away from here as soon as possible.

ZHIVOTA: You want to leave?

KLARA: Yes, I do. I can see that I'm just a nuisance to you all.

ZHIVOTA: That really is very decent of you, very decent. I've always been a great admirer of Swiss education.

KLARA: There is one thing, sir. I hope you won't think less of me if I ask something of you. I am not well off. I haven't even got enough money for my fare back to Switzerland. Might I ask for some help in that direction?

ZHIVOTA: If you really want to go, I'll buy first-class tickets for you!

KLARA: Thank you. Yes, I do want to go.

ZHIVOTA *(considers)*: Yes, I will give you the money for that! And, as you say … you're not well off … but how will you be able to earn a living?

KLARA: I don't know. I'll look about. I'll probably be able to find a job.

ZHIVOTA: Yes, but in the meanwhile, while you're looking for one?

KLARA: I don't know.

ZHIVOTA *(thinking)*: Look, I'll prove to you that I had a Swiss education, too. I'll be straight with you – I won't do you out of even ten paras. As soon as you wrote saying that you were coming I decided that I'd offer you twenty thousand dinars to go away. There! I won't go back on it now – that's what I'll give you!

KLARA: Thank you, but I don't wish to take your money. I'm not prepared to sell my happiness or my child's future. I'm not a blackmailer.

ZHIVOTA: God love us, of course you're not a blackmailer! You didn't ask for the money – I'm offering it to you freely.

KLARA: Thank you.

ZHIVOTA: Good! That's all right, then. Anyway, do you mind if I go off to the lawyers now and lay the complaint against you straightaway?

KLARA: By all means!

ZHIVOTA: Right! I'm off! If anyone asks for me, tell them I'll be back soon. *(Exit)*.

SCENE 6

*(*KLARA, *left alone, bursts into tears. After a pause,* **enter** MRS SPASOYEVICH *and* MRS PROTICH).

SPASOYEVICH and PROTICH *(in unison)*: Good day to you. We beg your pardon, but we would like to speak to the gentleman.

KLARA: Which gentleman? The young one?

SPASOYEVICH and PROTICH: No, the older one.

KLARA: He's just gone out, but he'll be back soon.

SPASOYEVICH and PROTICH: We'll wait for him, then.

SPASOYEVICH: We have reported yesterday's scandalous events to an Extraordinary Meeting of the Board of Management of our Day-Nursery.

PROTICH: And the Board has passed a Resolution which authorises us to demand satisfaction from the gentleman.

SPASOYEVICH: Otherwise we shall be obliged to take further steps.

PROTICH: Because he has not only insulted us ...

SPASOYEVICH: ... but he has insulted our whole Institution, the whole Nursery School Number Nine.

PROTICH: And you will understand, Madam ...

KLARA *(spiritedly)*: No, I'm afraid I don't. I don't know anything about it.

SPASOYEVICH: But you where there when it happened.

KLARA: Yes, I was, but I assure you that I had not the faintest idea what was going on. Please wait for the gentleman, and take it up with him when he gets back.

SPASOYEVICH and PROTICH: We'll wait, have no fear!

KLARA: Perhaps you'd like to wait in there, in the other room.

SPASOYEVICH and PROTICH: Thank you. *(As they **exeunt**, right, they continue to speak in unison)*: We must bring this matter to a satisfactory conclusion, because, after all ...

SCENE 7

*(**Enter** VELIMIR. He stops as he sees KLARA).*

VELIMIR: Klara?

KLARA *(coldly and distantly)*: Apparently you didn't expect to see me?

VELIMIR: What's the matter? Why that tone? *(She does not answer)* No, I didn't expect to see you, but I'm very glad you're here. I owe you an explanation for the situation that you and I find ourselves in.

KLARA: Isn't it a bit late? As far as I'm concerned you owed me that explanation four years ago.

VELIMIR: It was impossible then.

KLARA: And now it's superfluous. I've already been told the whole story.

VELIMIR: So much the better: we can speak freely. I am very, very sorry for the mess that I've got you in, through no fault of your own. I don't know how I can justify myself but, Klara, you and I have both turned out to be victims.

KLARA: Yes, victims of a deception which you perpetrated.

VELIMIR *(He is at first offended, but then speaks calmly)*: Against you, no – against myself, yes.

KLARA: Don't try to justify yourself: it's useless. Oh, Mother! Mother! It's all her fault!

VELIMIR: Why her?

KLARA: She thought you came from a wealthy family. It was maternal instinct, I suppose, but she was so concerned for her daughter's future that she literally pushed me into your arms.

VELIMIR: And now that you've found out that I'm a poor man, you are no longer in love with me any more?

KLARA: In love, no. In fact, I never loved you.

VELIMIR: Well, thank you for being so frank.

KLARA: I never loved you, but I didn't hate you, either. Now, though, I do hate you. I am so disappointed in you that it goes further – I never want to see you again. So far as I am concerned, there is no longer anything between us whatsoever.

VELIMIR: Klara, have you thought about this? Is that your final decision?

KLARA: Yes, it is. I've made up my mind. But it'll do you no harm – your girl-friend from childhood is waiting for you with impatience and longing.

VELIMIR *(upset)*: What did you want to bring that up for?

KLARA: Because it was something that helped me to make my mind up.

VELIMIR: Klara, you're upset and confused, and in that state one can say things that one doesn't mean. Hadn't we better continue this conversation later?

KLARA: There's nothing more to be said. Consider this conversation to be our last.

VELIMIR *(after a short hesitation)* Very well. Good bye! *(**Exit**, hurriedly)*.

SCENE 8

*(KLARA, who did not turn her head to watch Velimir leave, remains standing in deep thought. **Enter** BLAGOYE)*

BLAGOYE: Hullo! Is Grandpa in?

KLARA: He went out a short time ago to see the lawyers and lodge a complaint against me.

BLAGOYE: Yes, well, of course, he had to. You yourself admitted that you were in the wrong.

KLARA *(resignedly)*: Yes, I admit it.

BLAGOYE: I mean to say – kissing a strange man in public!

KLARA *(affronted)*: That, sir, was the father of my child.

BLAGOYE: Yes, that would normally be a mitigating factor, but in this case it's an aggravation.

KLARA *(coldly)*: Perhaps!

BLAGOYE: Yes, a child is always an aggravating factor. After all, even though the man is the father of your child, that doesn't alter the fact that he's a stranger. It often happens these days, you know – that a child's father is a complete stranger.

KLARA: Anyway, will it satisfy you if I admit I was wrong?

BLAGOYE: Certainly!

KLARA: Very well, I admit it.

BLAGOYE: Have you told Zhivota?

KLARA: Yes, I have.

BLAGOYE: Good! Now we can sort everything out. You've got nothing to worry about – just leave it all to me. Believe me, I shall look after you as if you were my own daughter, and make sure that you are able to leave here as soon as possible.

KLARA: Thank you very much – I'm grateful to you for taking the trouble. Now, if you don't mind, I'm very tired and I would like to have a rest.

BLAGOYE: Of course! Do go and have a rest! *(**Exit** KLARA, left)*.

SCENE 9

(Enter SOYKA *and* SOYKA'S HUSBAND*)*

SOYKA: Good morning!

BLAGOYE: Good morning to you!

SOYKA: My God! – did you see the danger I was in yesterday?

BLAGOYE: Yes, I saw.

SOYKA: D'you think Mr Zhivota will take that into consideration?

BLAGOYE: How d'you mean?

SOYKA: Well, you know how it is. Witnessing something in safety is one thing: being a witness in a dangerous situation is another matter.

BLAGOYE: You'll have to talk to Zhivota about that.

SOYKA: Yes, I want to – that's why I've come. By the way, do you think he would rather we made our depositions plain or coloured?

BLAGOYE: What's the difference?

SOYKA: Well, if we make a plain deposition we just say what happened, but if we make a coloured one we put in a lot of extra detail – such as, that the man cried out: "My darling, I can't live without you!" and that she, sighing deeply, said: "I am yours! Take me!"

BLAGOYE: Marvellous! It's like something out of a novel! Do you invent these things?

SOYKA: Yes, but only on request.

BLAGOYE: Oh, of course, on request! But you'd better wait for Zhivota and see what he wants.

SOYKA: Do you expect him to be back soon?

BLAGOYE: Yes, he's just gone to see the lawyer.

SOYKA: We'll wait, then.

BLAGOYE: You'd better go into that other room. This room's rather busy, people come in and out, and we don't want everybody to see you here – they'll say that you've been conspiring with Zhivota. Better wait in there.

SOYKA *(to her* HUSBAND*)*: All right. Come on, Sima! *(Exeunt into the same room, right, where* MRS SPASOYEVICH *and* MRS PROTICH *already are)*

SCENE 10

(Enter SLAVKA, *from the other room, left).*

SLAVKA: Hullo, Uncle Blagoye!

BLAGOYE: Hullo, dear! Is your mother in there?

SLAVKA: Yes, she is.

BLAGOYE: Is she by herself? I wanted a word with her.

SLAVKA: Yes, she's alone. Klara's in her room, packing. Tell me the truth, Uncle Blagoye, do you know why she's packing? What's happened?

BLAGOYE: How should I know? Your father may know. He'll be back soon, and we can ask him. When he comes, tell him I'm in with your mother.

SLAVKA: All right. *(Exit* BLAGOYE, *left)*

SCENE 11

*(*SLAVKA *rings the bell. Enter* MARITSA*)*

MARITSA: You rang?

SLAVKA: Maritsa, has Mr Velimir been?

MARITSA Yes, he was talking to you just now.

SLAVKA: No, I mean, after that?

MARITSA: Yes, he came back a little while ago.

SLAVKA: Did he talk to Mrs Klara?

MARITSA: Yes, they were in here together.

SLAVKA: That's all I wanted to know. Thank you, Maritsa. *(Exit, left)*.

MARITSA: Thank you, madam. *(She remains in the room, tidying various things)*.

SCENE 12

(Enter MRS DRAGA*)*.

DRAGA: Good morning!

MARITSA: Good morning, madam.

DRAGA: Is Mr Zhivota in?

MARITSA: No, madam, but he is expected back soon.

DRAGA: And Mrs Mara?

MARITSA: She's at home.

DRAGA: Please inform her that Mrs Draga is here, and would like to speak to her.

MARITSA: Yes, madam. *(She walks toward the door).*

DRAGA *(changing her mind)*: No! No, don't trouble her. It's really the older gentleman that I want to see: I'll wait for him, I think. Is the young gentleman in?

MARITSA: No, he's not in either.

DRAGA: And his wife?

MARITSA: His wife – who's that?

DRAGA: Why, the young Swiss lady, of course.

MARITSA: Oh, is she his wife?

DRAGA: Didn't you even know that?

MARITSA: To tell the truth, I just don't know what's going on. One moment she is his wife, and the next moment she isn't.

DRAGA: But you're a housemaid – surely you must know! Housemaids always know all the secrets in a house! Haven't you overheard any whispers?

MARITSA: No, madam.

DRAGA: And haven't you seen some things that you weren't meant to see?

MARITSA: No.

DRAGA: Not even through a keyhole?

MARITSA: I never look through keyholes.

DRAGA: What! But that's what keyholes in doors are for – so that housemaids can peep through them! You don't sound much of a housemaid to me. Anyway, may I wait here for the gentleman?

MARITSA: Madam, I think it would be better if you waited in this other room.

DRAGA: Very well. Please tell me as soon as he arrives. *(Exit, right, into the same room as the others have already gone into).*

MARITSA: Yes, madam.

SCENE 13

(Enter MILORAD, *rear).*

MILORAD: Maritsa, is my father in?

MARITSA: No, sir, but I think he'll be back soon.

MILORAD: Right! You can go now.

MARITSA: Sir, Mrs Klara asked me to tell her as soon as you came in: she wants to speak to you.

MILORAD: Klara! Good, tell her I'm here!

MARITSA: Yes, sir. *(Exit rear)*

SCENE 14

(Enter DR REISSER*)*

REISSER: Good day!

MILORAD: Good day to you, Professor Reisser.

REISSER: Excuse me, I have come to take my leave. I leave for Athens today later.

MILORAD: You want to see my father, of course?

REISSER: No, not your father, Milorad's father.

MILORAD: Yes, I thought so. I'm afraid he isn't in at the moment.

REISSER: I would very much like to wait for him.

MILORAD: Certainly! Perhaps you would like to wait in that other room – it's more comfortable. I'll tell you as soon as he arrives.

REISSER: Please do. *(Exit right, into the same room as the others).*

SCENE 15

(Enter KLARA*)*

KLARA: Excuse me, I wanted to talk to you.

MILORAD: By all means – I'm at your disposal.

KLARA: Thank you. I have been told everything, and I clearly understand the unfortunate position I am in.

MILORAD: So you'll understand, now, that it's not my fault that I'm your husband.

KLARA: No, I don't blame you, but you must be able to appreciate how difficult the situation that I am now in is. It's made worse by my being a foreigner – here I am, alone amongst strangers, with no one to turn to for help.

MILORAD: I sympathise with you, Klara, for what that's worth.

KLARA: I don't seek your sympathy. I didn't ask to see you for that reason: I asked to see you because I would like your advice.

MILORAD: My advice? D'you know, you're the first living creature that's ever asked me for advice! As it is, since you're sharing my name, you have every right to ask for my advice – and my protection.

KLARA: I have decided to go back to Switzerland. I shall only be staying long enough to make my formal confession of infidelity, so that you can obtain a divorce.

MILORAD: Do you really want to go? I mean – if you go, what will you do, how will you earn a living?

KLARA: I'm a qualified shorthand-typist. As you see, I can speak your language reasonably well. Perhaps I'll be able to get a job at the Embassy, or one of the Consulates.

MILORAD: Perhaps – but it's only perhaps. And how long might you have to wait before you get a job?

KLARA: Your father has very kindly offered to give me twenty thousand dinars for the journey, and to tide me over. I did refuse to take it at first, but I must say that it would be very useful in case I can't get work immediately.

MILORAD: What! My father offered you twenty thousand dinars! I'm flabbergasted! And he didn't demand that you give a lecture, or something, in return? I'd be wary of accepting that!

KLARA: But that's beside the point.

MILORAD: But?

KLARA: It's something different that I'd like your advice about. You and I are getting divorced. When it's completed I personally shall have the right to revert to my maiden name, and I intend to do so, but that will leave my child in a difficult position. Can you think of any way of getting round the problem of the boy having to go through life with a foreign surname – yours? That's what I wanted your advice about.

MILORAD: It was very sensible of you to come to me for advice. But first, I'd like you to answer one question – by getting divorced you will be able to abandon my name, but what about your relationship with your real husband? Will he be prepared to let you go off on your own?

KLARA: My relationship with him was never a real one and it no longer exists, any more than one exists between you and me.

MILORAD: But doesn't there exist that relationship which the poets call love?

KLARA: He never told me that he loved me, and I never told him that I loved him.

MILORAD: Well, that's what I usually do, but you …

KLARA: I know what you're going to say, but you'd be wrong. My dear departed mother had – how shall I put it – a very considerable influence over me. It was she who made me do what I did.

MILORAD *(ponders)*: So, the truth is, you didn't love him?

KLARA: No, I didn't, and I told him so, openly.

MILORAD: You told him?

KLARA: Yes, a few moments ago.

SCENE 16

SOYKA *(poking her head round the door, right)* Excuse me, is Mr Zhivota back yet?

MILORAD: Not yet.

SOYKA: Please tell us as soon as he arrives.

MILORAD: Yes, I will. (SOYKA *withdraws her head and closes the door).*

SCENE 17

MILORAD: You said that you were only staying here until you'd signed the divorce statement?

KLARA: That's right.

MILORAD: And you've agreed to go ahead with it?

KLARA: Yes.

MILORAD: And the other party?

KLARA: The other party? – that's you.

MILORAD: Yes, me.

KLARA: You're the petitioner – the accuser. Your father's just gone to the lawyer to get him to draft the divorce papers …

MILORAD: … which, of course, will only be valid when I sign them.

KLARA: Well, you are going to sign them aren't you?

MILORAD: Who says I'm going to?

KLARA *(surprised)*: But it's you who wants to be freed!

MILORAD: Freed from what?

KLARA: From me.

MILORAD: Look – you haven't imprisoned me, so it's up to me whether I get freed. And, anyway, how do you know whether I want to give you your freedom?

KLARA *(astonished)*: I don't understand …

MILORAD: You're being very casual about all this. You married me without asking me, and now you're divorcing me without asking me.

KLARA: But that's what you want, isn't it?

MILORAD: Have I ever said so?

KLARA: No, but your father has.

MILORAD: And are you married to my father?

KLARA: No, but …

MILORAD: Listen – you are married to me, and I don't want a divorce.

KLARA *(shocked)*: But … but … what does this mean?

MILORAD: It means that you are my wife, and you have to do what I say, not what my father says. *(KLARA is now so shocked and confused that she does not know how to compose herself).*

SCENE 18

MRS DRAGA *(opening the door, right, and poking her head round)*: Excuse me, has Mr Zhivota come back yet?

MILORAD: No!

DRAGA: Please let me know as soon as he does.

MILORAD: Yes, all right! (MRS DRAGA *withdraws her head and closes the door).*

SCENE 19

KLARA *(completely confused):* I don't know what you're talking about. I don't understand.

MILORAD: I'll speak plainly, so that you can understand. I will not allow you to go. I am your husband, and I have the right to forbid you. There! Is that clear?

KLARA: But why?

MILORAD: Why? I can't explain why. It's just what I want, that's all.

KLARA: But you *must* explain!

MILORAD: I don't know how to. The first time I saw you I said to myself: "My word, that's the most attractive woman I've ever seen!" True, I've often said that to myself whenever I've met a pretty woman, but I always forget it when the next one comes along, and I say just the same thing again. But with you, something quite different has happened. I've met other pretty women since I met you, and I haven't been in the least attracted to any of them. Nothing like this has ever happened to me before. I've tried to tell myself that I'm a scoundrel, but …

KLARA *(shocked):* What?

MILORAD: Yes – that's what I said. I said to myself: "You're a scoundrel – she's the wife of your oldest friend!" But now that I've heard from your own lips that you don't love him and that your relationship with him is over and done with, I can say openly that you are indeed the most attractive woman I've ever met.

KLARA: What are you saying?

MILORAD: I don't know how to put love into words. I've only ever associated with women to whom there was no need to talk about love. But what I have said to you is true: I mean it.

SCENE 20

MRS SPASOYEVICH *(poking her head round the door, right)*:
Excuse me … *(She sees* MILORAD, *gives a frightened squeal, and immediately withdraws her head and closes the door)*

KLARA *(startled)*: What's the matter with her?

MILORAD: Oh, that was just the woman I threw a cushion at – seeing me gave her a fright. *(After a short pause, he comes and stands in front of* KLARA, *whose head is lowered)* There! I've said it!

KLARA *(She thinks for a long time, and then raises her head)*:
Listen, you are making a big mistake. You are obviously a kind and good-hearted man, but your heart is leading you astray. What you think is love for me, or at any rate affection, is I'm afraid only sympathy. You have been moved by my sad situation – you feel sympathy for me, and that is all.

MILORAD: I don't know whether it is love or whether it isn't. But I am sure of one thing, and that is that I want you to be my wife. Come to think of it, that's rather an odd thing to say, seeing that you already *are* my wife!

KLARA: But, you must see, it would be dreadful for me to behave like that.

MILORAD: Why?

KLARA: It would make me feel ugly in myself.

MILORAD: How on earth can you say that? No woman in love is ugly!

KLARA: Not even if she comes into a family home like a robber and vandal, destroying everything that has been built up over the years?

MILORAD: But I was going to bring it to an end myself. I've already decided to free myself from the slavery that I've endured on account of that false diploma.

KLARA: No, no! Just think how I would appear in your family's eyes!

MILORAD: Do you think you appear any better as thing are? You don't have to give a damn for what Uncle Blagoye thinks, you know.

KLARA: Even so, this is all so sudden, so unexpected, and so strange, that I'm scared. I can't possibly decide. I greatly fear that I might be taking yet another rash and ill-considered step, and I've had enough of making mistakes like that.

MILORAD: Yes, it is unexpected – it's unexpected for me, too. If I'd had any inkling …

KLARA: All the same, my fear is that you have not thought about it sufficiently. You really must give yourself more time to consider. You can't take such a serious step as this until you looked at all the factors very carefully indeed. Do think about it seriously, please. I must go now. *(**Exit**, left, in haste.* MILORAD *watches her go, and remains looking in her direction for a long time. Then he sits down and lights a cigarette).*

SCENE 21

*(**Enter** ZHIVOTA, carrying a file of papers)*

ZHIVOTA: Good, you're here! I was going to tell you to wait for me.

MILORAD: Yes, and I have something to say to you.

ZHIVOTA: So much the better, but first of all you just sign this application and we can finish off the whole wretched business.

MILORAD: What application?

ZHIVOTA: The application for divorce – the lawyer's drafted everything.

MILORAD: Yes, that's easy enough, but before that I've got a suggestion for a scheme which would mean that you'd get ten thousand dinars and I'd get ten thousand dinars.

ZHIVOTA: Excellent! I like it! You're beginning to show signs of really being my own son! At last you're talking about making money instead of just spending it. Right! – what's the scheme?

MILORAD: It's right, isn't it, father, that you promised Klara twenty thousand dinars to go away?

ZHIVOTA: Yes, I am giving her something to leave us in peace.

MILORAD: Well, with my scheme we can both make a profit out of it.

ZHIVOTA: How?

MILORAD: Like this – I have decided that I am not going to sign that application for divorce, but that I am going to stay as I am, married to Klara. Therefore you don't need to give her the twenty thousand dinars. Instead, you can give me ten thousand and keep the other ten thousand for yourself. That way, we both make a profit.

ZHIVOTA *(greatly astonished)*: Stop! Stop! Just a minute! Didn't you sleep properly last night, for God's sake? Are you out of your mind? Have you still got a fuzzy head from that binge you had – the one I had to pay thirty dinars a glass for?

MILORAD: You heard what I said, and I mean it.

ZHIVOTA: I didn't hear – I didn't hear anything!

MILORAD: Then I'll say it again, more clearly. *(Speaking deliberately, in a loud voice)* I am not allowing my wife to leave me!

ZHIVOTA: Whose wife? Whose wife?

MILORAD: My wife.

ZHIVOTA: But when were you married?

MILORAD: On the day of our wedding.

ZHIVOTA: Now you just listen to me! Sober up! Pull yourself together! If you want to talk to me, talk sense!

MILORAD: I am talking sense.

ZHIVOTA: You're talking nonsense! – you're claiming someone else's wife as your own!

MILORAD: Do you say that Klara is not my wife?

ZHIVOTA: Of course she's not, you idiot!

MILORAD: Then how the hell can I divorce her?

ZHIVOTA: That's entirely another matter – that's nothing to do with you.

MILORAD: Listen, father! I *am* married to her, she *is* my wife, she is going to *remain* my wife, and that's that! Have I made myself clear?

ZHIVOTA: It's not at all clear.

MILORAD: What isn't?

ZHIVOTA: Nothing's clear. There's a darkness come over my eyes, and when that happens no one can see clearly. Do you imagine that I'd have worked, and slaved, and worried, and spent huge amounts of money, just so that you could turn round at the end of it all and twitter: "She's my wife"? No, my son, that is not going to happen! It's completely out of the question! I forbid it – d'you hear? – I forbid it!

MILORAD: Well, if that's so, you'd better divorce yourself from Klara, for I shan't.

ZHIVOTA: I shall disown you, do you hear me? – I shall disown you! You and Klara and Pepika can clear off and do what the hell you like! Let *her* look after you!

MILORAD: Very well, if that's your decision as a father, so be it!

ZHIVOTA: I shall disown you before God and before the world. I want the whole family to come here and hear me say it – now. *(He goes to the door)* Mara! Mara! Come here, quickly!

SCENE 22

(Enter MARA *and* BLAGOYE*)*

ZHIVOTA: Come here! Come here, and listen to this! *(To* MILORAD*)* Go on, tell them! They won't believe it from me!

MARA: What is it now, for goodness' sake?

ZHIVOTA *(to* MILORAD*)*: Tell them!

MILORAD: Tell them what?

ZHIVOTA: Mara, your son refuses to sign the application for divorce. He says Klara is his wife and he wants to keep her.

BLAGOYE: Well, I never!

MARA: Is it true, Milorad, dear?

MILORAD: Of course it's true! I'd rather have a good wife than a rotten diploma and, since I am already married to one why should I divorce her? I have a lovely wife …

BLAGOYE: … and you also have a child.

MILORAD: Yes, I have. And if only father would realise it, it's a saving for him. Firstly, he gets out of paying Klara twenty thousand dinars to go and, secondly, he gets out of paying for the wedding reception.

ZHIVOTA *(to* MARA*)*: There! You hear! Now he's mocking me!

MILORAD: I'm not mocking you, father. I'm saying she's a decent, honest, and good-looking woman.

MARA: And, Zhivota dear, she really is a very nice and respectable young woman..

ZHIVOTA: Now *you're* against me!

BLAGOYE: And, come to think of it, it wouldn't be at all a bad way of sorting out this whole horribly complicated affair that we've all got so tangled up in.

ZHIVOTA: It's your brain that's got tangled up, Blagoye! You don't know what you're saying! And her, too – your sister – muddled thinking must run in your family! What's happened to you all this morning? – have you gone mad, or are you drunk? Who would reject a government minister's daughter for this … this … Klara? A government minister's daughter brings kilometres with her, and viaducts, and tunnels, and what does Klara bring? – Pepika! *(To* MARA*)* And as for you and your "nice and respectable young woman" – this is all your fault! It's all your doing! You always spoiled the boy, and now you're wiping his nose for him! But you understand this, and let him understand it too – I will not allow it! So long as I have breath I will not allow it! *(Angrily)* I'll have you all committed to a lunatic asylum – Blagoye because he lost his wits when he dreamed up this plan, and you because you must be crazy for calling her "a nice and respectable young woman", and him for wanting to take on another man's wife. I'll see all of you – the lot of you – in the lunatic asylum before I'll allow this! I forbid it, do you hear? – I forbid it!

MARA: Zhivota, dear, do calm down!

ZHIVOTA: Calm down? It's you who should calm down – you – not me! If I calm down I'll go mad – and it'll happen – you'll see! There! Now I feel dizzy – everything's going round and round.

MARA: Come along, dear. Come into the other room and lie

down for a while. Have a rest!

ZHIVOTA: How can I rest with all of you on top of me? No, give me the key of that room *(He points to the door, right, of the room where all the other visitors are waiting)*

MARA: It's not locked.

ZHIVOTA: I know it's not locked: just give me the key. I'm going in there. I shall lock myself in, and I don't want anyone to disturb me. I need some peace and quiet. Let me have some peace and quiet or I shall go completely mad! *(He takes the key from MARA and goes to the door, right. He opens it and, as he is about to take a step inside, he stops and gives a despairing cry. Seeing him in the doorway, all those who are already inside the room start shouting. He leaps backwards, panic-stricken, slams the door shut and locks it. He only does it just in time).* Oh, my God! There's an ambush in there! *(To MILORAD)* Son, have you no pity on your father? You know I suffer with my heart. How could you have let me go into that wasp's nest? *(Those inside the room are heard shouting and banging on the door).*

MARA: Zhivota, for goodness' sake, you've locked them in!

ZHIVOTA: They're all in there – the whole damned lot of them! *(More shouting and banging).*

MILORAD: You can't keep them locked up. Give me the key.

MILORAD: Prove it, you say? Well prove it to her – say it to her face! *(He goes to the door, left, and calls)* Klara! Klara! Come here!

SCENE 25

*(**Enter**, all together, all those who were in the room, namely, MRS SPASOYEVICH, MRS PROTICH, SOYKA and SOYKA's HUSBAND, MRS DRAGA, and DR REISSER. They are all furious)*

DRAGA *(Goes to ZHIVOTA)*: You have deprived us of our liberty! We shall have something to say about that later, never fear, but first, sir, I have come to tell you that you can say goodbye to any idea of ever getting any of those kilometres.

(ZHIVOTA, *still sitting slumped on the sofa, looks dully at her, but says nothing).*

SPASOYEVICH and PROTICH *(in unison)*: And we, sir, have been authorised by last night's Extraordinary Meeting of the Board of Governors of the Nursery School Number Nine to demand satisfaction for the events of yesterday.

(ZHIVOTA *looks dully at them).*

SPASOYEVICH: At the very least, we require an apology.

PROTICH: An apology in writing.

(ZHIVOTA *says nothing).*

SOYKA: Sir, Mr Sima and I are here ... but ... we need to talk privately. Would you come into the other room with us?

(ZHIVOTA *just looks dully at her, but says nothing).*

REISSER: I have come to take my leave of you, sir. I am going on to Athens.

(ZHIVOTA *as before)*

ALL *(of those from the other room)*: Sir, you are very rude. We demand an answer ... *(etc).*

ZHIVOTA *(jumps up)*: What do you all want? What do you want from me? I've had enough! This is too much! Clear off and leave me in peace! I've got enough worries of my own!

SPASOYEVICH: and PROTICH: That is your affair.

ZHIVOTA: My affair, is it? Well, it's yours, too! I'll tell you all now, so that everyone can hear it – I'll tell you, so that can all laugh at my humiliation and my son's disgrace!

MILORAD: But, Father ... !

ZHIVOTA *(angrily)*: Listen, all of you! My son intends to take as his wife a cynical, immoral woman, who is no better than a trollop!

MILORAD: Father, what are you saying?

ZHIVOTA: I mean what I say, and I can prove it.

MILORAD: Prove it, you say? Well prove it to her – say it to her face! *(He goes to the door, left, and calls)* Klara! Klara! Come here!

SCENE 26

*(After a short pause, **enter** KLARA with Pepika, and SLAVKA)*

MILORAD *(to ZHIVOTA)*: Now then! Go on – prove it!

ZHIVOTA: I shall! Ask the lady what she has to say about *this!*
Now then, who is this .. *(he takes a piece of paper out of his
pocket and glances at it)* … this Johann Wolfgang Goethe of
hers, then?

REISSER *(hearing that name, raises his head and starts to speak
as if lecturing)*: Johann Wolfgang Goethe was a most famous
German poet and erudite author, whose works display a
tremendous breadth of imagination and the deepest
philosophical insight. Goethe was born in Frankfurt-am-Main
in 1749, and died at Weimar in 1832. His father was a Royal
Counsellor, Johann Kaspar Goethe, who was born in 1710 and
died in 1782, and his mother was Katerina Elizabeta Tekstor,
born 1731, died 1803. Goethe's literary genius earned him the
friendship of Duke Karl August of Weimar, who bestowed his
patronage upon him …

ZHIVOTA *(in despair and out of patience)*: Oh, for God's sake,
that's enough! *(To REISSER)* I've no time for lectures. The
roof's falling in on my head and all you can do is lecture me!
(To KLARA) Klara, answer truthfully – did you know this man,
Johann?

KLARA: But you just heard – he died eighty years before I
was born.

ZHIVOTA: Died … eighty years before … ? Oh my God! But I
put in the divorce application that she'd had an affair with
Johann Wolfgang Goethe!

MILORAD: And you expected me to sign it!

ZHIVOTA: Well, all right then! Let's leave this fellow Johann aside
– may God preserve his soul and may he rest in peace! One
should not speak ill of the dead. But what about Titulescu?
Aha! Who's he, eh? Ask her what she has to say about
Titulescu!

MILORAD: Why should I ask her, when I know myself who he is?

He's the Romanian Foreign Minister.[1]

ZHIVOTA: Titulescu is?

MILORAD and SEVERAL OTHERS: Yes! That's right!

ZHIVOTA: Heavens above! What's going on? My head's spinning
– I can't see straight – this is the end!

SCENE 27

(Enter VELIMIR*)*

ZHIVOTA *(As soon as he sees* VELIMIR *he leaps at him like a tiger
and tries to seize him by the throat)*: You! You! You devil! This
is all your fault! *(He raises his fist. General pandemonium).*

SLAVKA *(She runs and stands before her father to protect*
VELIMIR*)*: Father, he's not to blame!

ZHIVOTA: Oh yes he is! *(To* VELIMIR*)* But I'll have my revenge on
you, my lad! D'you hear? – I'll have my revenge – a terrible
revenge! I'm going to make you suffer! Here – you think this is
your wife, don't you? *(He points to* KLARA*)*. Well, she damned
well isn't – she's my son's wife! She's my daughter-in-law,
d'you hear! That's right, isn't it, Milorad?

MILORAD: Yes. That's right, isn't it, Klara?

KLARA *(She stands looking at each of them in turn, and when her
eyes meet* VELIMIR'S *she says decisively, even defiantly)*: Yes,
· that's right. *(She kisses* ZHIVOTA *and* MARA. *General
astonishment).*

SLAVKA *(to* VELIMIR*)*: Be brave!

ZHIVOTA *(to* VELIMIR*)*: That hurt, didn't it? *(*VELIMIR *laughs
and shrugs his shoulders)*. There now – that's it, then! It's all
over – I surrender. I thought that money could buy anything,
but I see now that it can buy everything except wisdom.
Maritsa, take that diploma down from off the wall, and take it
… *(*MARITSA *gets up on the table to take it down)* …

---

1. Nikolae Titulescu, the Foreign Minister of Romania from 1932 to 1936,
was well-known for travelling around Europe in his private custom-built
railway carriage.

MILORAD: ... to the attic.

ZHIVOTA: Yes, to the attic. Come, Mara, you and I must make peace after all that's happened to us. You too, Pepika, because you and I are reconciled. *(KLARA gives Pepika to ZHIVOTA, who takes him in his arms)* Maritsa, be careful not to damage the frame of that diploma. One day we're going to need it again, to put another diploma into it. One that has written on it, in large letters: "Doctor Pepika Tsviyovich!"

Curtain

Mrs Minister

Gospodja Ministarka

A Comedy in four Acts

If you have ever, from time to time, taken careful note of everything that is going on around you, and if you have sometimes discussed and become engrossed in considering the personal relationships which regulate the life of a society and the movements which bring that regulation about, you will surely have observed one clear straight line which can be drawn across a diagram of the life of that society. This line has been drawn by a combination of shortsightedness, inflexibility, cowardice, moral weakness, and all those other negative human characteristics under which individuals suffer, and to which society feebly surrenders.

Sociological mathematicians might call this line "the norm", while sociological physicists might describe it as a specific degree of heat or of cold, because it corresponds to that temperature above which living creatures rise through being warmed, and beneath which they sink through being chilled.

The life of practically the whole of our society adheres to this line. It is only those individuals who possess the moral strength and courage to overcome shortsightedness, inflexibility, and cowardice who can rise above the line. Such people do not wait for the mercury in the social thermometer to rise through being warmed by the ambient temperature, but find the necessary warmth within themselves through their own moral strength. Similarly, it is only those individuals who also have the moral strength to overcome shortsightedness and inflexibility, and to conquer cowardice, who sink below the line, for those members of society who do sink below the line of normality (some of them right to the very depths), possess within themselves a tendency to chill both the soul and the senses to freezing-point.

Anyone who is to rise above the line of normality in life, or to sink below it, must be individually courageous. It requires courage to be of noble, honourable, and elevated character, just as it does to be vile and wicked. Anyone who is to rise above the line, to be above the common herd, must have considerable moral strength and, likewise, anyone who is to sink below the line, to be below all others at the very nadir of society, to be a sinner, a burglar, a thief, a slanderer, a robber, or a murderer, must also be possessed of considerable moral powers. It takes as much courage to launch oneself into the air upon the unreliable apparatus of Icarus as to descend to the slimy ocean depths in a diver's suit.

Those people who would displace themselves either above or below the normal line of life must also be possessed of great energy, of much turbulence of the spirit, of huge passions and of strong emotions. The statesman stands in fear before the tribunal of history for setting his government and people upon a fateful path. The big financier stands with feverish excitement before the Exchange where, in a few moments, he may either triple his millions or lose everything. The general feels the racing of his heartbeat as he leads his armies into decisive battle. The poet is aroused by inspiration, the artist by the moment of creation, the scientist by the discovery of things hitherto unknown. They all feel the peaks of excitement, of strong emotion, and of great surges of the spirit.

But those who fall below the line of normality also feel such great excitement, emotion, and stirring of the spirit. The murderer experiences the peak of arousal as he thrusts his bloody knife into his victim. The robber shakes and trembles before the judge. The adulteress suffers the stamp of shame. The traitor beneath the gallows experiences the entire gamut of feeling, from agony and despair to self-abasement and apathy.

It is this region, the region of excitement, strong emotions, and great spiritual turbulence, whether above or below the line, which the dramatist explores most gladly, for he finds therein many deep sources which will provide rich and abundant material for him to use. It follows that most plays are concerned with this region of life.

However, it is much more difficult to look for and find material in the middle ground, in that part of society, and among those small-minded people who possess neither the strength nor the courage to depart from the mean line of life, whether upwards or downwards, among people who are too weak either to be good or to be bad, among people who are devoted immovably to their own petty attitudes, who are enslaved by outmoded traditions, and whose whole life is built on pusillanimity.

Life in this middle ground flows steadily and monotonously, like the hands of a clock on the wall. All movements here are small, quiet, unexciting, with no deep furrows or outstanding features but, rather, like the gentle ripples which spread across the surface of still water when a feather falls upon it.

In this middle ground there are no storms, no disasters, no earthquakes, and no conflagrations, for it is protected by thick walls against the tempests and whirlwinds which swirl around society. Its inhabitants live indoors, the streets are a foreign country to them, and events which shake continents are, for them, merely something to read about in the newspapers.

For the little people of this middle ground who cannot depart from the mean line of life there are no great happenings, no emotional upheavals, no strong sensations. "It's Aunt Savka's birthday today!" – amongst them that is a big event, and they all hurry and bustle about, they dress up, they buy bouquets, they write greeting letters, and they pay visits, for this is an event, a real event! "Uncle Steva's Mila has left her husband!" – "Oh, oh, oh!" cries the whole family, beating its collective breast: "What will people say?" But the most sensational sort of event in these humble circles is: "Daughter-in-law Zorka's had twins!" Sensational news like this passes from house to house; it is the sole topic of conversation, it is discussed and interpreted, and the subject occupies the entire interest of a whole family and neighbourhood.

Pera has been promoted, Djoka's ill, Steva's passed his exams,

Yova's moved, Mrs Mitsa's bought a new bedroom suite, Mrs Savka's had her hair cut short, Mrs Yulka's made a new dress of crepe-de-chine, Mrs Matsa's burned her cakes, and Anka's lost a hundred and seventy dinars at brag. These are the sensations, the emotions, and the events within this middle ground.

Well, I have taken by the hand a good wife and housekeeper from this middle ground, Mrs Zhivka Popovich, and led her suddenly and unexpectedly above her normal way of life. For such people, altering the weights in the scales of their normal lives can cause them to lose their balance so badly that they can hardly stay upright on their feet. Therein lies the content of *Mrs Minister* and the whole simple reason for the problems it reveals.

Branislav Nušić

CAST

SIMA POPOVICH

ZHIVKA *his wife*

RAKA *their [adolescent] son*

DARA *their daughter [aged 20]*

CHEDA UROSHEVICH *their son-in-law [*DARA's *husband]*

ANKA *their maid*

DR NINKOVICH *Permanent Secretary*
   at the Ministry of Foreign Affairs

PERA *a clerk in the Administrative Department*

RISTA TODOROVICH *a leather merchant*

PERA KALENICH

UNCLE VASA

AUNT SAVKA

AUNT DATSA

YOVA POP-ARSIN

UNCLE PANTA   } ZHIVKA's *Family*

MILÉ, PANTA'S *son*

SOYA, *a divorced woman*

UNCLE YAKOV

SAVA MISHICH

Mrs Nata Stefanovich

A Messenger *from the Ministry*

An English-Language Teacher

A Police Clerk

A Printer's Apprentice

A Dressmaker's Girl

A Photographer's Apprentice

First Policeman

Second Policeman

First Citizen

Second Citizen

**The action takes place [in Belgrade] at the turn of the
19th and 20th centuries.**

*Translator's note: I have not attempted to reproduce the extensive and
intricately detailed nomenclature of family relationships in which the
Serbian language abounds, but have reduced nearly all such titles to 'uncle',
'aunt', etc.*

Act One

An ordinary room in a town house. An old sofa, two armchairs, and some cheap dining chairs. Three doors, to rear, left, and right, and a window on the right. In the middle of the room a large table covered with a cloth.

SCENE 1

ZHIVKA *is standing behind the table, on which is spread out an old pair of her husband's trousers, which she is cutting down to fit her son. She has a tape measure hanging round her neck, and a large pair of scissors in her hand. She has placed the point of the scissors on her lips as she gazes thoughtfully at the trousers.* SAVKA *is sitting on a chair beside the table.*

SAVKA: What are you thinking about?

ZHIVKA: I'm trying to think how I can get round this bit that's all threadbare.

SAVKA: There's no way round it. You'll just have to patch it.

ZHIVKA: Maybe, but that means it won't last from Friday to Saturday.

SAVKA: He wears things out quickly, does he? Still, you know, as long as a boy's alive and healthy he's bound to wear things out.

ZHIVKA: It's not that he just wears them out, Auntie – he positively tears them apart them, like a wolf attacking a sheep. You make and mend for him, but nothing lasts more than twenty-four hours.

SAVKA: He's a very lively lad, then!

ZHIVKA *(continuing to measure and cut)*: It's very hard to cope
with. We're not well-off, you know: it's no joke trying to make
ends meet.

SAVKA: But Sima's well paid, isn't he?

ZHIVKA: No, he's not. By the time you've knocked off the tax,
and paid the rent, and bought fuel, there's precious little left.
It's hard, these days, to live on your salary, but that husband of
mine just doesn't understand. He takes no notice of what's
happening here at home – he's simply obsessed with politics.

SAVKA: That's right!

ZHIVKA: Other men struggle in politics and some, as they say, are
broken by politics, but at least they look after themselves.
Some sit on committees, some on boards, some on
conferences, but at least they all look after themselves
somehow. But that husband of mine doesn't understand. It's
always: "This won't do, it will harm the image of the Party"; or
"That won't do, the Opposition will kick up a fuss" – and so
on. All this, and we haven't paid the maid her wages for three
months, we haven't paid last month's rent, and we can hardly
afford even the bare necessities – milk, groceries and – well,
you know …

SAVKA: Times are hard.

ZHIVKA: That girl still hasn't brought in the coffee. The
impudence! – you have to tell her everything three times.
(She goes to the rear door) Anka! Where's the coffee?

ANKA *(offstage)*: Coming!

ZHIVKA: There! That's servants for you these days! You pay
them, and they do nothing!

SCENE 2

ANKA *(**Enters**, carrying the coffee on a tray)*: Here you are.
(She serves it).

ZHIVKA: I had to ask you for it three times.

ANKA: *(impudently)* Well, *I* haven't been sitting about chattering
– I've had work to do. *(**Exit**)*

SCENE 3

ZHIVKA *(after* ANKA *has left)*: Did you hear that! – I ask you!
There are times when I feel like taking these scissors and
cutting off her head! But it's no use – I just have to put up with
it. I haven't paid her for three months, so there's nothing I can
do about it.

SAVKA *(sipping her cup of coffee)*: Servants are like that
these days.

ZHIVKA: Aunt Savka, I asked you round to ask a favour of you.
Could you possibly lend us two hundred dinars?

SAVKA *(drawing back)*: But why me?

ZHIVKA: Well, you've got a bit in the Bank.

SAVKA: Oh, that … well, don't you go thinking that I'm going to
touch that. I didn't scrape that together just to give to other
people, I can assure you.

ZHIVKA: For goodness' sake, Aunt Savka, you're talking as if we
weren't going to repay you. We'll pay you back three months
from now, on the nail, with interest. Listen! – I'm absolutely
sure that I can make him get on some committee or other. The
Party's got plenty! Draga's husband Djoka is building an
extension to their house on Party funds, while all that husband
of mine can do with our house is mess it up.

SAVKA: Well, I don't know … can you be sure?

ZHIVKA: Sure of what?

SAVKA: That he'll get on a committee?

ZHIVKA: Do you think we'll let you down?

SAVKA: It's not that but, you know, I don't want to break in to that
money and, well, supposing he doesn't get on a committee …

ZHIVKA: It doesn't have to be a committee – there's lots of things.
And if, in the end, he can't get anything, well, we'll just borrow
the money to pay you back. You won't lose it.

SAVKA: Well, if it's only for three months …

ZHIVKA: Not a day longer!

SCENE 4

*(**Enter** RAKA, with ANKA following. RAKA, a secondary school boy, is in a dishevelled state. ANKA is carrying his cap and satchel)*

ZHIVKA: You wretched boy! Have you been fighting again?

RAKA: No, I haven't!

ANKA: Yes, he has! He's been fighting!

ZHIVKA *(to SAVKA)*: Just look at him – the state he's in! He looks as if he's been dragged through a hedge backwards!

ANKA *(putting the satchel on the table)*: And he's cut his hand.

ZHIVKA *(seizing RAKA's hand, which is wrapped in a dirty handkerchief)*: You wicked, good-for-nothing boy! *(To ANKA)* Bring some water to wash his hand. *(**Exit** ANKA). Now* do you still say that you haven't been fighting?

RAKA *(definitely)*: No, I haven't.

ZHIVKA: Well, what have you been doing?

RAKA: I've been on a demonstration.

ZHIVKA: Dear God! What are you talking about? What demonstration?

RAKA: Against the government.

ZHIVKA: What's the government got to do with you?

RAKA: Nothing. But that doesn't stop me shouting: "Down with the government!"

ZHIVKA: You stupid boy! You'll come to a bad end, that's certain! What were you thinking of, getting mixed up with a demonstration?

RAKA: It wasn't just me – everybody was there. There's fighting on the Terazije,[1] and the government has had to resign because a worker was killed and three more were injured.

ZHIVKA: Oh, my God! You'll lose your head one of these days!

---

1. Terazije (pronounced Te-ra-zi-yé) – a famous wide avenue in central Belgrade. The site (and name) of an ancient market, it is called "The Terazije", on the analogy of e.g. "The Mall" or "The Haymarket" in London.

ANKA *(Enters with a jug and bowl)*: Come on, Raka – come into the kitchen, where I can give you a wash.

RAKA: What do I need washing for?

ZHIVKA: You just go and have that hand washed! Get away with you! – you look like a rat-catcher's apprentice! *(She gives him a push and exeunt RAKA and ANKA)*.

SCENE 5

ZHIVKA: There! How can one begin to cope when he comes home every day with his clothes in tatters?

SAVKA: Oh well, I'll have to go now. I've got things to do. I won't disturb you any more.

ZHIVKA: Have you decided about that other thing?

SAVKA: What other thing?

ZHIVKA: You remember – the loan?

SAVKA: Oh, that! Well, to tell you the truth, I'd much rather not dip into that money, but if you really need it badly …

ZHIVKA: Oh thank you, dear Aunt Savka! I'll never forget you for this!

SAVKA: Shall I bring it round this evening?

ZHIVKA: Yes, please do – today! And, Aunt Savka, do be sure to come! I'm afraid I can't get away, otherwise I'd come round to you. Don't go to any trouble, but come whenever you like. You being on your own, you can drop in and have supper with us any time. Treat this house as your own.

SAVKA *(Walking to the door)*: I'll be back this evening, then. Goodbye!

ZHIVKA *(Accompanying her to the door)*: Good bye, Auntie! *(She returns to the table, finishes sewing the trousers, and folds them up)*.

SCENE 6

(Enter RAKA from the kitchen, cleaned up, and makes for the front door)

ZHIVKA: Where are you off to in such a hurry?

RAKA: Out!

ZHIVKA: You've been out of doors long enough already, you little devil! What about your schoolwork? Latin – grade 'D', Divinity – grade 'D', Mathematics – grade 'D'! You don't pay any attention to your lessons, only demonstrations, and you don't care if you're relegated a year!

RAKA: Well, father was relegated in the fourth year.

ZHIVKA: Don't you follow your father's example!

RAKA: All right, I'll follow yours.

ZHIVKA: Merciful heavens! – how ever did I give birth to such a wretched boy? Go on, then, get out!

*(**Exit** RAKA, running out of the front door just as CHEDA and DARA **enter**).*

SCENE 7

CHEDA *(He and his wife, DARA, are dressed for formal visiting)*: Well, here we are. We never got anywhere.

DARA: It was a waste of time.

ZHIVKA: What, didn't you find anyone at home?

CHEDA: Mother, this is the last time I take your advice. In future *you* can drag yourself round to this minister's wife and that minister's wife, paying visits here, there, and everywhere.

ZHIVKA: But it's you that needs the promotion, not me.

CHEDA: I know, but how could you send us to Mrs Petrovich when the woman wouldn't even see us?

DARA: She wasn't in.

CHEDA: Oh, yes she was! The maid was inside whispering for ten minutes before she came back to tell us that her mistress was "not at home".

ZHIVKA: Well, I really can't be blamed for that! I made enquiries through Draga and she told me that she had said: "By all means let them call. I haven't seen Madam Zhivka's daughter since she got married."

CHEDA: It's all very well her saying she hasn't seen Dara since she got married, but today she slammed the door in our face. And then ... that other one ... yesterday ... hadn't *she* seen Madam Zhivka's daughter since she got married?

DARA: Oh, don't go on so! She really wasn't in – I saw her soon afterwards in a cab.

ZHIVKA: There! You see! It isn't all as easy as you think, my lad. You often have to knock on the same door five or six times. Anyway, you must have seen that there are demonstrations going on in town, and the ministers are probably worried.

CHEDA: Well, even if the ministers are worried, why should their wives be?

ZHIVKA: That's just foolish talk. I know – Mrs Nata told me all about it. She said: "When my husband was a minister, and there was a crisis, it was nothing to him – he was as calm, damn him, as though there was nothing wrong. But I was absolutely beside myself with worry – I even found myself putting on one stocking inside out!" She said: "I would rather have pneumonia than face another ministerial crisis."

DARA: All this talking, and I haven't even taken my hat off yet. *(She goes towards the door, left)*. Mother, has the dressmaker brought my new dress yet?

ZHIVKA: No, not yet.

DARA: I'll send Raka to ask her about it *(Exit)*

SCENE 8

CHEDA *(lighting a cigarette)*: Things really can't go on like this.

ZHIVKA: No, they can't but, to tell you the truth, just one step in promotion wouldn't help you much – it wouldn't be enough to let you pay off your debts.

CHEDA: Why are you always dragging in my debts like this? I didn't run them up doing anything silly, but when one marries a woman with no dowry and tries to get a household going ...

ZHIVKA: We didn't force you to marry her. You always said that you loved her.

CHEDA: But you told me she had a 12,000-dinar dowry.

ZHIVKA: She has.

CHEDA: Well where is it? I'd very much like to see those 12,000 dinars.

ZHIVKA: You'll get them from the insurance company.

CHEDA: Oh, yes – but only when you and her father are both dead.

ZHIVKA: You'll just have to wait till then, won't you.

CHEDA: I may be dead myself by then.

ZHIVKA: That wouldn't be much of a loss.

CHEDA: Not for you, it wouldn't – you'd probably be able to get your hands on *my* insurance money.

SCENE 9

*(**Enter** PERA through the door, centre)*

PERA: Excuse me, I did knock twice.

ZHIVKA: Not at all, please come in!

PERA: Is Mr Popovich not in?

ZHIVKA: No.

PERA: He isn't at the office, either.

ZHIVKA: Are you one of his staff?

PERA: Yes, I'm Mr Popovich's clerk. I wanted to tell him that the Cabinet has resigned. I particularly wanted to be the first to tell him.

ZHIVKA: Is it certain?

PERA: Oh yes! Mr Popovich would have been told as soon as he arrived at the office.

ZHIVKA: Why, hasn't he been there yet?

PERA: Oh yes. He came in this morning, but he went out again almost immediately, as soon as he heard that the government was about to fall.

CHEDA: Well, that means that he knows already!

PERA: Certainly he does, but I still wanted to be the first to tell him. It's possible that he doesn't know that everyone's saying that our people are going to be called on to form the new government.

ZHIVKA *(pleasantly excited)*: Our people?

PERA: Yes, ours, and I wanted to tell him.

ZHIVKA: When you say "ours", who are you thinking of?

PERA: Well, "our people". Mr Stevanovich has already gone to the Palace.

ZHIVKA: Mr Stevanovich – really?

PERA: Yes, I saw him with my own eyes.

ZHIVKA: Oh my God! – wouldn't it be wonderful! You actually saw him yourself?

PERA: Yes, I did.

ZHIVKA: And he went to the Palace?

PERA: Yes!

ZHIVKA: Thank you! Thank you so very much for giving us the news.

PERA: I'm going to the Terazije now. I shall walk about a bit under the chestnut trees, and if I see anything I'll come straight back and tell you. But, please, when Mr Popovich comes in, do tell him that I was the first one to come and give him the news him that our people were going to form the new government.

ZHIVKA: We'll tell him!

PERA (as if seeking reassurance from Zhivka): Please, Mrs Popovich, don't forget to tell him that it was me – Pera from the Administrative Section.

ZHIVKA: Don't worry – I will!

PERA (by the doorway): If I see anything interesting, may I come back …?

ZHIVKA: Please do!

PERA: Permit me … (Exit).

SCENE 10

ZHIVKA: Oh, my dear son-in-law, I haven't kissed you since your wedding-day (She embraces him).

CHEDA: What are you so pleased about?

ZHIVKA: Don't you understand? You should be delighted as well. Raka! Raka!

CHEDA: But what's so wonderful … ?

ZHIVKA: "Ours"! Didn't you hear what the man said? He said: "Ours"!

CHEDA: What man?

ZHIVKA: That one who called …

CHEDA: Who, Pera, the clerk from the Administrative Section? As far as he's concerned "ours" just means the people who form the Cabinet. He'll have told everybody the same thing.

ZHIVKA: But he said Stevanovich had gone to the Palace.

CHEDA: Well?

ZHIVKA: Well! You can be promoted, and so can he …

CHEDA: Who?

ZHIVKA: What d'you mean, "who?" – Sima, of course!

CHEDA: But he's already Chief Secretary at the Ministry. How much higher can he go?

ZHIVKA: Government Counsellor – Director of Monopolies – Chairman of the Council – who knows? Aha, my lad! Whatever he feels like – there's time *(She goes to the doorway and shouts)* Raka! Raka!

CHEDA: What d'you want him for?

ZHIVKA: To go out and buy a newspaper. I'm bursting with curiosity. Raka! Raka!

SCENE 11

(Enter MESSENGER *from the Ministry)*

MESSENGER: Good morning, madam!

ZHIVKA *(stiffly)*: Oh! Good morning!

MESSENGER: Excuse me, but Mr Popovich sent me to get his top hat for him.

ZHIVKA: His top hat … ?

MESSENGER: Yes.

ZHIVKA *(unbelieving)*: You mean … his top hat?

MESSENGER: Yes, his top hat.

ZHIVKA: I'm sorry, I was just feeling a bit faint. Was it Mr Popovich himself who told you to come and get his top hat?

MESSENGER: Yes, it was.

CHEDA *(even he is becoming interested)*: Well, where is he now?

ZHIVKA: Yes, where is he?

MESSENGER: He's at the Ministry.

ZHIVKA: And did he tell you why he wanted his top hat?

CHEDA: Oh really! – why should he tell the messenger why he wanted it?

ZHIVKA: Oh Lord, I'm so confused! Where on earth is that Dara? Raka! Raka!

CHEDA *(by the door, left)*: Dara! Dara!

SCENE 12

RAKA *(**Enters** by the centre door)*: What d'you want?

ZHIVKA: Have you bought the newspaper? Oh, I didn't give you the money, did I! Now where has that Dara got to?

DARA *(**Enters** by the door, left)*: I was in the kitchen.

ZHIVKA: The top hat! Father wants his top hat!

DARA: Well, where is it?

ZHIVKA: The last time he wore it was at the Reception for the King's Birthday, and afterwards I put it in that room, on the chest of drawers.

RAKA: Oh no – I saw it in the living room, beside the stove.

ZHIVKA: Well, anyway, go and look for it! Quickly! Quickly!
*(**Exeunt** DARA and CHEDA)*

ZHIVKA *(to the MESSENGER)*: Was Mr Popovich in a good mood when he sent you for his top hat?

MESSENGER: No, not particularly.

ZHIVKA: Was he angry?

MESSENGER: No, he wasn't angry either.

DARA *(**Enters**)* It's not there!

CHEDA *(**Enters** after DARA)*: I can't see it anywhere!

ZHIVKA: What are you talking about – you can't see it? *(She runs to the rear door)* Anka! Anka! *(To everyone)* Well, don't just stand there! Go and find it!

CHEDA: What are you getting so upset for?

ZHIVKA: Of course I'm upset! The man only wears his top hat once a year, and now that he needs it nobody can remember where it is!

SCENE 13

ANKA *(Enters)*: You called?

ZHIVKA: Anka, do you know where the master's top hat is?

ANKA: It was on the chest of drawers, but *he (pointing at Raka)* took it to play with.

ZHIVKA: Not you again! Oh, you wretched, naughty boy!

RAKA: It's not true! I only took the box it was in, to make an aeroplane with, but I didn't take the top hat.

ZHIVKA: Well, where did you leave it?

RAKA: I don't know.

ZHIVKA: Well, go and look for it now! Find it! Find it! It's got to be found! *(Exeunt* ZHIVKA, ANKA, DARA, *and* RAKA *variously rushing about looking for the top hat, leaving only the* MESSENGER *with* CHEDA*)*

SCENE 14

CHEDA: Have you been in the Ministry long?

MESSENGER: A very long time, sir.

CHEDA: I suppose you're pretty used to seeing a change-over of ministers. Have you seen it happen a lot?

MESSENGER: Oh yes, I've seen lots of them come and go.

CHEDA: I expect you've developed quite a nose for appreciating the situation in advance?

MESSENGER *(flattered)*: Well, yes … of course. I knew three days ago that this government was going to fall.

CHEDA: Really?

MESSENGER: Oh, yes, I knew, even without reading the newspapers. As soon as I see that the Minister's constantly sending for the Head of Finance, and as soon as I see a whole lot of screwed-up documents in the waste-paper basket by his desk, I always say to myself: "He's getting ready."

CHEDA: And what do you reckon it means when he sends for his top hat?

MESSENGER: It means that he's been summoned to the Palace, and that he wants it in a devil of a hurry, too! I remember a while back, when I went and fetched a top hat for one of them, he just looked at it like a cow eyeing a dead calf and said: "Too late! Take it back!"

CHEDA *(flustered)*: Really! Is that so? *(He goes to the various doors and calls through them)* What's taking you all so long? Find that top hat!

SCENE 15

*(**Enter** ZHIVKA carrying the top hat and wiping it with her sleeve, followed by DARA and RAKA)*

ZHIVKA: That naughty, naughty boy – he'd filled it with walnuts and stuck it under the sofa! Who'd ever have thought of looking for it under the sofa?

CHEDA *(He seizes the top hat from ZHIVKA, thrusts it into the MESSENGER's hands and pushes him out)*: Go on, then! Run! You hold the fate of the nation in your hands! Hurry!
*(**Exit** MESSENGER)*

SCENE 16

ZHIVKA: Have you found something out?

CHEDA: No, but … I was just thinking … a crisis … the top hat …

ZHIVKA: And you can just stand there! Why don't you go?

CHEDA: Go where?

ZHIVKA: To the Terazije!

CHEDA: But that fellow Pera from the Administrative Section has already gone there.

ZHIVKA: How can you bear to hang around waiting for other people to bring you the news? Give me my hat – I'll go myself.

CHEDA: Where to?

ZHIVKA: To the Terazije!

DARA: For goodness' sake, Mother, you can't go there!

CHEDA: Oh, all right, then, I'll go!

RAKA *(appearing at the door)*: Me too!

ZHIVKA *(to CHEDA)*: And see that you don't go into any cafés!

Just walk about outside and keep your ears open, and as soon as you hear anything come back here and tell us. You know we'll all be waiting here on tenterhooks.

CHEDA *(putting on his hat)*: Don't worry, I'll be back! ***(Exit)***

SCENE 17

ZHIVKA *(sitting down, exhausted, on an armchair)*: Oh, my God, I hardly dare say it – but you know what it means when he sends for his top hat?

DARA: No.

ZHIVKA: It means he's been summoned to the Palace.

DARA: What – Father? But why summon him to the Palace?

ZHIVKA: Why? Are you a complete idiot? Oh, God! How could I have had two such unintelligent children? They're both as stupid as their father! *(Imitating DARA)* "Why summon him to the Palace?" Well, they certainly haven't summoned him to look after their chickens. You heard – the government's fallen and they're forming a new one.

DARA: You don't think …

ZHIVKA: What don't I think? Go on, tell me!

DARA: You don't think, perhaps, that they'll make father a minister?

ZHIVKA: I'm scared to think it, but I do. Look – he sent for his top hat, didn't he? Can't you see that I've got the fingers of both my hands crossed? I've been crossing them so hard that they hurt – I'm afraid I've strained them – but that's the least I can do for my husband.

DARA: Oh, if only it could happen! Cheda and I could …

ZHIVKA: Never mind that! I don't give a damn for Cheda.
  Oh, how happy you could have been if only you had listened to me … !

DARA: Listened to you about what?

ZHIVKA: It's just that … if your father should become a minister, and if only you weren't married to that creature, you'd be in a position to make a proper marriage with someone who's fit to be the husband of a government minister's daughter.

DARA *(angrily)*: For goodness' sake, Mother, what are you saying?

ZHIVKA: I've said what I've said.

DARA: But I'm perfectly happy!

ZHIVKA: Oh, you're all right, it's him that isn't.

DARA: Him?

ZHIVKA: Yes, him! Your husband! He's uneducated, he doesn't know any languages, he's got no prospects, and he just isn't suitable …

DARA: Well, I love him, and you don't have to. If I'm happy, what's it got to do with you?

ZHIVKA: Oh, I know you so well! If anyone attacks *him* you take it as a poke in your own eye.

DARA: That's right! I do!

SCENE 18

PERA *(**Entering** by the rear door)*: Excuse me, I …

ZHIVKA *(leaping up as if scalded)*: What is it? Is there any news?

PERA: Yes.

ZHIVKA: Come on, then!

PERA: I've seen him.

ZHIVKA: Who?

PERA: Him, Mr Popovich. I saw him going to the Palace wearing his top hat.

ZHIVKA *(excitedly)*: Are you sure it was him?

PERA: Of course I'm sure! I saw him as clearly as I see you. I said: "Good morning" to him.

ZHIVKA: And he?

PERA: He said: "Good morning" back.

ZHIVKA: And do you know why he was going to the Palace?

PERA: Of course I know. All our people have been summoned there.

ZHIVKA: Do you think they'll make the decisions today?

PERA: Today? – they've made them already! They've probably all signed by now.

ZHIVKA *(Aside, to* DARA*)*: Fingers crossed, Dara! *(Aloud)* Is it
possible that they've already signed?

PERA: I'll go now and wait for them to come out. I'll be able to tell
what posts they've got from the expressions on their faces. But,
please, do be sure to tell Mr Popovich that I was the first
one who came and told you that he had been to the Palace.
And I'll …

ZHIVKA: Yes, yes! Come back the moment you hear anything.

PERA: Pera, the clerk from the Administrative Section. *(He bows
and **exit**).*

SCENE 19

ZHIVKA *(Returning from the door)*: Dara, my child, I can hardly
hold the tears back. *(She starts crying)* But you … aren't you
excited?

DARA: Yes, of course I am but, frankly, I can't believe it's true, yet.

ZHIVKA: Oh, Dara dear, put your coat on and we'll go the
Terazije and wait for him.

DARA: No, Mother! You know that wouldn't do!

ZHIVKA: You're right. Come to think of it, it would never do,
would it? If he's already a government minister, it would be
ridiculous for *me* to be seen *walking*.

DARA: It's not that, it's the crowds.

ZHIVKA: But I'm bursting with impatience – I can hardly hold
myself in! And where's that wretched husband of yours, may
I ask – why hasn't he come back? *(She goes to the window)* He's
gone into some café, I'll be bound, and doesn't give a damn
about us here, all dangling on tenterhooks. *(She paces about
nervously and crosses herself)* Oh, if only I could be changed
into a little fly, so that I could buzz right inside the Palace and,
with my own ears, hear the King saying to Sima: "I have
summoned you, Mr Popovich, to offer you a Portfolio in the
Cabinet!" And that silly fellow of mine, instead of saying:
"Thank you, your Majesty!" will probably start stammering,
or something. Oh, I just *know* the fool is going to make a mess
of it!

DARA *(going to her)*: Mother! For goodness' sake!

ZHIVKA: Oh, my dear daughter, nothing else matters so long as I can turf that Mrs Dara out of her official government carriage, even if only for a day. She's stuck to that carriage as tight as a postage stamp and imagines that nobody can get her away from it. Well, you just see – I'll unstick her from it, all right! Today – this afternoon – you and I are going to be riding in that ministerial carriage!

DARA: Now, mother, you mustn't count your chickens before they're hatched …

ZHIVKA: I'm not so bothered about Mrs Draga. At least she's a well brought-up woman: her father was a senior civil servant. But as for that Mrs Nata! What's the country coming to if a woman like *that* can finish up as a government minister's wife? Her mother used to rent out rooms for bachelors, and she made the beds for them …

DARA: Don't go on so, mother, you could be a government minister's wife too.

ZHIVKA: What's that got to do with it? There's a lot of difference between me and Nata. My mother was a seamstress in a military tailors' shop, but she brought me up decently. I passed three grades at elementary school, and I could have gone further if I'd wanted to. If I hadn't been respectable your father wouldn't have married me – he was already a civil servant when we were married, you know.

DARA: Oh yes? They do say, mother, that he *had* to marry you.

ZHIVKA: That's the sort of thing people like that husband of yours would say. Anyway, why the devil hasn't he come back yet, with some news? But, of course, he'll be tucked away in some café by now. *(Remembering)* Just a minute … where are the cards? … You were playing with them last night.

DARA: They're in the drawer.

ZHIVKA *(Taking out the cards and shuffling them)*: Now we'll see what the cards have to say. The last time Sima was up for promotion everything turned out just exactly as the cards foretold – it was incredible. There! – that Widow card's got between mine and Sima's! *(Deals out the cards)* One, two, three, four, five, six, seven .. News! *(To herself)* Knocking ... soon ... money in the evening! *(Aloud)* I know – that means Aunt Savka's bringing it ... All true ... bed! *(She picks up the two lower rows and starts to cover the cards)*

DARA: Why are you covering your card?

ZHIVKA: To see whether I shall be a minister's wife.

DARA: But, mother, you should cover father's. Surely the main thing is whether *he's* going to be a minister.

ZHIVKA: You're right! Now then. Ten of Hearts ... great happiness! My goodness, Dara dear, I really do think that it's all coming out in the cards ... !

SCENE 20

(Enter ANKA with a DRESSMAKER'S GIRL carrying a dress wrapped in a white cloth)

ANKA: The dressmaker's girl's here with your dress ...

ZHIVKA: Take it back, I don't want to try it on.

DARA: But, mother, why not?

ZHIVKA: I, er ... bring it this afternoon ...

DARA: It's nearly that now.

ZHIVKA: I want her to bring it back later, because ... well ... because I don't know yet what sort of trimming I shall have on it. If it's *one* thing, I'll have silk trimmings, and if it's *another* thing, I'll have satin. There!

GIRL: What shall I say to my mistress?

ZHIVKA: Tell her that if it's *one* thing I'll have silk trimmings ...

DARA *(Interrupting)*: Don't tell her anything – just bring it back later!

(Exeunt ANKA and the GIRL)

SCENE 21

ZHIVKA: Oh, dear! Now ... all of a sudden ... my right eye's started twitching.

DARA *(looking out of the window)*: Here's Cheda.

ZHIVKA: Is he running? Is he looking pleased? Is he waving his handkerchief? Call out to him – ask him what's happening!

DARA: He's just coming in.

ZHIVKA: I just know that he's bringing some good news! I can tell – it always means good news when my eye starts twitching.

SCENE 22

(Enter CHEDA)

ZHIVKA *(The moment he appears in the doorway)*: Well?

CHEDA: Hold on!

ZHIVKA: If you don't tell me at once I'll faint!

CHEDA: Give me a chance, and I'll tell you everything in order.

ZHIVKA: Just *tell* us – stop messing about!

CHEDA: Well, as I was coming back I was just thinking …

ZHIVKA *(Seizing him by the throat)*: Tell us! Is he or isn't he? Is he or isn't he?

CHEDA: Stop it! As I said, I was just thinking. Father can arrange for me to have a Loan for Economic Purposes from the Classified Lottery Fund, instead of a dowry. That way I can renegotiate my debts, and then …

ZHIVKA: Dara, my head's started swimming. Will you get this husband of yours to say "yes" or "no", or I'll hit him with this chair!

DARA: Oh, Cheda, for goodness' sake tell us!

ZHIVKA: Yes or no?

CHEDA: Yes.

ZHIVKA: "Yes" what?

CHEDA: Yes, he's a minister.

ZHIVKA: But *who*? Damn and blast it! – *who's* a minister?

DARA: Is it Father?

CHEDA: Yes.

DARA *(Thrilled, she embraces him)*: Oh, Cheda, my darling!

ZHIVKA: Children, hold me! *(She falls, exhausted with emotion, on to a chair).*

CHEDA: So, as I was saying, your father can arrange for me to have a loan of 12,000 dinars for Economic Purposes from the Classified Lottery Fund and that can represent your dowry. I'll easily be able to pay off my debts with that and, as a premium, he can arrange for me to be promoted by three grades.

ZHIVKA *(Jumping up)*: What are you talking about – "father this" and "father that"? Hasn't it occurred to you to wonder about somebody else?

CHEDA: Well, yes, I had wondered who else would become a minister.

ZHIVKA: What about me?

CHEDA: What about you?

ZHIVKA: You have the impertinence to ask that? *I* am *Mrs* Minister! *(She smiles broadly with satisfaction)* Oh, my word, I can hardly believe my own ears! You say it, Dara, you say it!

DARA: Say what?

ZHIVKA: Just say it – call me what everyone's going to have to call me now.

DARA: "Mrs Minister!"

ZHIVKA *(To* CHEDA*)*: Now you say it!

CHEDA: All right, but first you can call me "The Minister's Son-in-law", so that I can hear how that sounds.

ZHIVKA: First of all, "son-in-law" is nothing and, secondly, frankly, you don't look much like a proper one to me.

CHEDA: Oh, really! Well you look like …

ZHIVKA *(Facing him boldly)*: Like what?

CHEDA *(Mumbling)*: Like … er …

ZHIVKA: Come, come! You'd better learn your language lessons, starting at paragraph seventy-six.

CHEDA: Oho! Now you're talking as though *you* were the minister.

ZHIVKA: I may not be the minister, but I am Mrs Minister, and sometimes that's much more important – and don't you forget it!

DARA: Oh, Cheda! – Mother! Stop quarrelling! The way you're

carrying on isn't what you expect in a government minister's household!

ZHIVKA: You're right, it isn't. And that's because you don't expect to find uneducated slobs like him in a government minister's residence.

SCENE 23

(Enter RAKA, *running)* Mama, have you heard? They've made Papa a Minister!

ZHIVKA *(Kissing him)*: And who told you that, dear?

RAKA: The other boys told me, and now they're calling me "The Minister's Piglet"!

ZHIVKA: The little devils! Anyway, you won't have to mix with riff-raff like that any more.

RAKA: Why, who'll I have for friends?

ZHIVKA: From now on you'll be associating with the British Consul's children.

RAKA: They aren't just calling me the Minister's Piglet – they're calling my mother names, too.

ZHIVKA: Don't they know that your father's a government minister?

RAKA: Of course they know, that's why they're ragging me.

ZHIVKA: You are to write down for me the names of those impudent children, and we'll have them all arrested and transferred – the children, *and* the rest of their class, *and* their teacher. There has got to be Law and Order in this country, and people have got to know whose mothers they can call names, and whose they can't!

RAKA: Anyway, Mama, d'you know what I like best about Papa being a minister?

ZHIVKA: Eh? What?

RAKA: Because from now on every time he smacks me I shall just start a demonstration, and we'll all go round shouting: "Down with the government!"

ZHIVKA: May you be struck dumb, you wicked boy!

RAKA *(shouts)*: Down with the government!

ZHIVKA: If you can't say anything sensible, just shut up!

RAKA: Oh, I forgot to tell you – Father's on his way.

ZHIVKA: Is he coming? Why didn't you say so, you little imp, instead of talking nonsense? *(She becomes flustered)* Now, children, children, don't you upset me. Stand here, behind me! Oh, my God! – who'd have imagined it: he went out this morning as an ordinary man, and now he's coming back as a Government Minister. Now, just stand still and don't annoy me!

SCENE 24

(Enter POPOVICH, wearing his top hat)

ZHIVKA *(kisses him)*: My Minister! *(He takes his top hat)*

CHEDA and DARA *(embracing him)* Congratulations!

RAKA *(loudest of all)*: Down with the government!

ZHIVKA *(She jumps as if she had been scalded, then hits RAKA on the head with Popovich's top hat, stunning him into silence)*: Shut up, you little devil! How in hell could I have given birth to a creature like you?

POPOVICH: Now, now, Zhivka, steady on!

SCENE 25

(Enter PERA who, when he sees Popovich, becomes embarrassed)

PERA: Oh, excuse me … I, er … I came to tell you that you had become a Minister.

POPOVICH: Mr Pera, I know.

PERA: I know that you know, but I still wanted to be the first to tell you.

POPOVICH: Thank you very much.

ZHIVKA: Mr Pera, are you going back to the Ministry now?

PERA: At your service, Madam Minister.

ZHIVKA: Kindly make arrangements for the Ministerial Carriage to be here, outside the house, at exactly four o'clock this afternoon.

POPOVICH: What do you want it for?

ZHIVKA: Don't bother me, for goodness sake! I want it so that I can ride in it from the Kalemegdan to Slavia[1] and back, three times, and then I shall be able to die peacefully. Arrange it, Mr Pera!

PERA: Yes, Madam Minister. *(He takes his leave, bowing)* Pera, the clerk from the Administrative Section ...

Curtain

1. Kalemegdan to Slavia *(Slavija)*. Kalemegdan is the old fortress and public park at the northern end of Belgrade, whilst Slavia is the name of a major square and meeting of roads about a mile south. These two landmarks effectively constitute the boundaries of central Belgrade, the route between them passing directly through the Terazije and other main streets.

Act Two

The same room, but now full of furniture in ostentatious bad taste.

SCENE 1

CHEDA: *(He is sitting by a small table, speaking on the telephone which stands on it)* The Minister's lady is not in at present ... no ... what? ... I'm afraid I don't know when she is receiving visitors. – Oh, she asked you to come? ... that's different. Please come whenever is convenient, I'm sure she will be back soon. – Who's calling? ... Dr Ninkovich, Permanent Secretary at the Ministry of Foreign Affairs ... Very well, I'll tell her... Yes, do come! Good bye. *(He puts the telephone down)*.

Enter PRINTER'S APPRENTICE, *carrying several packets.*

APPRENTICE: Here you are, the visiting cards.

CHEDA: Have they been paid for?

APPRENTICE: Yes. *(He hands over the packets)*

CHEDA *(surprised)*: Good lord! How many are there?

APPRENTICE: Six hundred.

CHEDA: Six hundred !!

APPRENTICE: That's how many the lady ordered.

CHEDA: Very well. Thank you. *(**Exit** APPRENTICE)*

SCENE 2

*(*CHEDA *opens one of the packets, takes out a visiting card and,
when he looks at it he laughs out loud. At that point* DARA **enters**
from the other room)

DARA: What's so funny?

CHEDA: This is a scream. Just look!

(He hands her the visiting card)

DARA *(reading)*: "Mrs Minister Zhivana Popovich" *(Speaks)*
   What on earth … ?

CHEDA: You might well ask! See how she calls herself
   "Mrs Minister" as if it were some sort of title!

DARA: Well, since she won't take anyone else's advice, she must
   have made it up herself.

CHEDA: And that's not all – she's ordered six hundred. How
   many years does she think she's going to be a minister's wife
   for? Or perhaps she imagines that her visiting cards are to be
   distributed among the population like a proclamation.

DARA: And look – she calls herself "Zhivana".

CHEDA: Oh, of course. "Zhivka" is far too vulgar a name for a
   government minister's wife! Anyway, where's she been all
   morning?

DARA: She's gone to the dentist.

CHEDA: Oh, why?

DARA: I don't know – to have her teeth seen to, I suppose. She's
   been going every day for the last four days.

CHEDA: Someone who said he was the Permanent Secretary at
   the Ministry of Foreign Affairs was asking for her on the
   telephone, by the way.

DARA: Have you spoken to my father?

CHEDA: I have, but I didn't get anywhere. It was a lucky gust of
   wind that blew him into becoming a Minister, but he just
   wasn't born to it. Ministers are born, not made, you know. Can
   you believe it? – he wants to be a government minister and still
   be honest! That's ridiculous! I said to him, politely: "You
   can't, just as you can't provide me with a dowry for my wife,

but now you've got a good opportunity to provide me with a "Loan for Economic Investment from the Classified Lottery Fund". Of course, in fact these "economic investments" are not invested in the economy and they don't get repaid to the government.

DARA: And what did he say?

CHEDA: He said that he would not soil his hands with it, and that he wished to remain an honourable man.

DARA: But that's fine! How can you hold that against him?

CHEDA: It's all very well in theory, but it doesn't work in practice.

DARA: Well, can't you think of some other idea?

CHEDA: I'll think up something later, perhaps, if necessary, but I've got to finish this first.

DARA: There's nothing else for it – you'll have to speak to Mother again.

CHEDA: If only it were possible to talk to her properly.

SCENE 3

(Enter ZHIVKA *with, following her, a* PHOTOGRAPHER'S APPRENTICE *carrying a dress wrapped in a white cloth, which he places on the table).*

ZHIVKA: Very well, you can go now! *(Exit* APPRENTICE*)*

DARA: Where have you been with that new dress?

ZHIVKA: I've been having my photograph taken. I've ordered twelve ordinary prints, and one extra large one for the photographer's shop window. I've been to the dentist, too. Has anyone called?

CHEDA: They brought your visiting cards.

DARA: Mother, why on earth did you want six hundred of them?

ZHIVKA: Why not? We've got a large family, and I'll have to give one to every one of them as a souvenir and, in any case, they'll be all used up within three years. Anyway, my children, have you noticed anything special about me?

CHEDA: No, nothing.

ZHIVKA: What about when I smile? *(She smiles)*

CHEDA: A gold tooth!

DARA: Really, mother! That tooth was perfectly good!

ZHIVKA: Yes, I know.

DARA: Well, why have a gold crown put on it then?

ZHIVKA: Because! Anyway, what sort of a question is that? That Mrs Draga has a gold tooth; that Mrs Nata has *two* gold teeth; and even that Mrs Roksa, the priest's wife, has a gold tooth – so why shouldn't I?

CHEDA: Yes, one can see the sense in it – it would never do for a government minister's wife to be without a gold tooth!

ZHIVKA: Exactly! So, when cultured people come to visit, and when I laugh in the course of conversation, I won't be put to shame.

CHEDA: Indeed!

ZHIVKA: I can't decide whether it would look better if I had another gold tooth – perhaps one on the right hand side as well.

CHEDA: Yes, it might have the advantage of lending a certain … symmetry to the face.

ZHIVKA: Has anyone telephoned?

CHEDA: Yes. A Dr Ninkovich.

ZHIVKA: Did he say he would call?

CHEDA: Yes, he did.

ZHIVKA: Good!

DARA: Who is he?

ZHIVKA: He's the Permanent Secretary at the Ministry of Foreign affairs. Dara, my dear, would you please take this dress and hang it up in the wardrobe. Just a minute – would you take my hat as well. *(She takes it off)* And now I'd like to have a word or two with your husband.

CHEDA: Fine! I'd like to have word or two with you, too.

*(**Exit** DARA, carrying the dress and the hat).*

SCENE 4

CHEDA: Mother, I have decided to put things right once and for all.

ZHIVKA: That's good, because I, too, have decided to put things right once and for all.

CHEDA: I have decided that you are going to have to talk to Father today ...

ZHIVKA: Wait! Wait until I have told you what *I've* decided. What I have decided, my dear son-in-law, is that I am going to take my daughter back.

CHEDA: What d'you mean – take her back?

ZHIVKA: Exactly what I say. And I would be obliged if you would now, in a civilized and gentlemanly manner, quit this house and leave your wife.

CHEDA: What ?!

ZHIVKA: Just that, and it should not surprise you. I want you to leave this house and I want her to leave you as well.

CHEDA: Just that? And may I ask why, pray?

ZHIVKA: Why? Because she is not for you. Her situation is now quite different from what it was when you married her.

CHEDA: Is that so? And who says so, may I ask?

ZHIVKA: And she now has the opportunity to find a far better marriage-partner than you.

CHEDA: For goodness' sake, what? ... say that again!

ZHIVKA: Why must you go on behaving as if you were so surprised? I can now find a much better husband for her, and that's that.

CHEDA: Oh, now I understand.

ZHIVKA: And you've got nothing to complain about. Just think who you are and what you are – an absolute good-for-nothing.

CHEDA *(offended)*: Really, Mrs Minister! ...

ZHIVKA: Yes. Now that we are having a friendly and frank discussion, I can tell you that you are a total and absolute wastrel. What have you ever accomplished? – nothing! You've got no education, you've got no languages. You've been sacked from your job three times. Isn't that right?

CHEDA: Please …

ZHIVKA: I suppose you're going to say that if you were such a wastrel we wouldn't have let you marry our daughter. The fact is, you hooked her at a time when we weren't in a good position. She wasn't getting any younger, and she fell blindly in love with you – we were wrong to let it happen at all. Be that as it may – if a thing can be put right it must be put right.

CHEDA: But what thing are you going to put right?

ZHIVKA: Not you, that's certain! – but the whole thing. That's why I thought of getting rid of you.

CHEDA: Oh, really! It was *you* that thought of it, was it?

ZHIVKA: Yes, it was. We'll get rid of you and marry Dara off to someone who's worthy of her.

CHEDA: What a marvellous plan! All made up without, of course, consulting those concerned, but never mind. And what would you say, Mrs Minister, if I told you that I absolutely refuse to agree to any of it?

ZHIVKA: If you are an intelligent man, and if you think about it in a grown-up way, you will see that it is in fact to your advantage. If you agree to it in an amicable and civilized way, I could see to it that you get a step in promotion.

CHEDA: I'm not selling my wife for a step in promotion.

ZHIVKA: All right then, if you must make difficulties, two steps in promotion.

CHEDA: Listen to you – bargaining as if we were in the market-place! Now please tell me – do you seriously mean all that you've been saying?

ZHIVKA: I certainly do! The dentist that I've been going to for my tooth also operates as a match-maker and he's already been in contact with someone.

CHEDA: But how can he have been approaching other men, while I'm still alive?

ZHIVKA: Make no mistake, I'm not letting a triviality like that get in the way of such a golden opportunity.

CHEDA: Good God! And may one be permitted to ask who this prospective son-in-law is?

ZHIVKA: He's an honorary consul.

CHEDA: What?

ZHIVKA: That's right, the honorary Consul of Ni ... Ni ... Just a moment, please *(She takes a slip of paper out of her handbag and reads)* "The Honorary Consul of Nicaragua."

CHEDA: God Almighty! And who's he, when he's at home?

ZHIVKA: A gentleman of rank in the diplomatic corps and, as such, a suitable husband for a government minister's daughter.

CHEDA: Oh, I am pleased! And what on earth is that ... "Nicaragua"?

ZHIVKA: What Nicaragua?

CHEDA: That one – your future honorary son-in-law!

ZHIVKA: Whatever it is, he's the Consul of it.

CHEDA: He's only an honorary consul. He can't just make a living from that – nobody can. He must have some other occupation.

ZHIVKA: Yes, he's a leather merchant.

CHEDA: Phew! He must stink a bit.

ZHIVKA: Better than you! You're nothing! – you don't even stink or smell beautiful. It would be a lot better if you were a leather merchant.

CHEDA: Yes, it would be very convenient, wouldn't it, seeing that your Raka needs new soles on his shoes every week!

ZHIVKA: Bah! Look at the soles of *your* shoes!

CHEDA: And may I be so bold as to ask what this Nicaragua's name is?

ZHIVKA: What Nicaragua, damn you?

CHEDA: This new son-in-law.

ZHIVKA: Oh, him! His name is Rista Todorovich.

CHEDA: Really? – Rista? Oh, that's absolutely marvellous! And you say the dentist is the match-maker.

ZHIVKA: Yes.

CHEDA: Well you tell your match-maker that he had better come and discuss things with me. Tell him that he and I will get on very well together, because we are both in the same business. I also know how to pull teeth out.

ZHIVKA: You?

CHEDA: Oh, yes indeed! I pull all the front ones out at the same time, but I pull the back ones out one by one. Mind you, when I'm pulling a single one out I make all the others rattle. So, please tell your dentist to come and see me.

ZHIVKA: There's no point – the arrangements have already been made. The bridegroom is coming to see the girl today.

CHEDA: What girl?

ZHIVKA: Why, your wife, of course.

CHEDA: This Nicaragua's coming *here* to see her?

ZHIVKA: Of course.

CHEDA: Well, isn't that just marvellous! Look, you'd better tell the girl to get dressed up. And do you expect *me* to get dressed up too?

ZHIVKA: It's no concern of mine. You can go off and get married on your own account, if you want to, but just leave us alone.

CHEDA: Oh, you're quite right – I shall get married on my own account. *(Picks up his hat)* I'll invite you all to the wedding! *(Exit)*.

SCENE 5

ZHIVKA *(She goes to the telephone, takes out of her handbag a piece of paper with a telephone number written on it, and speaks)*: Hallo? Exchange? Please give me *(reads)* 5872 ... Hallo ... Is that Mr Peshich the photographer? ... It is? ... Mrs Minister Popovich here. Can you tell me, please – I forgot to ask – when the photographs will be ready? ... Really ... or even sooner? ... Well, do please make sure that they turn out well. It's occurred to me, you know, that some foreign newspapers might want to print my photograph, so it must be a good one. You know what foreigners are like! ... Good bye.

SCENE 6

*(**Enter** LANGUAGE TEACHER. She is a mature lady in a tweed suit, with short hair, and wearing glasses. She bursts into the room, very upset, **followed** by RAKA, who is wearing a white sailor suit with short trousers, with his bare knees showing)*

TEACHER: Oh! Oh! It's shocking!

ZHIVKA: What's the matter?

TEACHER: Madam, it is quite, quite impossible to work with this boy. He is such an ignorant, impudent, and badly behaved child that I simply can't put up with it any longer.

ZHIVKA: But what's he done?

TEACHER: You ask him, Madam! I can't bring myself to repeat the things he said.

ZHIVKA: *(to RAKA)* Speak up, then! What have you been saying to her?

RAKA: Nothing!

TEACHER: Well! That is the limit! I could have stood it but, just imagine, he insulted my mother!

ZHIVKA: You horrid boy! What d'you mean by insulting the English language teacher's mother?

RAKA: I didn't!

ZHIVKA: Oh, yes you did, you little wretch! Why should she try to teach you and educate you, when you insult her mother? Come on – out with it! Why did you do it?

RAKA: It was when she made me pronounce the word *"rationalisation"* ten times.

ZHIVKA: Well pronounce it!

RAKA: It's all very well – it's very hard. Why doesn't *she* say: *"Peter Piper picked a peck of pickled peppercorn"* ten times![1] Let's hear *her* try to say it ten times, and I bet she'd insult *my* mother *and* my father!

---

1. The original is a well-known Serbian tongue-twister: *"Ture bure valja, bula Ture gura; niti Ture bure valja, niti bula Ture gura."*

TEACHER: Well!

ZHIVKA: Get out, you little brute! What sort of behaviour is that?
I badly want him to learn English so that he can play with the
British Consul's children, but the way things are going he
could end up insulting the British Consul and *his* father.
Outside, you little devil – get out of my sight!

RAKA *(Going to the door)*: Why should I have to break my jaw
over your silly English language, anyway? *(Exit)*

ZHIVKA: I am so sorry about that. Please come again tomorrow.

TEACHER *(flustered)*: Oh, no, it's impossible to work with him.

ZHIVKA: Do please come. I'll deal with him, don't worry.

TEACHER: Oh, very well. At your service. *(Exit)*

SCENE 7

ZHIVKA: *(going to the door, left)* Dara! *(Louder)* Dara!

DARA *(Enters)*: What is it? Has Cheda gone?

ZHIVKA: Yes, he's gone. I've arranged matters with him.

DARA: Arranged what matters?

ZHIVKA: I have informed him that with immediate effect he is
relieved of all his duties.

DARA: What duties?

ZHIVKA: His duties as a husband.

DARA: I don't understand a word you're saying. Ever since you
became a Minister's wife you've been talking like some
government official. What have you relieved him of?

ZHIVKA: I told him that from today he is no longer your husband.
Now do you understand?

DARA: What !! But … why …?

ZHIVKA: Because an excellent opportunity has arisen for you.

DARA: Opportunity? … Mother! … What are you talking about?

ZHIVKA: An excellent opportunity. A gentleman of rank, one who
will make a suitable husband for you. He's the Honorary
Consul of Ni … Ni … I can't remember what he's the Consul
of, but that doesn't matter to you. He is also a businessman,
Rista Todorovich.

DARA: But, Mother, for God's sake! – I'm married!

ZHIVKA: Oh yes, but we can soon get that set aside. Surely you can see for yourself that he is quite unsuitable for you? He's nothing and nobody, a man whose only occupation is being a son-in-law.

DARA: But, Mother, he's a civil servant!

ZHIVKA: Huh! What sort of a civil servant? Sometimes he's employed and sometimes he isn't. Haven't we had to bend over backwards to save his job for him three times already? In spite of that you let yourself become infatuated with him. We gave in to you, and ever since we've been beside ourselves with worry. Well, we've suffered, but we're not going to suffer any more. Indeed, we don't deserve to have to suffer any more.

DARA: For God's sake, Mother, what are you saying? Aren't you going to ask me what I want – don't I count?

ZHIVKA: No, I'm not asking you. Wait until you've seen the bridegroom – then I'll ask you

DARA: Never mind the bridegroom. Ask me first of all whether I'm prepared to leave my husband.

ZHIVKA: He's no sort of opportunity for you.

DARA: But he was before I was a minister's daughter, wasn't he!

ZHIVKA: Not even then.

DARA: Well, he is for me.

ZHIVKA: Then you wrap him up in cotton wool, put him under your pillow, and look after him, because I won't – he's no use to me. And understand this – from this day forward he is no longer my son-in-law!

DARA: But he's my husband!

ZHIVKA: Maybe, but wouldn't you rather be rid of the good-for-nothing wastrel that he is?

DARA: Only if I knew he was being unfaithful to me.

ZHIVKA: Well, he is unfaithful to you!

DARA: Who says so?

ZHIVKA: He's a man, isn't he? Men are all unfaithful to their wives. That's Nature.

DARA: If I knew that …

ZHIVKA: Oh, as long as we're living in this world you'll find out, all right!

DARA: Well, I'm telling you I don't believe it, so there!

ZHIVKA: You'll see!

DARA *(bursting into tears)*: It's not true – you're just making it up!

ZHIVKA: Oh, no I'm not! – and why are you crying?

DARA: You don't think I'd be laughing after all you've said, do you? Of course I'm crying! *(**Exit** to her room, still sobbing)*.

SCENE 8

*(**Enter** ANKA in the doorway)* Excuse me, madam, Mr Pera the clerk is here to see you.

ZHIVKA: Ask him to come in.

(ANKA withdraws and ushers in PERA)

PERA: Will you permit me?

ZHIVKA: Please come in.

PERA: I have come back only to ask whether there is anything I can do for Madam Minister?

ZHIVKA: No, thank you. There's nothing I require at present.

PERA: And I do beg Madam Minister not to overlook me. All I wish is that Madam Minister should bear me in mind.

ZHIVKA: Well, as it happens, I've just thought of something. Do you know my son-in-law?

PERA: Certainly – I know him well.

ZHIVKA: Good! Well do you know anything, as it were, personal about him? For instance, has he, perhaps, got a woman … how shall I put it … on the side? Or anything like that?

PERA: I really don't know, madam.

ZHIVKA: What d'you mean, you don't know? Men know these things – they're always talking about things like that amongst themselves.

PERA: I'm sorry, but I'm not one to know about such things.

ZHIVKA: Maybe not, but you can at least keep your ears open, can't you?

PERA: Believe me, Madam Minister, I've heard nothing and, frankly, I just don't believe that he's like that.

ZHIVKA: What d'you mean, you "don't believe he's like that"? Of course he's "like that" – he must be! You must, surely, have heard something about him?

PERA: No, I haven't, truly.

ZHIVKA: I simply can't believe it!

PERA: Well, madam, the truth is that he's only been a poor civil servant up to now, on low pay and – you know how it is – women are expensive, so a poor civil servant on low pay couldn't afford one, even if he wanted to.

ZHIVKA: What you're saying would mean that every poorly-paid civil servant must always be faithful to his wife. And that certainly isn't true!

PERA: I don't say he must be. There are some on low pay that manage it one way or another.

ZHIVKA: What d'you mean "one way or another"?

PERA: Well … oh, madam, please excuse me – it is embarrassing to speak of such things to you …

ZHIVKA: Never mind that – tell me!

PERA: Well … for instance … if there should happen to be a young housemaid, or suchlike, in the house … because, even on low pay …

ZHIVKA *(strikes her forehead)*: Of course! And to imagine that I never thought of that! But of course, it's obvious! I really am most grateful to you – you have given me an excellent idea.

PERA: I am glad to be of service to you in any way I can. You will, I hope, keep me in mind?

ZHIVKA: I will – don't worry.

PERA: Please remember my name – Pera, the clerk from the Administrative section. *(**Exit,** bowing)*

SCENE 9

*(*ZHIVKA *rings the bell.* **Enter** ANKA)*

ANKA: You rang?

ZHIVKA: Yes. Come over here – a bit closer *(She looks searchingly at* ANKA *from head to toe)*

ANKA: Why is Madam looking at me like that?

ZHIVKA: We'll come to that. Anka, tell me, do men consider you to be attractive?

ANKA: Really, madam! How would I know?

ZHIVKA: Well, can you tell me whether men are inclined to run after you?

ANKA: Oh, madam, how can I put it? – men are men, they run after anything in a skirt.

ZHIVKA: That's true. And so I wonder … Anka, would you be prepared to do something very special for me, for which I shall reward you handsomely?

ANKA: Certainly, madam. What sort of thing?

ZHIVKA: I want you to … to make yourself attractive to my son-in-law.

ANKA: Lawks!

ZHIVKA: Never mind the "Lawks!" – can you do it?

ANKA: But, crikey, madam, why me? I'm not that sort of girl. Oh, you must think very badly of me!

ZHIVKA: On the contrary, if you'll do what I ask I shall think very highly of you.

ANKA: But how can I? – your son-in-law's a married man!

ZHIVKA: Of course he is – if he wasn't married I wouldn't have asked you to do it.

ANKA: I don't know, madam – you might be just testing me?

ZHIVKA: Why on earth should I want to test you? This is important to me, that's all. And, I promise you, Anka, if you pull it off I'll give you two steps in promotion.

ANKA: What promotion?

ZHIVKA: No, not promotion – I got mixed up. No, I shall give you an increase in pay, and I shall get my husband to award you a thousand dinars for Economic Purposes from the Classified Lottery Fund.

ANKA: That would be wonderful!

ZHIVKA: Well, do you think you can get him interested?

ANKA: I'm not sure, but you know what they say: "All men are the same"!

ZHIVKA: Precisely!

ANKA: Only, madam, I must please ask you to tell me exactly what you require of me – what I'm to do, and how far you want me to go.

ZHIVKA: It doesn't bother me – you can go as far as you like. The most important thing, as far as I am concerned, is that you should get my son-in-law into your bedroom, and that I should catch him in there with you.

ANKA: That you should catch him in there? Oh, madam, I'd be taking an awful risk!

ZHIVKA: What risk? What are you talking about?

ANKA: I'd be risking my good name. It'd be bound to come out afterwards, what happened, and I'd be blamed.

ZHIVKA: Don't you worry about that, that's my concern.

ANKA: Are sure you don't want anything more than that – only that he should come into my room?

ZHIVKA: Well, it might be as well if you could get him to take his coat off, so that I can catch him there without his coat on.

ANKA: Only his coat?

ZHIVKA: Isn't that enough?

ANKA: That'll be easy – I'll light the stove.

ZHIVKA: What now, in April?

ANKA: Yes, that's the point! Right then! – all you want is for me to get him to come into my room and take his coat off.

ZHIVKA: That's good enough for me.

ANKA: Once again, I must beg of you, madam, that it shouldn't come out afterwards that I had seduced the young lady's husband away from her, otherwise my reputation would be ruined.

ZHIVKA: I told you, you don't have to worry about that.

ANKA: But won't the young lady be angry with me?

ZHIVKA: In this household I am the only one who has the right to be angry, and no one else.

ANKA: Very well, madam, if that is what you wish …

ZHIVKA: And do you think you can do it?

ANKA: Goodness me, there's no telling what may happen! I hope
I can do it and, after all, you know, men do give in more easily
than women.

ZHIVKA: You understand, of course, that it mustn't look as if it
had been planned. And, another thing, it must be done as soon
as possible.

ANKA: You may depend on me, madam, I'll do the best I can.

ZHIVKA: All right. Now off you go! – and keep me informed.

ANKA: Yes, madam *(Exit* ANKA. ZHIVKA *sits down on an
armchair with a satisfied expression on her face).*

SCENE 10

(Enter UNCLE VASA, *from outside).*

VASA: Good morning, Zhivka!

ZHIVKA: Oh, it's you, Vasa! What do you want?

VASA: What do I want? Why, who's the most likely person to
come and see you, if not me? I met Mrs Vida, Draga's mother-
in-law, on the way here, and she said to me: "You must be very
proud, Mr Vasa, now that you are part of the family of a
government minister!"

ZHIVKA: Oh, and why should *you* be proud of that?

VASA: But of course I'm proud! As your uncle, I'm your closest
relative, aren't I? So of course people congratulate me. Do you
know, Zhivka, I was sitting in a café the other day, with some
friends, and I just happened to mention that I was going to
drop in on my niece "the government minister's wife, you
know", and everyone at the table immediately doffed their caps
and said: "Bless you, Mr Vasa!" and "We're honoured, Mr
Vasa!" and "Shall we see you tomorrow, Mr Vasa?" And, to tell
you the truth, I enjoyed it as much as if I was having my belly
scratched!

ZHIVKA: That must have been very agreeable.

VASA: I've been waiting for so long for somebody in our family to

… to … what's the word? . . to get ahead, to be noticed, to stand out and be admired. So far, there's been nobody at all. I had thought that Yova Pop-Arsich might get ahead. He was very bright as a boy, and had a gentlemanly air about him. And I remember I always used to say: "That Yova of ours will go far!" – but, of course, he finished up in prison doing hard labour. And then we had high hopes of Christina, Datsa's daughter. She was very pretty and looked as if she had been born to be a lady. She was good at school too, but – well, she made a bit of a mistake, didn't she, and it was bad luck that her nine months were up just at the very time when she was due to sit her final exams. After that I had completely given up hope when, all of a sudden, *you* shot ahead and became a government minister's wife. As I said to my Kata: "Good for Zhivka!" I always said that someone in our family would be sure to rise as high as that one day.

ZHIVKA: Yes, but I don't see what the fact that I am a Minister's wife has got to do with the family.

VASA: Zhivka, what are you saying? Don't you think you ought to take some notice of your family?

ZHIVKA: In what respect?

VASA: Well, to look after them! What have you become a government minister's wife for, if it isn't so that you can look after your family? You can't say that it will put you to a lot of trouble, or that you can't do it. It's not as though any of us wants to be made a Government Adviser, or a Bishop, or anything like that – there are just a few little little things, a few minor requests, that we want you to attend to for us.

ZHIVKA: Oh really, and how can I possibly cope? – there are far too many of them.

VASA: Now, don't be like that, Zhivka! And just you listen to what I have to say. Remember this – there's nothing in the world that can blacken a person's name as effectively as a family can. Nothing can throw mud, and spread vilification and slander like a family can. They say that it's damaging when the newspapers run somebody down – hah! when it comes to doing damage the newspapers aren't in the same league as families! So you'd better make an effort to get on with your family. In any case, it's only right and proper. Every government minister puts looking after his family first and foremost, and the country second. For, after all, the Family is the backbone of the State..

ZHIVKA: Do you really think that I'm going to take responsibility for the whole family?

VASA *(takes a piece of paper out of his pocket)*: Oh, there aren't really all that many. Here you are – I've made a list for you and, you see, there are only nineteen of us on it.

ZHIVKA: Only nineteen! For God's sake, Vasa, that's a whole regiment. Who've you put in it?

VASA *(reads)*: There's Aunt Savka.

ZHIVKA: Oh yes, Aunt Savka. She lent me two hundred dinars, and now she's pestering me for it. Well, I'll repay her the two hundred dinars, and that's all I'm going to do for *her*.

VASA *(reads)*: There's Soya.

ZHIVKA: She's out! She called me an old gossip.

VASA: No, Zhivka, don't be like that! She said it a long time ago, before you became a Minister's wife, and I swear to you that she certainly won't say it now. Anyway, you can't take literally everything that's said within the family. You even used to say things about me – that I was a pub crawler and a swindler – but, there, I didn't take it to heart. I admit that, after that, I didn't come and see you any more, but the moment you became a government minister's wife I was the first to hurry round and congratulate you.

ZHIVKA: And who else is on the list?

VASA: Aunt Datsa and her daughter Christina.

ZHIVKA: Is she the one that took her exams?

VASA: Yes.

ZHIVKA: Well, what does she want? She's passed her exams – so good luck to her.

VASA *(reads)*: Pop-Arsa's son Yova

ZHIVKA: The one who went to prison?

VASA *(reads)*: Yes. Then there's Pera Kalenich.

ZHIVKA: Who on earth's he?

VASA: I don't know him, actually, but he's says he's part of
the family.

ZHIVKA *(pondering)*: Pera Kalenich? Frankly, I've never heard
of anyone by that name in the family.

VASA: Nor I, Zhivka, but he said to me: "Uncle Vasa, we are
related."

ZHIVKA: Well, was he related before I became a minister's wife,
or only after?

VASA: I'd never seen or heard of him before.

ZHIVKA: Very well, Uncle Vasa, what do you want me to do with
this list of people?

VASA: To receive them.

ZHIVKA: Receive who?

VASA: Why, them – the family. You should receive them all, ask
them what they want, and see what you can do for them.
They were all disappointed that you wouldn't see them when
they called.

ZHIVKA: You mean, I should receive everyone on this list? But
that would take ten days, and I'm already so busy that I hardly
have time to take a break for a bite to eat.

VASA: Maybe, but you'll have to see them. If the worst comes to
the worst I could, if you like, gather them together and you
could receive them all at the same time. How would that do?

ZHIVKA: Yes, I suppose that would be possible. But won't they
be offended if I receive them all at once, in such a crowd?

VASA: I'll tell them that it's the only way, at present. And
later, when they're leaving, you can tell them that you'll see
them separately some other time.

ZHIVKA: All right, they can come tomorrow afternoon.

VASA: Tomorrow then, good! And thank you Zhivka – they've
been pestering me dreadfully. I am your nearest relative, you

know, and they were all saying: "Uncle Vasa, what's wrong? – why won't Zhivka see us?" They were crowding round me as if *I* was the government minister's wife myself! I'll go now, immediately, and tell them about the reception. Right, then! – until tomorrow!

ZHIVKA: All right.

VASA: This will be the best way, you know. I'll collect them all together, the whole family, and you'll do what you can for them or, if you can't do anything, then promise them something. You know how it is – even a mere promise is often good enough. Right, then! Give my love to Dara and her husband. Good bye! *(Exit)*.

SCENE 11

(After VASA *has left,* **enter** ANKA, *carrying a visiting card which she gives to* ZHIVKA*)*

ZHIVKA *(reading the card)*: Ah, Mr Ninkovich. Ask him to come in.

*(***Enter*** NINKOVICH *and* **exit** ANKA *after ushering him in.*
NINKOVICH *is very elegantly dressed, his clothes perfectly brushed and ironed. He is wearing white spats, he has gloves on his hands, and he has a flower in his button-hole).*

NINKOVICH: Madam, I kiss your hand! *(Kisses her hand)* I took .the liberty, upon your invitation …

ZHIVKA: I am most grateful to you for coming. Please sit down. I do hope that I haven't inconvenienced you …

NINKOVICH: Not at all! I am honoured!

ZHIVKA: I wished to ask you whether you could do something for me.

NINKOVICH: Madam, you may rely on me to be of service to you. *(He speaks French with an appalling accent)*: *Je suis tout-à-fait à vôtre disposition.*

ZHIVKA: They tell me that you know all the … how shall I say … rules …

NINKOVICH: The rules and conventions of high society. *Le bon ton du grand monde.* Oh, madam, high society is to me as Nature itself – it is an atmosphere without which I cannot live or breathe.

ZHIVKA: Well, you know, I am under an obligation to receive the best people. I expect to come into contact with all the current leading politicians and foreign ambassadors, so I wish to give a cultured impression.

NINKOVICH: That is a most admirable ambition and, believe me, you were absolutely right to turn to me.

ZHIVKA: Yes, people said that.

NINKOVICH: Mrs Draga, when she was the wife of a Minister, was unwilling to take the slightest step without consulting me. I designed the bill of fare for her dinners – *le menu de dîner* – she decorated her boudoir in accordance with my taste, I arranged all her parties, I chose all her toiletries. I possess, you will appreciate, an exquisitely refined taste. *Un goût parfait.*

ZHIVKA: Well, I'm thinking of having a new evening dress made – what do you suggest?

NINKOVICH *(Looks at her appraisingly)*: *Grisâtre* – a pale grey, which shades into sky blue, *crêpe de chine*, with something a little pink, perhaps a fringed sleeve and lapel, or perhaps pockets of the same shade … I'm not sure, we shall see … it will need a certain *nuance.*

ZHIVKA: Will you come to the dressmaker with me?

NINKOVICH: With pleasure!

ZHIVKA: And what else do you recommend in the way of culture?

NINKOVICH: Ah, yes! Culture – that is the most important thing. *C'est la chose principale.*

ZHIVKA: I had a gold tooth put in only this morning.

NINKOVICH: An excellent idea – it is *chic* and adds charm to the smile.

ZHIVKA: Do, please, tell me all about high-class culture and everything that I must do to achieve it. I shall do whatever you say.

NINKOVICH: Do you know any card games?

ZHIVKA: I know Beggar-my-neighbour.

NINKOVICH: Ah! ... You will have to learn to play Bridge.

ZHIVKA: Learn to play what?

NINKOVICH: Bridge. It is not possible to be a cultured lady without Bridge. Naturally, you will wish to invite the Diplomatic Corps to your house, but the Diplomatic Corps without Bridge simply is not the Diplomatic Corps.

ZHIVKA *(pretending to be offended)*: No, obviously!

NINKOVICH: Madam smokes, of course?

ZHIVKA: No. I can't stand smoking.

NINKOVICH: I'm afraid that it will be necessary for you to learn that, too. A cultured lady who does not smoke cigarettes is something that one could not even imagine.

ZHIVKA: Oh dear, I'm afraid I'll cough until I choke.

NINKOVICH: Well, you know, one has to suffer a certain amount in order to be cultured. *Noblesse oblige*. And there is one other thing, madam, if you will permit me to ask.

ZHIVKA: Has it got to do with being cultured?

NINKOVICH: Very much so, madam. Only, the question is ... how shall I put it? .. you will not, I hope, think the less of me for asking you a question of considerable delicacy. *Une question tout-à-fait discrète*.

ZHIVKA: Please continue!

NINKOVICH: Has madam got a lover?

ZHIVKA *(astonished and insulted)*: Eh? What sort of a woman do you take me for?

NINKOVICH: I did warn you that it was a very delicate question, but the fact is that if you wish to be a cultured lady with a position in high society, *une femme du monde*, it is absolutely necessary to have a lover.

ZHIVKA: But I'm a respectable woman, sir!

NINKOVICH: *Excellent!* That is what makes it so interesting. If a disreputable woman has a lover, that's of no interest at all.

ZHIVKA: Have I really got to do it?

NINKOVICH: I can assure you madam, that it is only possible for you to be a cultured lady, a lady with a position in high society, *une femme du monde*, if you play Bridge, smoke cigarettes, and have a lover …

ZHIVKA: Oh, my God! Bridge is one thing, and so is smoking, but having a lover ..!

NINKOVICH: Well, madam, you asked for my advice and I felt duty bound to give it to you openly and truthfully. Of course, it is a matter for you whether you follow it. You can, if you wish, do without Bridge, do without cigarettes, and do without a lover, but you will then be a minister's wife quite without culture.

ZHIVKA: What about Mrs Draga – did she play Bridge?

NINKOVICH: Yes, of course! She learned it.

ZHIVKA: And did she smoke cigarettes?

NINKOVICH: Naturally!

ZHIVKA: And … the other thing?

NINKOVICH: Yes, madam, indeed she had a lover.

ZHIVKA *(overcome by curiosity)* Who was it?

NINKOVICH: It was I!

ZHIVKA: You? And was Mrs Nata cultured?

NINKOVICH: Very much so!

ZHIVKA: And who was her lover?

NINKOVICH: It was also I.

ZHIVKA: But … how? … did you take them in turns?

NINKOVICH: As soon as a Cabinet resigns, I resign.

ZHIVKA: What, you mean you only do it as long as the person is in power?

NINKOVICH: Exactly, madam! A minister's lady only has to be cultured as long as she is in power. After she relinquishes power she no longer has any need to be cultured.

ZHIVKA: Do you know, I never thought of that.

NINKOVICH: In the meantime, nothing could be easier. Of all the things I have told you about, the hardest is Bridge. Because, after all, what is there to smoking? – you just cough a bit and that's it. And what is there to having a lover? – you just compromise yourself a bit, and that's all. But, believe me, Bridge is a very difficult and complicated game. *Un jeu compliqué, mais très distingué.*

ZHIVKA: But, Mr Ninkovich, I wish to remain a respectable woman.

NINKOVICH: Well do so, there is nothing to prevent you!

ZHIVKA: But how can I "do so", and at the same time play Bridge? Can I play Bridge, and still be a respectable woman?

NINKOVICH: Why not?

ZHIVKA: No, no … not Bridge – I didn't mean that. To tell you the truth, my head's in such a whirl that I don't know what I'm saying! None of the things you've told me had ever entered my mind.

NINKOVICH: You see, madam, it's important to have a lover, not for its own sake, but for the sake of appearances. You have to be compromised if you are to be a cultured lady in high society. *Voilà, ça c'est le principe fondamental !*

ZHIVKA: But how do you suggest I am to be compromised?

NINKOVICH: It is necessary that, at your very first party, you should be the subject of conversation between some of the ladies – it doesn't matter who. One lady, let us say, will whisper discreetly to the lady next to her: "Have you heard what they are saying about Mrs Zhivka?" "No, what?" says the other lady. "You won't believe it," whispers the first lady, "But I have heard from a reliable source … just think of it! – that Mrs Zhivka has seduced Mr Ninkovich away from Mrs Natalia!"

ZHIVKA: Yes, that's the sort of thing they'd say.

NINKOVICH: But it's quite possible that there will be some who will try to defend you. "Oh no, I don't believe it. It can't be true. I know Mrs Zhivka and she's not that sort." Of course, it will be essential to shut *their* mouths.

ZHIVKA: What? Silence the people who are defending me?

NINKOVICH: Certainly! They *must* be silenced. You may ask how? Well, it is very easy and simple. *D'une manière bien simple!* You must badger my minister to promote me, and to do it at once. Of course, the minister will say: "But he was promoted only two months ago." But you say: "Yes, but that was under the previous government – he ought to be promoted under this government." Why all this, you ask? Because, madam, that would be the most effective way of shutting up those who try to defend you, and once they have been silenced the gossip can spread without hindrance.

ZHIVKA: Well, is it all just a matter of gossip, and nothing more?

NINKOVICH: *C'est ça!* That is all! *C'est suffisant!*

ZHIVKA *(pondering)*: If it's only a matter of gossip … but that way, it seems to me, I would only be thought to be disreputable by other people, whereas I shall actually remain respectable?

NINKOVICH: Why not? That's quite possible. *Ça va aussi.*

ZHIVKA: This "culture" is a queer business. In the old days, women were respectable outwardly and disreputable in private, but nowadays it's the other way round! All right, then, will you be my lover too?

NINKOVICH: That, madam, is a matter of taste for you. A matter of … how shall I put it … *une question de vos sentiments intimes!* But, if you ask my advice, you should take someone who is thoroughly experienced.

ZHIVKA: Thoroughly experienced in what?

NINKOVICH: Well I, for instance, know every possible way of compromising you in short order. In addition I know how to arrange matters so that they have a particular pattern – *une forme speciale* – to the extent that, in the end, even you will start to doubt your own respectability. And, above all – *et ça c'est la chose principale* – as soon as the Cabinet resigns, I fully understand that it is my duty to resign also. On the other hand you can, if you wish, make enquiries about me, but I am confident that you will receive nothing but the most glowing references.

ZHIVKA: Oh Lord! What's going to happen to me? If only I had died yesterday I wouldn't have had to live through today.

NINKOVICH: No, but if you had died yesterday you wouldn't be a minister's wife today.

ZHIVKA: That's true. *(After a pause for reflection)* Well, what do you think?

NINKOVICH: Oh, it's all very simple. *C'est simple comme tout!* As far as Bridge is concerned, you must practise; as far as smoking is concerned, you must practise that as well, and as far as having a lover is concerned, you've no need to practise at all.

ZHIVKA: What d'you mean "I've no need to practise"? You must have a very low opinion of me.

NINKOVICH: Madam, you would be able to see much more clearly how I intend to proceed if we were to put the business in hand straightaway.

ZHIVKA *(frightened)* What business?

NINKOVICH: This is my plan: Bridge, for instance – you can start learning that tomorrow. As for smoking, you can make use of this now. *(He takes out his cigarette case and offers it to her).* And as for a lover, that too ...

ZHIVKA: And that, too, I can make use of now, eh? Oh, you've got round me somehow, but it looks to me as though I lose my reputation in the end.

NINKOVICH: *Oh, pardon! Mille fois pardon!* I would not, of course, dream of overstepping the bounds of propriety by pressing you to accept the advice that it was my duty to give you, if you are still anxious about it. If there is anything at all in the advice I have offered which you find disagreeable, I am always prepared to withdraw. But you did want me to acquaint you with the rules and manners of high society ...

ZHIVKA: Well, yes. I can quite see that you are not to blame, but you know ...

NINKOVICH *(standing up)* May I take it, madam, that you would consider any further advice from me to be superfluous?

ZHIVKA: No, wait a moment! I can see that it must be as you say. It's not that I don't understand, but ... you know ... it's not easy to play fast and loose with one's own reputation.

NINKOVICH: Just as you please.

ZHIVKA: So be it. All right, let's start on the Bridge tomorrow. And as for the cigarettes, here, let me have one.

NINKOVICH *(Offers his cigarette case)* Please … *(*ZHIVKA *takes a cigarette out of the case and puts it on the table).*

ZHIVKA: And as for … *that* … couldn't we wait a bit?

NINKOVICH: If you are nervous it would be better not to think about it.

ZHIVKA: Oh Lord! … But in the end, I suppose, what must be must be! Very well, then. You may consider your duty as commencing from today.

NINKOVICH: What duty?

ZHIVKA: Well … *that*! … your duty as a lover.

NINKOVICH: Thank you. *(He gently kisses her hand)* I assure you that you will find me entirely satisfactory.

ZHIVKA: Well, it's all in the lap of the gods now. If that's being cultured, then cultured we will be!

NINKOVICH: Just one more question. Do you wish me to write love letters to you or not?

ZHIVKA: What sort of love letters?

NINKOVICH: Ah! Well, some ladies very much like receiving, each day, a small letter on scented pink paper, full of amorous words and phrases.

ZHIVKA: Well, fancy that! I've never received anything like that in my whole life.

NINKOVICH: *C'est comme vous voulez.* If it would please you, I am at your disposal.

ZHIVKA: Would you just send me one to start with, please, so that I can see what it's like, and if I approve I'll order some more from you.

NINKOVICH: Certainly! – as soon as I get back to my office. You shall receive a love letter within the next ten minutes. *(He prepares to leave)* And now, my darling, I kiss your hand. *(Kisses her hand). Ma chère amie! (Going to the door he turns and blows her a kiss)* Mwah! Mwah! *(Exit)*

SCENE 12

(ZHIVKA *remains, in a bewildered state. She looks, alternately, at the door through which* NINKOVICH *left and at the audience, as if to say: "Now see what's happened to me!"*

Enter ANKA *from outside. She is wearing a pretty new dress).*

ANKA: Madam is alone?

ZHIVKA: Yes, alone …

ANKA: You look a little upset, madam … not yourself. What is it?

ZHIVKA: Frankly, I'm bewildered. God alone knows what's going to happen! You know, Anka, it's not easy being a government minister's wife. I hadn't realised how hard it was going to be. I'm going to lie down and have a rest – my head's spinning. *(She gets up to go)* What about you – anything?

ANKA: Well, as you see, I've put a new dress on.

ZHIVKA *(As she goes to the bedroom door she murmurs)* Mwah! Mwah! *(Exit).*

SCENE 13

(ANKA *watches her go, astonished. Then she goes over to a mirror and, moistening her fingers at her lips, she smooths her eyebrows and arranges her hair).*

(Enter CHEDA *from outside)*

CHEDA: What are you doing by the mirror?

ANKA *(coquettishly)*: I'm making myself look nice, sir!

CHEDA: Oh, indeed!

ANKA: I'm young, you know, and some might even find me attractive, mightn't they?

CHEDA: Indeed, they might.

ANKA: But, for instance, you, sir, have never paid me much attention.

CHEDA: But why should I have paid attention to you?

ANKA: For goodness' sake, you're a man, aren't you!

CHEDA: I know I'm a man, but …

ANKA: And you know what they say – men are all the same.

CHEDA: Maybe, Anka, but you must know that I am an honourable man.

ANKA: I've generally found that honourable men are the ones who pester me the most.

CHEDA: You may be right. Actually, you know, I'm not all that honourable.

ANKA *(very coquettishly)*: That's rather what I thought. *(She moves towards him)*.

CHEDA: Oho! *(He touches her cheek)* You're being very nice to me today, Anka.

ANKA: I dreamt about you. Oh, my! – it was such a lovely dream.

CHEDA: Anka, I'd love to hear about your dream, but not now – later. Things are in such a state at the moment that real life must come before dreams. Would you please, my dear, look and see if my wife's about anywhere. I've got to speak to her.

ANKA: All right, but you'll let me tell you about my dream later?

CHEDA: I certainly will!

ANKA *(going out of the room)*: Believe me, it was a *very* interesting dream! *(Exit)*

SCENE 14

CHEDA *(watching Anka go)*: My word! *(Enter DARA)*

DARA: Where've you been?

CHEDA: Me? To see a lawyer.

DARA: What d'you want a lawyer for?

CHEDA: To ask him whether there is any law in existence by which a woman can marry someone while she's still married to someone else.

DARA: That's silly – you didn't even need to ask.

CHEDA: Didn't I just! Hasn't your mother spoken to you?

DARA: Yes, what about it?

CHEDA: Hasn't she told you that you've got to become Mrs Nicaragua?

DARA: Yes, but surely you're not taking that seriously!

CHEDA: I most certainly am taking it seriously, considering that

Nicaragua is coming here tomorrow to look you over.

Dara: He can look *me* over as much as he likes, the question is whether I'm going to take any notice of *him*!

Cheda: All right, but what did you say to your mother when she spoke about marriage?

Dara: I told her that am married already, that I have a husband, and that I have no intention of leaving him.

Cheda: And what are you going to say to him?

Dara: To who?

Cheda: To Nicaragua.

Dara: I shall say exactly the same to him.

Cheda: Good for you! She thinks that just because she's a government minister's wife she can give orders that her son-in-law is to relinquish the duties which he has hitherto performed as a son-in-law, and that he is to be transferred elsewhere. God alone knows where she is minded to send me. She thinks that she can just swap one son-in-law for another, as she pleases. Well, she can't – it's not going to happen!

Dara: I simply cannot believe that she means it seriously.

Cheda: Oh, she means it seriously, I assure you. The match-maker is already in touch with the bridegroom – everything has been arranged! Are you aware, by the way, who the match-maker is?

Dara: No.

Cheda: It's the dentist – the one who put in her gold tooth. Just think of it! – she goes to the dentist and as she sits down in the chair she says: "I have come for you to change my tooth and, while you're at it, would you change my son-in-law as well!" Thank you very much! And if she can do that, what next? Will she go back to the dentist and say: "Now I've come for you to drill my son-in-law and put a filling in him"?

Dara: Goodness, Cheda, what nonsense you do talk!

Cheda: But she could, dear, she's capable of anything! It's obvious that she's completely gone out of her mind since she became a minister's wife.

DARA: She can't make me do anything I don't want to.

CHEDA: Are you quite sure of that?

DARA: I am, just so long as she can't prove that you're being unfaithful to me.

CHEDA: What! Me? Where on earth did you get that idea?

DARA: She said that she'd be able to prove it .

CHEDA: There! I told you that she was out to have me drilled and filled, and you didn't believe me.

SCENE 15

*(**Enter** MESSENGER from the Ministry)*

MESSENGER: A letter for Mrs Minister Popovich.

CHEDA *(carelessly)*: Give it to me.

MESSENGER: I was ordered to deliver it to the lady personally.

DARA: All right, I'll send her in.

CHEDA: I'll make myself scarce – I don't want to meet her.

*(**Exeunt** DARA, left, and CHEDA, right).*

SCENE 16

*(**Enter** ZHIVKA, after a short interval)*

ZHIVKA: A letter for me?

MESSENGER: Yes, from Mr Secretary Ninkovich.

ZHIVKA *(pleasantly surprised)* Aha! *(She takes the small pink envelope and sniffs it. A look of satisfaction spreads across her face)* Thank you! *(The MESSENGER bows, and **exit**).*

SCENE 17

(ZHIVKA first of all laughs out loud, childishly. Then she opens the letter and sits down on an armchair to read it, but before doing so, as if suddenly remembering something, she gets up and goes over to the table where she had put the cigarette which she had taken from NINKOVICH. She takes the cigarette, returns to the armchair, and sits down again. Then she lights the cigarette and begins to read the letter, holding it in her left hand and the cigarette in her right

hand. However, after her first puff at the cigarette she is overcome by a fit of coughing and retching so severe and noisy that it arouses the whole household. Variously, and through various doors **enter** DARA, CHEDA, RAKA, *and* ANKA. *They all gather round the chair to help* ZHIVKA, *who is still coughing uncontrollably.* DARA *holds her right hand, with the cigarette still in it, and* CHEDA *holds her left hand, with the letter in it.* ANKA *thumps her back, and* RAKA *forces a glass of water into her mouth.* CHEDA, *holding her left hand, notices the letter in it and starts to read it, taking no notice of* ZHIVKA's *sufferings. As he reads it through, a look of malicious satisfaction spreads across his face).*

Curtain

Act Three

The same room as in the previous Act.

SCENE 1

*(*PERA *is waiting in the doorway, with his hat in his hand, while* ANKA *goes into the room, left, to announce him. After a short while* ANKA ***re-enters****)*

ANKA: The Minister's lady is very busy: she can't see you.

PERA: I see. Thank you very much. My profound respects to Madam Minister. Indeed, there is really no need for her to waste her precious time on me. Only, please be so good as to tell the lady that I came to ask her not to overlook me.

ANKA: Very well, sir, I'll tell her.

PERA: You do know my name, don't you.

ANKA: Yes. You're Mr Pera, the clerk.

PERA: Not just "Mr Pera the clerk" – please say to her: "Mr Pera the clerk from the Administrative Section."

ANKA: All right, I will.

PERA: Yes, please do. Good day! *(**Exit**)*

SCENE 2

*(*ANKA *goes straight over to the mirror.* ***Enter*** UNCLE VASA*)*

VASA: Good morning. Is your mistress in?

ANKA: Yes.

VASA: Actually, the person I really want to see is Cheda, her son-in-law. On Madam's instructions, I have some business to do with him.

ANKA: That's funny, I've got some business to do with him on
    Madam's instructions, too.

VASA: I wonder if it's the same thing you and I have to do?

ANKA: Have you got to get him to take his coat off?

VASA: Who?

ANKA: Her son-in-law.

VASA: Take his coat off!… what are you talking about?

ANKA: Oh, obviously your business with him's not the same
    as mine.

VASA: Well, anyway, is he in?

ANKA: Yes.

VASA: Call him, please.

ANKA: Very well! *(Exit)*

SCENE 3

*(*VASA, *noticing a cigarette box on the table, takes one out and slips
it into his cigarette case. After that,* **enter** CHEDA*)*

CHEDA: Good morning, Uncle! You wanted to see me?

VASA: Yes, I want to have a serious conversation with you.

CHEDA: Are you here as an emissary from the minister's wife?

VASA: Not as an emissary, as an uncle. I am your uncle, aren't I?

CHEDA: Yes, you are.

VASA: Well, then!

CHEDA: So what's this serious matter that you want to talk to talk
    to me about, on behalf of your niece?

VASA: You will already know what Zhivka's intentions are with
    regard to Dara. You have to admit that she's her mother, and
    Dara's her only daughter, and she has to look after her.

CHEDA: What d'you mean – "look after her"?

VASA: What I say – look after her. You can see that for yourself –
    you're an intelligent man. Dara isn't a child any more, she's
    grown up, she's twenty years old, and it's time that she thought
    about getting married.

CHEDA: What the hell are you talking about – "getting married"?
    For God's sake – hasn't she been married to me for two
    years now?

VASA: Yes, she has. Look, I'm not the sort of character who says that things are not what they are. Only …

CHEDA: Only what?

VASA: Only, we don't count that as a marriage.

CHEDA: What d'you mean – you "don't count it"?

VASA: Well, it's like this. Suppose you and I were playing noughts and crosses, shall we say. We play one game, and I say: "I tell you what, Cheda, let's not count that game – let's start again."

CHEDA *(pretending to be persuaded)* Ah, I see!

VASA: Well, there you are, then!

CHEDA: So you say that this game of noughts and crosses that we've been playing for the last two years doesn't count?

VASA: That's right. We just take a sponge and wipe the slate clean. D'you understand now?

CHEDA: Oh, I understand, all right!

VASA: There you are, then! That's what I wanted to talk to you about. You're a sensible and reasonable chap. I'm sure we can easily come to an agreement.

CHEDA: I hope so.

VASA: After all, my dear fellow, you just tell me this – what do you want a wife for, anyway? When you think about it in a mature and grown-up way, you will see there is no real need for one. I can understand it if you say that you need a house, or if you say that you need a taxi-cab, or if you say that you need a winter coat. All those things I can understand, but if you say that you need a wife, then, frankly, I don't understand it at all.

CHEDA: Well, that may be so … at your age.

VASA: Oh, when I was younger I had even less need of one.

CHEDA: That's true, too.

VASA: Of course it's true, and so, you see, I ask you, as an intelligent man, why do you need a wife?

CHEDA: Why indeed! – I don't need one at all, do I?

VASA: No, you don't.

CHEDA: That's right. Well, Uncle Vasa, could you now please explain to me, so that I can understand clearly, why it is that Nicaragua needs a wife?

VASA: What Nicaragua?

CHEDA: The one that "needs" to take my wife. I'm only asking, you see – why does he need a wife?

VASA *(somewhat put out)*: Him? Well, … how shall I put it? … there are, you know, some people who take things that they don't need. There really are such people.

CHEDA: Oh, there are, indeed!

VASA: But you're not one of those people. You're an intelligent man and, if you do as I tell you, you'll find that it'll be much better for you to leave your wife. You don't really need a wife, do you? – you said so yourself. So, since you don't need her, leave her! Now, I've got to ask you, on behalf of Zhivka, are you going to leave Dara or aren't you?

CHEDA: Is that all that you've got to ask me on behalf of Madam Zhivka?

VASA: Yes, that's all.

CHEDA: Well, you can tell Madam Zhivka that I am *not* going to leave Dara.

VASA *(astonished)*: Not? I can't believe it – I didn't expect this of you. I took you for a sensible man. Well, in that case, I can tell you – there is something else. Zhivka said to me that if you agreed to go quietly you'd get a step in promotion, as a reward. Just think of it – promotion! So, you see, you've got to choose which you'd rather have – a wife, or promotion!

CHEDA: Actually, I'd rather have my wife *and* a step in promotion.

VASA: That's pie in the sky – you can't have your cake and eat it.

CHEDA: Oh, I haven't finished. I'd like even more to have my wife and *two* steps in promotion.

VASA: What! At this rate of bidding you'll tell me that you want two wives and four steps in promotion! It's no use, my friend – what cannot be, cannot be! No, you just listen to me, and then think about it, in a mature and grown-up way. Look, you can easily get a wife any time, but getting promotion's quite another matter, and any intelligent man will make sure that he first of all grabs hold of the thing that's more difficult to get, won't he! Come, now, my good fellow, you're a practical sort of chap who's not interested in mere theories. And, when you think about it in a mature and grown-up way, a wife is just something theoretical, while promotion is something really practical, isn't it!

CHEDA: Listen, Uncle Vasa, I've heard everything you've had to say from beginning to end. I greatly admire and respect you, Uncle, so I will be completely open and honest with you when I tell you, in confidence of course, what I my conclusions are. This is what I have decided to do. Firstly, that dentist, the match-maker – I'm going to smash his teeth down the back of his throat. Secondly, that Nicaragua – I'm going to rip his ears off. And thirdly you, my dear Uncle – I'm going to bust your nose!

VASA: Cheda, my boy, you astonish me! I don't see what my nose has got to do with all this.

CHEDA: You shouldn't poke it into things that aren't your concern.

VASA: All right, all right, I won't in future. But don't you start complaining if things turn out in a way that you don't like!

CHEDA: And what's your latest plot?

VASA: We haven't been plotting but, you know how it is, I am Zhivka's closest relative, so she's bound to turn to me for advice. And, as a person experienced in these matters, I shall say to her: "Zhivka, why don't you have the fellow transferred to Ivanitsa,[1] and listen to him squeal!"

CHEDA: And that'll be your advice to her?

VASA: Indeed – she wouldn't have thought of it herself.

CHEDA: Very well, Uncle, then you'd better go out today – now! – and buy yourself some sticking plasters for your nose, while I get the cases out so that I can pack for the journey to Ivanitsa with my wife.

---

1. Ivanitsa *(Ivanjica)*. A small, remote town in the hills of southern Serbia.

Vasa: But Dara would be mad to go there with you – her father a government minister in Belgrade, and her stuck miles away in Ivanitsa!

Cheda: Listen to me! You go and tell your niece, the minister's wife, to come here now, so that we can settle this account once and for all.

Vasa: Oh, I can't do that. Zhivka specially told me to inform you that from this moment onwards she does not acknowledge you as her son-in-law, that she will no longer talk to you informally as a member of the family and that, if you have anything to say to her you will have to come as a stranger, submitting your visiting card, and requesting an interview – and she will concern herself only with formal matters.

Cheda: Those are her orders, eh? Didn't she say that I'd have to come wearing a top hat?

Vasa: Yes, of course, you'll have to wear a top hat.

Cheda: And gloves, naturally?

Vasa: Yes, and gloves.

Cheda: Very well. Tell her that I'm going to get dressed up to call on her. *(Exit)*

SCENE 4

(Vasa shakes his head, unhappy about the prospect of personal injury to himself, and gingerly feels his nose, muttering. Then he takes a cigarette from the table, puts it in a cigerette-holder and lights it)

(Enter Zhivka, in the doorway)

Zhivka: Vasa!

Vasa: Come in, come in!

Zhivka: Has he gone?

Vasa: Yes, he's gone.

Zhivka *(entering)*: Well, what did he say?

Vasa: Frankly, nothing. Oh, you should have heard, Zhivka! I spoke to him in a calm and sensible way, and if it had been anyone else he'd have been convinced, but he was a stubborn as a mule.

ZHIVKA: So, he won't go quietly?

VASA: No, he certainly won't! He was even threatening to rip people's ears off, bash their teeth down their throat, and bust their noses! He even told me to go out and get some sticking-plasters, because his final threat concerned *my* nose.

ZHIVKA: Oh, well, if he won't go quietly we'll just have to turn the screw a bit more.

VASA: I told him that.

ZHIVKA: I shall make arrangements today for him to be transferred to Ivanitsa.

VASA: I told him that, too.

ZHIVKA: And what did he say?

VASA: He said he'd even go to Ivanitsa, but that he'd take his wife with him.

ZHIVKA: Pie in the sky!

VASA: I told him that as well.

ZHIVKA: What?

VASA: That – "pie in the sky".

ZHIVKA: He imagines that I don't know how to get the better of him. Hah! I've mixed together all the ingredients, and I'm only waiting for Anka to light the stove. Then his goose will be well and truly cooked. Dara will reject him and will never want to see him again. You'll see and hear it all, God willing, today. And did you tell him that I no longer consider him to be my son-in-law?

VASA: Yes, and I told him that if he had anything to say he'd have to approach you formally.

ZHIVKA: Good!

VASA: Zhivka, I'll have to go now to collect the family.

ZHIVKA: Oh, the family again!

VASA: I told them yesterday that they'd all have to gather at this time at Aunt Savka's, so that I can bring them here together. It wouldn't be right to disappoint them.

ZHIVKA: Oh, very well. Bring them just this once, and we'll get the wretched business out of the way. Only please don't let them stay too long, because my new son-in-law is coming to see us today.

VASA: Don't worry, I'll tell them that they'll have to be brief. *(Exit)*

SCENE 5

(When he has gone, ZHIVKA *rings the bell.* **Enter** ANKA*)*

ANKA: Yes, madam?

ZHIVKA: What are you doing, for goodness' sake, Anka? You seem to be making heavy weather of it. It's not as though simply getting a man to come to your room was some sort of specially difficult task imposed on you by God.

ANKA: No, it's not a specially difficult task, I agree, but you know how it is, one has to have an opportunity, and with so many people in the house I haven't had a chance to get him alone.

ZHIVKA: Listen, Anka! It's very important for me that you should do it today if you possibly can.

ANKA: All right, madam, I'll approach him openly. I have already laid the groundwork, you know.

ZHIVKA: Never mind the groundwork – get up close, and get on with it! These things work better when you get up close!

ANKA: Very well, madam!

SCENE 6

*(***Enter** POLICEMAN, *dragging a reluctant* RAKA *by the hand)*

POLICEMAN: I humbly beg your pardon , Madam Minister, but the Inspector told me to bring this …

ZHIVKA: You little devil! What have you been up to now?

POLICEMAN: Begging your pardon, Madam Minister, he punched the British Consul's son on the nose with his fist and insulted his father, and my Chief said …

ZHIVKA: What!! Oh! Oh! – I think I'm having a stroke! Anka! Anka! Bring me a glass of water – quickly! *(*ANKA *runs out)* Punched him on the nose! … insulted his father! … the British Consul's son! God damn and blast you, you little villain! You'll be the death of me – you'll drive me into an early grave! *(ANKA returns with a glass of water, which ZHIVKA drinks)*. To think that I should live to see a policeman bringing a criminal into my house! Oh! Oh! Anka, get him out of my sight! *(ANKA comes forward and takes RAKA from the Policeman)*.

POLICEMAN: May I go now?

ZHIVKA: Yes, constable, and please tell your Chief that I shall ... tell him that I'm going to break every bone in the little brute's body.

POLICEMAN: Yes, madam! *(He salutes and **exit**)*

SCENE 7

ZHIVKA *(to RAKA)*: You little beast, what the hell have you been playing at? Tell me!

RAKA: Nothing!

ZHIVKA: What d'you mean, "nothing"? D'you call punching the British Consul's son on the nose "nothing"? And even if it might have been an accident, and your fist just happened to slip on to his nose, that's one thing – but what did you want to insult his father for?

RAKA: He started it!

ZHIVKA: That's nonsense! I don't believe it. He's a well brought-up boy.

RAKA: He did! He swore at me. I just said to him, politely: "Get out of my way or I'll bash you up!" and he said to me: "Orlrite!" and "orlrite" in English means that he's cursing my father.

ZHIVKA: That's not true.

RAKA: Oh yes it is! – I remember it from my lessons.

ZHIVKA: Well, if he said "orlrite" to you, why didn't you just say "orlrite" to him?

RAKA: Because he wouldn't have understood me. Anyway, I didn't. I just said to him, quite politely: "Shut up, you rotten swine!" and he said: "Orlrite!" again. Well, I couldn't take any more of that, so I just punched him on the nose and cursed his father.

ZHIVKA: Wretched boy! don't you understand that his father's English? It wasn't the father of one of our own people that you were cursing – it was an English father, and that's different. Oh, God preserve us, what am I to do with you? Anka, take him away – take him out of my sight, before I pluck him like a chicken. Get him out of here! *(Exit* ANKA *taking* RAKA *with her).*

SCENE 8

ZHIVKA *(Picks up the telepone and speaks into it)*: Hallo … exchange? The Ministry of Foreign Affairs, please … Is that the Ministry of Foreign Affairs? Yes … may I speak to Mr Ninkovich, the Secretary … Yes! … Tell him that Mrs Minister Zhivka wishes to speak to him. *(Pause)* Is that you, Mr Ninkovich? *(Pause)* Good! It's been signed … yes, I congratulate you on your advancement. So, I have kept my word, you see. But I have to say it didn't go completely smoothly. The minister objected, saying that you'd already been promoted three months ago. But I kept on at him and wouldn't give him any peace. I even persuaded my husband to get involved. Yes, yes, he got involved, too. *(Pause)* Anyway, there was one other thing that I wanted to ask you. My son, Raka, who's at Secondary School, was in the playground today with the British Consul's son. I'd sent him there specially because, you know, that's the sort of company that he ought to be keeping now … Yes! Well, just imagine, he punched the British Consul's son on the nose and insulted his father! *(Pause)* Yes, yes, I realise that it's all most unfortunate, but what can I do? I'm very angry. Punish him? – I shan't just tell him off, I'll break his bones, but the most important thing is to smooth over the affair with the British Consul, so that he will not be offended. I wanted to ask if you could possibly go and see him and suggest to him, on my behalf, that he shouldn't

take it too seriously – boys will be boys, you know! *(Pause)*
And there's something else that might be said. He must be an
intelligent man, and I'm sure he wouldn't want there to be a
diplomatic incident between two governments over a nose
and, as far as the insulting of fathers is concerned, you could
tell him that in our language that doesn't mean anything rude
at all – it's just like saying "Good morning" in English. Indeed,
you might tell him that is our national custom for people to
insult each others' fathers. Of course! Well, thank you very
much. Please go and see him straightaway, and then come and
tell me how you got on. What? … ah … Mwah? Mwah? – well,
all right here's a "Mwah" for you – but please do this little
thing for me. Good bye! *(She replaces the receiver)*.

SCENE 9

ANKA *(Enters, in a hurry)*: Madam, he wants to go out again!
ZHIVKA: Who?
ANKA: Raka.
ZHIVKA: He's not going anywhere – I'll break his legs! Just let
    him wait – I'll teach him manners! He thinks he's just going to
    get a telling-off – he'll find out .. ! *(Exit, hurriedly)*

SCENE 10

CHEDA *(speaking from inside his room)*: Anka, are you alone?
ANKA *(coquettishly)* Yes, I am!
*(Enter CHEDA. He is formally dressed in a black suit, with a top
    hat on his head. He is carrying a bouquet of flowers)*.
ANKA: My word! What are you all dressed up like that for?
CHEDA: For you, Anka. This is my wedding outfit.
ANKA: Oh, I am pleased! And are you going to come to my room
    dressed like that?
CHEDA: Yes, that's why I put it on.
ANKA: Truly?
CHEDA: I'll tell you when I'm coming.
ANKA: Will it be today?

CHEDA: Yes, this very day.

ANKA: Now, perhaps?

CHEDA: All right, in a minute. But first I must ask you to announce me to Madam Minister.

ANKA *(surprised)* Announce you to the mistress?

CHEDA: Yes, please. And give her my visiting-card. *(He takes it out and hands it to her)* I'll wait in the hall.

ANKA *(confused)*: But … but … you'll wait? … I'm to announce you? … I don't understand this at all!

CHEDA: Please persuade Madam to see me. Tell her I'm here on official business.

ANKA: All right. And afterwards?

CHEDA: And afterwards – I think we understand each other!

ANKA: I'm going! *(**Exit**. CHEDA watches her go and then **exit**, rear).*

SCENE 11

*(**Enter** ZHIVKA and ANKA. ZHIVKA is holding the visiting-card in her hand)*

ZHIVKA: And he gave you this?

ANKA: Yes, your son-in-law did. He's waiting in the hall.

ZHIVKA: Tell my son-in-law to clear off! I won't see him.

ANKA: But he said he was here on official business.

ZHIVKA: I'm not disposed to do official business today, so there! I can't see him.

ANKA: But, madam, if you don't see him you'll spoil everything.

ZHIVKA: How?

ANKA: He said that after he'd seen you he'd come and see me in my room.

ZHIVKA: That's what he said?

ANKA: Yes.

ZHIVKA: Very well, tell him to come in, I will receive him! *(ANKA **exit** into the hall).*

SCENE 12

*(**Enter** CHEDA, looking very serious. He bows in the doorway)*

CHEDA: Do I have the honour of addressing Madam Minister?

ZHIVKA *(scornfully refusing to look at him)* Yes. Be seated.

CHEDA: I am most grateful. Please excuse me for taking the liberty of disturbing you ...

ZHIVKA: On what account, sir?

CHEDA: I have come upon very delicate business, madam, and I would be obliged if you will listen carefully to what I have to say.

ZHIVKA: Very well, say it!

CHEDA: You see, madam, life is a very complicated business. Nature has created living things but has not laid down the rules by which its creatures conduct their relationships with each other. Instead it has allowed them to evolve and develop individually, in many varying environments and circumstances. In consequence it is a normal phenomenon, not mere chance, that conflicting interests so frequently arise in all sorts of ways.

ZHIVKA: Do you imagine, sir, that you are giving a lecture, or have you anything to say to me?

CHEDA: I beg your pardon, madam, but that was a necessary introduction to the matter in question.

ZHIVKA: Very well – now kindly proceed to the matter in question.

CHEDA: It is this, madam. I have a friend, a young man with a good future ahead of him. He is anxious to get married, and he has entrusted me with the task of match-maker. He is confident that I shall carry out that task discreetly and properly.

ZHIVKA: What possible interest is your friend or your match-making to me?

CHEDA: I will explain. He has been thinking about marrying for a long time now, but finds it very hard to make up his mind. He has always said to me: "If I do finally decide to get married, I shall only marry a mature woman."

ZHIVKA: All right, if he wants to marry a mature woman, let him do so. Why on earth are you telling me about it?

CHEDA: Because, madam, he is deeply in love with *you*.

ZHIVKA: What !!

CHEDA: He considers you to be mature …

ZHIVKA *(leaps to her feet)*: Cheda!

CHEDA: He said to me only today, with tears in his eyes: "Cheda, they know you in that household. I beg of you to go now to Madam Zhivka and offer her my hand in marriage!"

ZHIVKA *(barely able to restrain her anger)*: Cheda! Be silent! Cheda!

CHEDA: And I replied, gently: "But she is a married woman." But he said: "What does that matter? These days it is quite all right to marry a married woman." So I said: "But she is a respectable woman."

ZHIVKA *(shouting)*: I am, I am!

CHEDA: I told him that, but he said: "If she were respectable, she wouldn't accept my love letters."

ZHIVKA *(her anger turning to fury)*: Shut up! Damn and blast you! Shut up, you bastard! If you utter another word I'll smash your head in!

CHEDA: So I said to him: "Well, Mr Ninkovich, I know you've written a love letter to her, because I've read it."

ZHIVKA: Who's read it?

CHEDA: I have!

ZHIVKA *(screaming with rage)*: Get out!

CHEDA *(stands up)*: Very well, then, but what shall I say to the bridegroom?

ZHIVKA: He can go to the Devil – and you too!

CHEDA: He would like to come and look you over.

ZHIVKA: Cheda! Haven't you heard that, being who I am, I've the power to have you sent away to "look over" Ivanitsa?

CHEDA: I'll go gladly, why not! But before that I must go to Mr Minister Sima Popovich and ask him to leave his wife because she has received an offer of marriage.

ZHIVKA: Get out of my sight, before you receive something you won't like!

CHEDA: Madam, do calm down! As you have seen, life is a very complicated business. Nature has created living things but has not laid down the rules by which its creatures conduct their relationships with each other ...

ZHIVKA *(In a paroxysm of fury, she seizes various things from the table, books, boxes, the bouquet of flowers, and bells, a cushion from the chair, and anything else that comes to hand, and hurls them about)*: Get out, you bloody swine! Get out! *(CHEDA bows formally in the doorway and **exit**)*

(ZHIVKA collapses, exhausted, on the sofa and when she has recovered somewhat she junps up and goes to the doorway, left)

ZHIVKA: Dara! Dara! Dara!

SCENE 13

*(**Enter** DARA, in haste)*

DARA: What is it?

ZHIVKA: Dara, my child, I swear to you that I'll kill him!

DARA: Kill who?

ZHIVKA: That husband of yours!

DARA: For God's sake, why?

ZHIVKA: Imagine! He dared – he had the impertinence – to mock me! I'll kill him and I don't care if I go to prison with hard labour! – I'll go down in legend as a woman who murdered her son-in-law.

DARA: But, Mother, what on earth has he done?

ZHIVKA: He came to propose marriage to me!

DARA: How could he do that?

ZHIVKA: As a match-maker.

DARA: Mother, what's the matter with you – what are you talking about?

ZHIVKA: What I said – he came as a match-maker with a proposal of marriage for me.

DARA: What, with your husband still alive?

ZHIVKA: The very idea!

DARA: How could anyone propose marriage to a woman whose
husband is still alive?

ZHIVKA: You're muddling it up with your situation. Your case is
quite different.

DARA: How can you pretend that it's different?

ZHIVKA: Because ... because I say it is! And even if it isn't, it's
going to be! I wouldn't have him for my son-in-law if he was a
Crowned Head. You wait and see!

DARA: You're off again!

ZHIVKA: Yes, because I'm never going to let him in my house
again. I tell you – this very day you're going to come to me on
bended knee and beg me to save you from that scoundrel!
You'll see! As my name's Zhivka, you'll be on your knees to
me later!

SCENE 14

(Enter VASA)

VASA: Zhivka, they're here!

ZHIVKA: Who?

VASA: The family!

DARA: Oh Lord – I'm off! *(Exit DARA)*

VASA *(opening the door, rear)* Come in! *(Enter an assortment of
various comic types in old-fashioned clothes. The older ladies,
SAVKA and DATSA, are wearing unfashionable skirts and
blouses, and SOYA has a hat decorated with birds' feathers.
There are also AUNT SAVKA, AUNT DATSA, YOVA POP-ARSIN,
UNCLE PANTA with his son MILE, UNCLE YAKOV, SAVA
MISHICH, and PERA KALENICH. They all approach ZHIVKA,
the women kissing her cheek and the men her hand).*

SAVKA *(kissing ZHIVKA)* You'll have forgotten me, Zhivka.

DATSA *(kissing her)*: Oh Zhivka, dear, I haven't seen you for ages!
You're looking very well. Ach ... ach ... *(she spits)* Good luck!

PANTA: You know, Zhivka, nobody is more pleased at your good
fortune than I am.

YAKOV: I did call, Zhivka, but it appeared you were busy.

SOYA *(kissing her)*: My dearest Zhivka, I've always loved you the most of all the family.

ZHIVKA *(after everyone has kissed her, or her hand)*: Thank you very much for coming. Please sit down. *(The older ones sit, the rest remain standing)* Please forgive me for receiving you all together like this. I know it's not the right way of doing it, but you simply can't imagine how busy I am. I never dreamed how hard it would be being a government minister's wife. But, God willing, you shall all come again another time.

VASA *(who has remained standing, and now comes beside Zhivka)*: Yes, of course we shall see you again. This is just ... well, we'll see you again, anyway.

ZHIVKA: How are you, Aunt Savka?

SAVKA *(offended)*: Well enough ...

ZHIVKA: There, there! I know you're upset, but please don't think that I'd forgotten you. And you, Aunt Datsa, how are you?

DATSA: Please forgive me, my dear. When I said to my Christina: "Let's go and see Zhivka. We ought to go and congratulate her, for if the family doesn't, who will?" But she said: "No, Mama. We haven't been inside her house for over a year, and if we go now everyone will say we've come running just because she's now a government minister's wife." It's true that we haven't been to see you, but that was because you'd said nasty things about Christina, but I said to her: "Let people say that we've only come running to her because she's a government minister's wife, but who's going to come running anyway, unless it's her nearest and dearest!"

ZHIVKA: And you, Uncle Panta, I haven't seen you for a long time. How are you?

PANTA: To tell you the truth, Zhivka, none too well: everything's topsy-turvy. But things are looking up for me a bit, now that you're in the government. I'm sure you'll cherish and look after your own.

VASA: Of course, who will if she won't!

ZHIVKA: I haven't seen you for a while, Soya.

SOYA: Funnily enough, people say they see a lot of me. You can't please some people. If I stay cooped up at home they run me down, and if I go out in company they run me down. But what does it matter if people run one down as long as one's dear family sticks up for one!

VASA: Yes, indeed, who would, but the family?

DATSA *(aside, spitefully)*: Nobody gets slandered unless there's a reason why.

SOYA *(annoyed)*: Just as you say, Aunt Datsa. I wonder why people say things about your house, if there's no reason why?

DATSA: It's people of your sort that say things like that!

SOYA: I am who I am, even if I haven't passed the Matriculation examination.

DATSA *(jumping up angrily)*: You've been examined by half the population, you bitch!

SOYA *(jumping up likewise and thrusting her face at Datsa's)*: That's as maybe, but I haven't even sat my Final examinations!

DATSA: Oh! Let me get at her! … *(She grabs at Soya's hair)*

VASA *(He gets between them and separates them)* For shame! Can't you hold a civilised, family conversation for five minutes? *(The other men come round and pull them apart)*.

DATSA: What, when there are creatures like that in the family?

SOYA: You keep your own front doorstep clean before you go chucking mud at other people!

VASA: Calm down, I say! You should be ashamed of yourselves – and you pretending to belong to the family of a government minister!

ZHIVKA *(to VASA)*: There! I told you.

VASA: Yes. Before, they were saying: "Come on, Uncle Vasa, please take us round to Zhivka's." And what happens? – they disgrace themselves, and me! Come on, now, you two, get back into your place, and when you get out into the street again you can pull each other's hair out by the roots if you want to. *(They separate and sit down)* I beg your pardon, Zhivka. It was just a little family discussion.

ZHIVKA: It wasn't very pleasant, but ... *(wishing to get down to business)* And how are you, Uncle Yakov?

YAKOV: Well, you know how it is when one has to live in bits. God knows what will become of me – I had a bit of education, a bit of time as a trader, and a bit as a civil servant. It all came to nothing – I got nowhere. Still, I've always consoled myself with the thought: "Just wait, Yakov, your day will come!" I'm still waiting, but nothing changes.

ZHIVKA: And you, Sava?

SAVA *(He is a corpulent man with a large belly)* Don't ask. I'm drained with worry.

ZHIVKA: What about?

SAVA: About injustice. I've been dogged by injustice all my life. I'll tell you all about it.

ZHIVKA *(To Pera Kalenich)* But ... *(surprised)* you .. ? *(To Vasa)* Is this gentleman one of the family?

VASA: He says he is.

KALENICH: Certainly, I'm one of the family.

ZHIVKA: Well I don't remember you.

VASA: Nor I. Perhaps you do, Savka ...? *(ALL look at Kalenich)*

SAVKA: No, I don't know him as one of our family.

DATSA: Nor I. *(SEVERAL OTHERS, shrugging their shoulders, say the same).*

KALENICH: I come down on my mother's side.

SOYA: Well, I'm in the female line, but I don't recognise you.

DATSA *(through clenched teeth)*: That's a wonder!

VASA: But how do you come into the female line, whose are you?

KALENICH: My mother died twelve years ago, and when she was on her deathbed she said to me: "Son, I am not leaving you all alone in the world. If you ever need anything, go and see Aunt Zhivka, the government minister's wife, for she is your kin."

VASA: What was your deceased mother's name?

KALENICH: Mara.

VASA: And your father's?

KALENICH: Kersta.

VASA: Well, I have to say, I don't know of any Mara or Kersta in the family.

ZHIVKA: Nor do I.

KALENICH: The trouble is that previously we were not called Kalenich, but Markovich.

VASA: Markovich? I've never heard the name.

KALENICH: Anyway, that makes no difference. I'm sure that you are my kin, and I won't budge from that. I'd rather die than disown my family ties.

VASA: There's no need to go that far, but …

ZHIVKA: But when he says …

VASA: Yes, when he says he is, he may be.

ZHIVKA: Well, then, how are you?

KALENICH: I'm all right, thank you, Auntie. I'm glad to see you are looking so well. You look positively radiant.

VASA: Zhivka, we all know that you must be very busy. Hadn't we better get on with the matters in hand? Right, now, you people, come up one a time and say what it is that you wish for, and we'll see if it can be granted or not.

PANTA: If nothing can be done for us now, I can't see that it ever will be.

VASA: Each of you say what it is you most desire, and I'll write it down. Then Zhivka can look at it and see what is possible and what is not possible.

DATSA: Where there's a will there's a way. The question is whether she can do things for everyone when some of us are not exactly …

SOYA *(interrupting)*: I've only one thing to ask of you, Zhivka, and that's that you help me take my Matriculation exams.

DATSA *(angrily)*: There she goes – sticking her tongue out again!

VASA: Be quiet, I say!

SAVA: Behave yourselves! If you annoy me any more I'll smack you both in the mouth.

KALENICH: Listen, Aunt Datsa, and you, Soya! As you can see, Aunt Zhivka has been kind enough to receive the whole family, and it's right and proper that she should. Now we should tell her our desires and ask her to fulfill them for us. I'm sure that Aunt Zhivka is very busy, and you all know how kind-hearted she is. But for those reasons we should respect her and her home, which is now a ministerial home. If we're going to behave like this, quarrelling amongst ourselves, we shall bring disgrace upon this house. So I would ask you both to restrain yourselves.

DATSA *(to those nearest to her)*: How on earth can I be that fellow's aunt?

SAVKA: I don't know. I don't know who he is, either.

DATSA: Nor I!

PANTA *(to* YAKOV, *who is sitting beside him)*: Do you know who he is, for God's sake?

YAKOV: I've never seen or heard of him before in my life.

VASA: So, now, let's forget that and get on with the business in hand. Zhivka hasn't got all day.

ZHIVKA: You're right – I haven't got much time. I'm expecting some important visitors from the Diplomatic Corps to call shortly.

VASA: Exactly! Now then! *(He takes a pencil and paper)* Aunt Savka, what do you want to ask of Zhivka?

SAVKA *(still feeling offended)*: Let Zhivka ask me herself, and I'll tell her.

ZHIVKA: Oh, Aunt Savka, I've had it up to here with you and your two hundred dinars. It's going too far, Vasa, if she can't talk reasonably, like a family member, instead of always being spiteful.

SAVKA: I'm not being spiteful, I just want what is mine.

ZHIVKA: Very well, you shall have it. Vasa, write down that she's to have what I owe her. There you are!

VASA *(after he has written it down)*: What about you, Datsa? Is there anything you want to ask of Zhivka?

DATSA: Only for my Christina, not for me. I wanted to ask you,

Zhivka, to make arrangements for the child to be allowed back into school and to be accepted for her exams, because at present she's stranded half way. Yes, she has sinned, I admit – and I'd be obliged if a certain person would refrain from coughing – I admit it, I say, but everybody's sinning these days, the teachers as well as the pupils. And she didn't sin because of anger or dishonesty, but because of learning. Would that certain person stop coughing!

VASA: Soya, stop coughing!

DATSA: Yes, because of learning. She and one of her friends were studying for their Matriculation examinations together, and she went into a room with him and they spent the whole day learning – in fact, they wore themselves out with learning. And afterwards ... he passed, but she got stuck half way, as it were. So I am asking you, Zhivka, to give orders that it should all be forgotten.

KALENICH (now apparently accepted as free to delve into family matters as if he had always been involved in them): How long ago was this?

DATSA: Last year.

KALENICH: A twelvemonth. Well, even the most serious crimes are forgotten after twelve months, let alone minor sins like this. Write it down, Vasa – to be forgotten!

ZHIVKA: And you, Yova? You went to prison with hard labour, eh?

YOVA: Yes, Aunt Zhivka, I did serve a sentence of hard labour and, since I faithfully fulfilled my duty to the government in the process, I think I've now got the right to ask the government to fulfil its duty to me.

ZHIVKA: How?

YOVA: By giving me a government job.

ZHIVKA: But it was having a government job that got you hard labour.

YOVA: Aunt Zhivka, every man alive does wrong sometimes, and I have paid the due penalty for my wrong-doing. And believe me, Aunt, I don't complain about being sent to prison –

I learned a great many things there that it would be hard for anyone to learn elsewhere. It would be a very good thing if all candidates for government employment were sent to prison first, and only given jobs after they had finished their sentences.

YAKOV: For goodness' sake, why?

YOVA: I mean it, Uncle Yakov. I now know the criminal law better than any High Court judge! There isn't a single university professor who can interpret the criminal law as well as those who have been sentenced under it. Convicts all know the wording of complete Sections by heart, and they know what they mean, and they know how to exploit various Sections. I'm sentenced, let's say, under Section 235, in conjunction with Section 117(a) – but mitigating circumstances must be taken into consideration under Section 206! And so on – I know all the Sections, so why doesn't the government make use of my knowledge?

KALENICH: Exactly! Write down, Uncle Vasa, that Yova Pop-Arsin is to be given a job so that the government can profit from his knowledge!

ZHIVKA: And what about you, Uncle Panta?

PANTA: To tell you the truth, Zhivka, I'm not asking anything for myself. I shall get by just as I've always got by, but I do have this boy *(indicating* MILE, *a young man, who is standing behind him).* Somehow or other God did not see fit to give him any gift for book-learning – he was expelled permanently from every school he went to. He can't settle down to any trade, or to any sort of job. So I wanted to ask you if you could please arrange for him to be enrolled in the Government Cadet College.

ZHIVKA: To learn what?

PANTA: Oh, anything will do so long as the government takes him in and maintains him. They can make him into a veterinary surgeon, or a musical bandmaster, or a professor of theology, or a pharmacist – anything you like, provided he becomes a Government Cadet.

KALENICH: Clearly, it would be a shame if the government rejected such a bright lad. Write it down, Uncle Vasa – Government Cadet!

ZHIVKA: And you, Soya?

SOYA: Zhivka, may I tell you what I want in private?

ALL *(protesting)*: Oh no! Do the same as us! Ask her openly!

DATSA *(her voice is heard above the rest)*: *We* have nothing to hide, but she … *(*VASA *cuts her short with a look).*

SOYA: Oh, anyway, why should I try to hide anything? – it's not my style. Zhivka, you know that I divorced that lousy husband of mine. Well, he remarried, but I was left on my own because the Court unfairly ruled that I couldn't marry again, and I don't think that's right. Well, of course I lost the case because, being so young … *(*DATSA *coughs loudly)* … they put me in the hands of the Church authorities, and *they* all looked askance at me. Even the lawyer who represented me said one thing to me in private, but another in Court – so, obviously, I lost the case. So I wanted to ask you, Aunt Zhivka, to get that ruling overturned so that I can marry again. There, you see, I'm not asking for the Earth, and if certain persons can't stop coughing, a fat lot I care! They're all mouth, and nothing else!

KALENICH: That can certainly be done. The lady feels the need to get married, but is prevented by certain formalities. Uncle Vasa, write down that Soya should remarry without the formalities.

SOYA: That's all I want.

ZHIVKA: And you, Uncle Yakov?

YAKOV: I tell you, Zhivka, I just never get anywhere. I should have been educated when I was younger, but it didn't happen. I was a civil servant for a while, but I got nowhere. I tried being a trader, but everything went wrong. But I always said to myself: "Just wait, Yakov, your day will come!" And now, lo and behold, it has! What I'd like is for you to arrange a Concession for me like, for instance, a logging concession in the State forests. I reckon, you see, that if I can't get my hands on anything else, at least I might get hold of a concession.

KALENICH: You can certainly get one of them, and it won't cost the government anything. It wasn't the government that planted the forests, so why should they complain if they're cut down. That's fine! Write it down, Uncle Vasa – he's to cut down a State forest, because, after all, what's the use of being a government minister's relative if you can't cut down a forest or two?

ZHIVKA: And you, Sava?

SAVA: Zhivka, I'll be brief. As your close relative, I appeal to you to arrange for me to have a government pension.

ZHIVKA: But you've never been a civil servant, have you?

SAVA: No.

ZHIVKA: And you've never had any sort of government employmentt?

SAVA: No, I haven't.

ZHIVKA: Well then, why should I arrange a government pension for you?

SAVA *(excitedly)*: Why? – as a citizen! Lots of people have got government pensions, so why shouldn't I?

VASA: Yes, but look, Sava – they'd all been in government jobs.

SAVA: But if I'd had a government job I wouldn't have needed to come to Zhivka to ask for a pension, because I'd have gone to the government for one. What's the use of her being a minister's wife, if she can't do this for me?

KALENICH: This is all a bit complicated. Uncle Vasa, write down: "Pension for Uncle Sava", and Aunt Zhivka and I will put our heads together later to see if it can be done. *(To Zhivka)* Now, please allow me, Aunt Zhivka, to submit my request also. I was dismissed from my employment a year ago. There were a few files missing from my drawer, as result of which the business of the Department was disrupted. I don't see that I was to blame for, after all, even human beings can get lost, so why shouldn't files? Anyway, some other files had gone missing from my drawer earlier and nobody made a fuss, but this time a wretched Inspector came pestering me and very nearly had me prosecuted. Well, the matter's been over and done with for a year now, and I've been waiting all that time for it to be forgotten. I don't really know whether or not it has been forgotten yet, but now that Zhivka's a government minister's wife, she can give orders for it definitely to be forgotten. I ask only that the injustice which was done to me should be put right, and that I should get my job back. However, I must stress that I couldn't accept just taking my job back – I need compensation for the injustice that was done to me. I would have to be promoted, in return for which I would be prepared to overlook the injustice which I suffered. There, that's all I ask. Uncle Vasa, please write it down: "Pera Kalenich to have his job back, with compensation." *(He peers at Vasa's note)* Have you written: "With compensation"?

VASA: Yes, yes!

KALENICH: Good! And now, Aunt Zhivka, allow me, on behalf of the whole family, to thank you sincerely for listening to our requests, and to ask you to give your personal attention to fulfilling them. As you can see, they are all modest requests, which you are in a position to fulfil and, by doing so, to give much happiness to your family and let them all long remember you with gratitude.

ZHIVKA: Yes, very well. I will do what I can. After all, why shouldn't I?

KALENICH: We will now say goodbye, then. We have already taken up too much of your time. *(He kisses her hand, and everybody gets up ready to leave).*

ZHIVKA *(remembering)*: Just a moment, I want to give you all my visiting card as a souvenir. *(She takes a box from the table and hands out visiting cards to all of them).* There you are … there … as a souvenir.

SOYA: I'll stick it in the frame of my mirror.

YAKOV: Oh, thank you very much.

KALENICH: May I have two, please.

SAVKA *(stiffly after everyone has received a visiting card)*:
Good bye, Zhivka!

ZHIVKA: Now, now, don't be so sensitive!

DATSA *(kissing her)*: Look after yourself, Zhivka!

PANTA: Please arrange it for me!

SOYA *(kissing her)*: Do a good deed for me, Zhivka!

SAVA: Please don't forget, Zhivka!

YAKOV: Farewell! *(All these comments come one after another as they prepare to go).*

KALENICH *(kissing her hand)*: Now at last I understand what my dear sainted Mother meant when she said to me on her deathbed, twelve years ago: "Son I am not leaving you all alone in the world. If you ever need anything, go and see Aunt Zhivka, the government minister's wife, for she is your kin."!

SOYA *(following the others, all of whom have by now gone to the door)*: If nothing comes of my request, I shall still take my matriculation exams.

DATSA: You've been taking them ever since you began to walk!

SOYA: Pooh! You're just all mouth! *(She and DATSA start quarrelling and, once ALL THE FAMILY except VASA are out of the house and the door closed behind them, the sounds of their shrieking and fighting are heard from outside, together with the shouts of those trying to separate them).*

ZHIVKA *(to VASA)*: Hurry, Vasa, they're fighting!

VASA: The bitches! *(Exit hurriedly).*

SCENE 15

ZHIVKA *(Sinking, exhausted, into an armchair)*: Phew!
(Enter ANKA, running, from outside)

ANKA: Madam, two of your relatives are fighting!

ZHIVKA: Let them fight – what do I care? I'm exhausted – I feel as if I'd spent the whole day digging trenches. I'm going to lie down for a while. See that nobody disturbs me. *(Exit to her room. ANKA goes to the outer door and opens it a little. The noise of fighting slowly fades into the distance).*

SCENE 16

*(After a certain interval, **enter** CHEDA. As he opens the door he comes face to face with ANKA. He is still formally dressed)*: Ah, what a happy meeting! Have you been waiting for me, Anka?

ANKA: Of course.

CHEDA: Well, you go to your room now, and I'll come in a moment.

ANKA: Truly?

CHEDA: Just go in, I'll be there!

ANKA *(offering her cheek)*: Give me a kiss then – on account, like.

CHEDA *(kisses her)*: There! Lovely! That's just for now!

ANKA: I'll go and wait, then! *(Exit)*

SCENE 17

*(*CHEDA *lights a cigar. After a certain interval, **enter** RISTA TODOROVICH. He appears in the doorway, dressed formally in a wedding suit similar to Cheda's. He is carrying a bouquet of flowers).*

RISTA: May I come in?

CHEDA: Please do!

RISTA: May I have the honour of introducing myself – Rista Todorovich, leather merchant.

CHEDA *(surprised)* Who did you say?

RISTA: Rista Todorovich, leather merchant.

CHEDA: And also the Honorary Consul of Nicaragua?

RISTA: Yes, that's correct.

CHEDA: But this is remarkable! Well, I really am very pleased indeed to make your acquaintance.

RISTA: And to whom do I have the honour … ?

CHEDA: Just a moment, Rista, my dear fellow – will you allow me to call you "Rista"? – just wait a moment while I have a good look at you! *(He moves back and looks him up and down).* Well, who would have thought it? So here you are, Rista! Oh, I am pleased!

RISTA: And to whom do I have the honour … ?

CHEDA: Who, me? You want to know who I am? I am .. how shall I describe myself? … I, my dear chap, am Uncle Vasa, Zhivka's Uncle Vasa!

RISTA: Oh, you're Uncle Vasa, are you? I'm delighted to meet you. Actually, I had thought that you'd be a bit older.

CHEDA: No. I'm not.

RISTA: I've heard a lot about you, and it is a great pleasure to make your acquaintance.

CHEDA *(looking closely at him from all sides)* Well, you're a bit of a card, aren't you! Look at what a trim figure you've got! – quite the Nicaraguan ladies' man, eh? *(He pats Rista's stomach)* Who'd have thought it? I'd imagined you quite differently. *(*RISTA *laughs in a friendly way)* Well, you sly dog, I know why you've come.

RISTA *(shyly)*: Well, yes …

CHEDA: You like our Dara, then?

RISTA: You know how it is.

CHEDA: Oh, yes, I know, all right!

RISTA: It's not only that I like her, but it's also important for me to form ties with upper-class society, on account of my position.

CHEDA: Naturally! And, believe me, the more I look at you, the more I think that she will like you, too. I was worried that she might not, but now that I've met you … I expect all the girls fall for you!

RISTA *(flattered)*: So they say!

CHEDA: I bet they do! I'm sure our Dara will like you. You say that you like her?

RISTA: Yes, I do.

CHEDA: And it doesn't worry you that she's been married before?

RISTA: No, why should it? I mean to say, if I buy a house, the fact that that someone else owned it before me doesn't worry me at all.

CHEDA: Exactly. The old owner moves out and you move in.

RISTA: That's right.

CHEDA: Who'd have thought that you would be one to regard life in such a philosophical way! Well, in that case we should be able to settle the matter quickly and easily. There don't seem to be any obstacles in the way.

RISTA: No.

CHEDA: There is just one thing that concerns me a little – how are we going to get rid of that other wretched fellow?

RISTA: Who?

CHEDA: Why, her husband. He's been making a damned nuisance of himself, you know.

RISTA: What, didn't Madam Zhivka tell you? Oh, his goose is already prepared, and all that remains is to cook it!

CHEDA: Eh?

RISTA: Yes. Madam Zhivka has arranged for her housemaid to entice him into her bedroom, and once he's in there she and Dara will burst in on them, with witnesses.

CHEDA: My word, what a brilliant plan! Ha, ha, ha … he'll be caught like a rat in a trap! One moment he's nibbling the bait, and the next moment… bang! Caught! Ha, ha, ha!

RISTA *(joins in, laughing heartily)*: Ha, ha, ha!

CHEDA: And then?

RISTA: Then? . . well … Dara has already said that if she believes he's unfaithful to her she will immediately reject him.

CHEDA: That's marvellous! Only I'm afraid that there is just one thing that might rather spoil this ingenious plan.

RISTA: What's that?

CHEDA: The fact is, you really shouldn't have come here today, before we've dealt with Dara's husband …

RISTA: But Madam Zhivka asked me to come today.

CHEDA: … because, you know, it really would be *especially* unfortunate if he were to find you here.

RISTA *(somewhat disturbed)*: What d'you mean? Why "especially"?

CHEDA: "Especially" because he has sworn that he's going to kill you like a dog, and he's bought a large-calibre revolver, the sort they use to shoot bulls with.

RISTA *(frightened)* What for – to shoot me with, for God's sake.?

CHEDA: Oh yes, just that, and he's sworn to do it – he swore it before me. But, of course, you mustn't show fear – you can't afford to look cowardly, can you? Anyway, I've seen the revolver myself – he showed it to me – and I'm quite sure that it holds no more than six bullets. He's bound to miss you with some of them. You can be fairly sure that at least four of his shots will miss.

RISTA: But … but what about the other two?

CHEDA: Well now, surely you can put up with a couple of bullet-wounds for the sake of love and for the honour of Nicaragua!

RISTA: Why on earth should I be shot twice for the honour of Nicaragua? Listen, Uncle Vasa, don't you think it might be as well if I left now and came back some other time?

CHEDA: Yes, perhaps it would be as well … *(he looks out of the window)* Oh dear, oh dear! I'm afraid it's too late now – much too late!

RISTA *(frightened)*: Why, for God's sake?

CHEDA: He's here! He's just coming into the house.

RISTA *(even more frightened)*: Who?

CHEDA: It's him – with his revolver!

RISTA *(now terrified)*: Oh what shall I do? Uncle Vasa, what shall I do?

CHEDA: I'll have to hide you somewhere until I can get rid of him.

RISTA *(trembling violently)*: Where can I hide?

CHEDA: I don't know … Hang on, I've got an idea! *(Rings the bell)*

RISTA: Where?

CHEDA: Be quiet and don't ask questions – there's no time!

SCENE 18

(Enter ANKA*)*

ANKA: You rang?

CHEDA: Anka, my dear, do me a great favour, and I'll be in your
   debt. And you know how I'll repay you!

ANKA: Yes?

CHEDA: Take this gentleman into your room and lock the door.
   Don't ask why, but be quick – there's great danger!

RISTA: Very great danger! Quick, show me the way – I'll pay
   you well!

ANKA *(to Cheda)*: And afterwards?

CHEDA: Afterwards – you know already!

ANKA *(to Rista)*: Come on then – quickly! *(Exeunt* ANKA *and*
   RISTA, *hurriedly)*

SCENE 19

CHEDA *(He bursts out laughing, and then goes to the open window
   and shouts, beckoning with his hand)*: Raka! Raka!

(Enter RAKA *from outside)*

RAKA: What is it? Oh, brother, what are you all dressed up like
   that for?

CHEDA: I'll tell you a secret, but only if you'll promise not to tell
   anyone else. Here, I'll give you a dinar if you'll promise
   faithfully not to tell anyone that I'm going to see Anka in her
   bedroom! *(He gives Raka a dinar)* Now, don't tell anyone,
   d'you understand? I expect your mother would give you two
   dinars to tell her, but you'll be a lad of strong character, won't
   you, and you won't tell her, because you promised! You won't
   tell, will you?

RAKA: Of course I won't!

CHEDA: Good! *(Exit)*

SCENE 20

RAKA *(at the doorway, left)*: Mama! Mama!

(Enter ZHIVKA*)*

ZHIVKA: What is it?

RAKA: Brother Cheda gave me a dinar to be a lad of strong character and not to tell you where he is now. Give me two dinars and then I'll be a lad of even stronger character, and I'll tell you.

ZHIVKA: Speak up! Where is he?

RAKA: Two dinars, or I won't tell.

ZHIVKA *(giving him two dinars)*: Now, you little wretch, where is he?

RAKA *(pocketing the money)*: He's there – with Anka, in her room.

ZHIVKA: Are you telling the truth?

RAKA: Yes. He's just gone in.

ZHIVKA *(elated)*: Oh, my dear, dear boy! *(She kisses him)* Here's two more dinars.

RAKA: Orlrite!

ZHIVKA: Go and call Dara – quickly! *(*RAKA *exit, right)*.

SCENE 21

ZHIVKA *(speaking on the telephone)*: Hallo … 7224, please … Is that the Police Station? I wish to speak to the Inspector, please … That's you? This is Mrs Zhivka, the Minister's wife. Please send round a clerk and two constables to my house immediately – as a matter of the utmost urgency. Yes, urgently … well, no, it's not an actual robbery, but it's like one .. And tell the clerk to bring the forms for interrogating suspects, and two members of the public as witnesses. Please make sure that he brings two citizens, without fail. Yes, now, at once – it's very urgent! Yes! *(Replaces the receiver)*.

SCENE 22

(Enter DARA *from the room, left, with* RAKA *following)*

ZHIVKA: Dara, my dear daughter, I've called you so that you can prepare yourself. Be strong, my child, so that you can withstand the blow that you are about to receive.

DARA: Oh, what now? – and why this solemn lecture?

ZHIVKA: I told you that you would eventually come to believe how cruelly that good-for-nothing husband of yours is deceiving you. Well, my daughter, the moment has come for you to see the proof of it with your very own eyes. Your husband has gone into our Anka's bedroom, with improper intent!

DARA: I don't believe it.

ZHIVKA: Raka, tell us, where has my son-in-law Cheda gone?

RAKA: It'll cost you a dinar!

ZHIVKA: Get out, you greedy little pig! D'you think this is a joke?

RAKA: I'm not saying anything for free! *(Exit)*.

DARA: Come on, then! *(Starts to go toward Anka's room)*.

ZHIVKA: No, wait! I've arranged something more.

DARA: What?

ZHIVKA: You'll see.

SCENE 23

(Enter, in haste, POLICE CLERK, TWO POLICEMEN, *and* TWO CITIZENS*)*

CLERK: Madam Minister, the Inspector has sent us here urgently, in response to your instructions. I have also brought these two members of the public with me.

ZHIVKA: Excellent! Now, everybody, come with me!

(ALL exeunt toward Anka's room, with ZHIVKA leading, DARA following, and the rest behind. For a certain time the stage is empty, but then the rear door is slowly and carefully opened and CHEDA pokes his head through the opening, looking and listening. Suddenly, from off-stage, left, an uproar is heard, with people shouting and women screaming. CHEDA immediately withdraws his head and shuts the door. Immediately afterwards ALL re-enter, led by the CLERK, who is holding RISTA (now in his shirtsleeves), and followed by the others).

ZHIVKA *(collapsing with fatigue on an armchair)*: Nicaragua! Damn you, Nicaragua! – what the hell were you doing in there?

RISTA *(bewildered)*: I don't know ... I ... it must have been Fate!

ZHIVKA: Fate! You sneak into the maid's room, you lock the door, you take your coat off, and you call it "Fate"? And anyway, for God's sake, why take your coat off?

RISTA: It was hot – she'd lit the stove.

DARA *(to* ZHIVKA*)*: So this is the honourable "gentleman" whom you intended that I should marry? Well, thank you very much indeed, Mother!

CLERK *(to* ZHIVKA*)*: Madam, do you wish me to take this gentleman in for interrogation?

ZHIVKA: Interrogation? Oh, God willing, he'll be interrogated all right, but in the next world, not this one! If anyone's going to take him in for interrogation, it's going to be me! Now, speak up! – what were you doing in there?

RISTA: Uncle Vasa sent me.

ZHIVKA: Uncle Vasa? It's him, is it, that's wrecked everything? Oh, Vasa, you fool! Now you've well and truly taken care of the whole family!

SCENE 24

(Enter CHEDA, *carrying Rista's coat. He offers to help him on with it)*

CHEDA: Here, put your coat on or you'll catch cold!

RISTA *(who, when he sees Cheda, looks as if he has been struck by lightning)*: Uncle Vasa, help me! Help me! *You* made me hide in the maid's room!

ZHIVKA *(astonished)*: What? You think that *he's* Uncle Vasa?

RISTA: Yes, of course I do.

ZHIVKA: Oh, the devil! – he could worm his way out of anything! Cheda! … *(turning to the* CLERK*)*. Kindly write down exactly what I say, and file it. *(She raises three fingers)* Cheda, I swear to you before Almighty God and these witnesses, that the order transferring you to Ivanitsa shall be signed this very evening!

CHEDA: Even better, why not transfer me to Nicaragua?

Curtain

Act Four

The same room.

SCENE 1

Piled up on the chairs, left, are a great many bundles of newspapers, some tied up as for wholesale distribution. In other parts of the room various articles of men's and women's clothing, hats, and other things, are strewn on the chairs. DARA is busily packing them into a large travelling trunk, and going in and out of the side rooms to fetch more.

*(**Enter** ANKA from outside. She is carrying yet another bundle of newspapers)*

ANKA: Here you are, madam. I'm afraid I only managed to buy twenty copies. *(She puts them down with the others).*

DARA *(continuing her packing)*: That's no concern of mine.

ANKA: I wanted to mention it, because the mistress told me to go to all the newsagents and buy up all their copies of today's paper, but more copies keep arriving at every shop I go to, after I've left. I don't know whether I should, perhaps, just stand in the doorway? …

DARA: Don't ask me. Just do whatever she told you.
*(**Exit** for more things to pack).*

SCENE 2

*(**Enter** RAKA from outside, carrying a dozen or so copies of the newspaper)*: There! I could only find twelve. *(He puts them down).* What about you, Anka?

ANKA: I only got twenty.

RAKA: That's a lot!

ANKA: Mr Pera from the Administrative Section's doing the best, he's bought three hundred so far.

RAKA: Gosh! And Uncle Vasa?

ANKA: Only eighty . Anyway, Raka, have you any idea why she wants us to buy so many copies of the same newspaper?

RAKA: Oh, I know, all right!

ANKA: Why, then?

RAKA: Because there's an article in the newspaper ridiculing her, and she wants to buy them all up so that nobody can read it.

ANKA: Oh, how dare they ridicule a government minister's wife?

RAKA: They're ridiculing her because of *that*.

ANKA: What d'you mean, "that"?

RAKA: That business of yours.

ANKA: What d'you mean – what business of mine?

RAKA: Do you want me to read it?

ANKA: Yes, please.

RAKA *(takes a copy of the newspaper, unfolds it, and sits down in an armchair)*: Pass me one of those ministerial cigarettes, please.

ANKA: My! You've got a cheek, smoking in the house! *(She passes him a cigarette)*

RAKA *(lighting it)*: I don't usually, but it's the done thing to smoke a cigarette while one's reading the newspaper. *(Reads)*: "In a certain region of China … " *(Speaks)*: Look out that Mother doesn't come in and catch us, otherwise we'll both be in trouble!

ANKA: All right. Go on!

RAKA *(reads)*: "In a certain region of China, even today, they practise a strange custom whereby if a man loves a married woman he can propose marriage to her even though she has a husband still living. An example of this occurred recently in the house of the mandarin Si-Po-Po." *(Speaks)* By "the mandarin Si-Po-Po" they mean my father, Sima Popovich.

ANKA: Oh my!

RAKA *(continues to read)*: "His wife, a horrible old woman … "
(He looks round, and speaks): That "horrible old woman" is my
mother. Make sure you look out for her, or she'll make
mandarins of us!

ANKA: Oh dear, oh dear! … *(She looks around)*

RAKA *(continues to read)*: "His wife, a horrible old woman, has
aroused the amorous passions of Ni-ni-ko … "

ANKA: Who's he?

RAKA: I don't know – some Chinaman … ah! … *(reads)*: "… the
amorous passions of Ni-ni-ko, the Permanent Secretary at the
Ministry of Foreign Affairs! … "

ANKA: Oh, I know who he is. Go on!

RAKA *(reads)*: "The way that the love between them is expressed
is that she wangles promotion for him, and he sends love
letters to her."

ANKA: Oh yes, I do know who he is!

RAKA *(continuing to read)*: "This Ni-ni-ko is a pretentious
nincompoop who makes love to the wives of all the mandarins
while they are in power so that, through their husbands, these
foolish women will arrange promotion for him. He even sent a
match-maker to the house to propose to the old woman at the
same time as a malodorous Chinese stinker called Ka-Ra-Gua
turned up to propose to her married daughter." *(Speaks)*:
Do you know who "Ka-Ra-Gua" is?

ANKA: No, who?

RAKA: It's that fellow you had in your bedroom.

ANKA: But why do they call him "Ka-Ra-Gua"?

RAKA: I don't know.

ANKA: Poor man, he wasn't to blame.

RAKA: Oh, really! Then why did he take his coat off?
Here – it says in the paper that he took his coat off.

ANKA: Does it really say that? Well, for goodness' sake, a man can
take his coat off perfectly innocently, can't he?

RAKA: Oho! If I'd been in your bedroom and had taken my coat
off …

ANKA: Well, what then?

RAKA: Then I'd have taken my trousers off!

ANKA: Saucy monkey! Grow up first! You should be ashamed of yourself!

RAKA: And do you know what they're calling you in the paper?

ANKA: Surely they don't mention me?

RAKA: They do!

ANKA: What do they call me?

RAKA *(Looks for the passage and finds it)*: Housemaid A-Ki-Ka. *(Laughs)* A-Ki-Ka!

ANKA: Is there any more? Go on!

RAKA *(Reads)*: "But, of course, even in China these love affairs do not always run so smoothly. For instance … "

SCENE 3

(Enter DARA, bringing in some more clothes, and folding them)

DARA: What are you doing, sitting there reading the papers? If Mother catches you she'll give you what for!

RAKA: We're looking out for her. Hey, Dara, can you tell me who Ni-Ni-Ko is?

DARA: I haven't the faintest idea, and I suggest that you clear off before Mother finds you. And you, Anka, you should be doing some work, not reading the newspapers.

ANKA: I was only bringing in the newspapers that I'd bought.

RAKA: Me too. D'you know why I only managed to buy a dozen copies? – it was because that Karagua is offering to pay twelve paras a copy, so everyone's selling them to him. And I only managed to get the ones I did by shouting at the newsagent: "You must sell them to me, because I'm the mandarin's son!"

DARA: You little devil!

RAKA: No, I meant to say "minister's son"!

DARA: You'd better go out and buy some more, if that's what Mother told you to do.

RAKA: You're right! *(To ANKA)* Come on, A-Ki-Ka! *(Exit)*

ANKA: Does Madam wish me to help?

DARA: I don't need any help, thank you.

ANKA: Very good, Madam. *(Exit)*

SCENE 4

(Enter CHEDA *from outside)*

CHEDA: Still packing? You're really taking this seriously, aren't you?

DARA: What else can I do?

CHEDA: It's amazing how fast everything's happened! The order transferring me to Ivanitsa was only signed last night, and first thing this morning I was relieved of my duties.

DARA: When have you got to go?

CHEDA: I've no idea what your mother has arranged. Quite possibly she'll give orders in the course of today that I'm to go tomorrow. It all depends on your mother's orders.

DARA: Well, let's hope it is tomorrow – I'll be ready by then.

CHEDA: Are you really sure you want to come with me?

DARA: Yes, I am. To tell you the truth, I can't stand this ministerial business any more. The place has become a madhouse ever since Father was made a minister.

CHEDA: I agree.

DARA: And I can't bear the shame, either. After what's appeared in the newspapers I hardly dare go out of the house – I can't look people in the face. I want to go to Ivanitsa, if only to escape their silly grins.

CHEDA: Especially as it's such a huge scandal. The whole of Belgrade is shaking with laughter, you know.

DARA: It's dreadful!

CHEDA: The newspapers are selling like hot cakes.

DARA *(pointing)*: Mother has bought up most of them.

CHEDA: She imagines that the fewer people read the papers the fewer will know about the scandal, but she doesn't realise that they've printed not three, but six thousand copies today.

DARA: Oh, my God!

CHEDA: Not taking into account the fact that at least four people will be reading each copy.

DARA: And does everybody know that it's our family that they're talking about?

CHEDA: They most certainly do. They know it from the names, but in particular from the fact that the only one of the current crop of ministerial wives who has a married daughter is Madam Zhivka.

DARA: And haven't you been able to find out who wrote the article?

CHEDA: Oh, I've found out, all right.

DARA: Really? Who was it?

CHEDA: I'll tell you if you'll promise not to tell your mother.

DARA: Why all the secrecy?

CHEDA: Because it's a very big secret.

DARA: Go on, then, tell me! Who wrote it?

CHEDA: I did.

DARA: What!! *(She drops the dress she was holding)*.

CHEDA: As I said, I wrote it.

DARA: Oh, Cheda, what have you done?

CHEDA: Let her find out that I'm capable of hurting people, too!

DARA: How could you do it? How could you?

CHEDA: In the same way as she could just pack me off to Ivanitsa!

DARA: Have you no heart? – she's my mother!

CHEDA: Has she no heart? – sending her own daughter off to Ivanitsa!

DARA: You've brought shame on us, on the whole family.

CHEDA: Me? God save us, *she*'s the one who's done that.

DARA: My God! My God! I don't know where I am any more! I don't know what to think! *(She bursts into tears)*

CHEDA: But can't you see for yourself, my dear, that it was high time somebody stood up to her? Can't you see that she's turned this place into a madhouse? Leaving aside that she's tried to marry you off even though you are a married woman, she's made a complete fool of herself by taking on a lover.

DARA: It can't be true!

CHEDA: But it is. I've read the fellow's love letters myself, with my own eyes. And she did arrange for him to be promoted. You just go out into the streets and you'll hear for yourself how everybody's laughing at her!

DARA *(wringing her hands)*: My God!

CHEDA: You may be able to bear the disgrace, but I can't. I'm ashamed to appear in public – everyone's nudging each other and whispering and giving sly winks …

DARA: But surely it would have been better to have told her all this – to have had a serious talk with her?

CHEDA: Have a serious talk with *her*! Some hope! You tried to talk to her, didn't you? – and all she did was set up that farce with Nicaragua!

DARA: It was you that did that.

CHEDA: Yes, but I did it to save both of us. If I hadn't done it your mother's plot would have worked – I'd have finished up in Anka's room with no coat on, and you'd have found yourself alone in a room with Nicaragua. Would that have been better?

DARA: Well …

CHEDA: Go on, tell me – would that have been better?

DARA: Well, all right, so be it, but why did you have to broadcast it all in the newspapers?

CHEDA: To make her draw back. To make her see sense before it was too late.

DARA: But do you think that it will help to change things?

CHEDA: I certainly hope so. Since this morning the scandal has spread like wildfire all over Belgrade. It's even possible that it will bring your father's position into question.

DARA: His position?

CHEDA: Oh yes. There's a lot of talk about it outside. Some say that after this it will be impossible for him …

DARA: Poor Father!

CHEDA: Yes, I'm very sorry for him myself, but it's all his wife's fault.

DARA: What! Do you really think that Father …

CHEDA: I can't be sure, but it's quite possible. He has been compromised, and that can have unfortunate consequences.

DARA: But that would be dreadful!

CHEDA: Frankly, to tell you the truth, I think the opposite – I think it would be for the best, because if things had been left to go on as they were, God knows how many more even worse idiocies she'd have got up to. Don't you see, my dear, what a terrible thing that woman has done? Don't you see that she's the one who has brought ridicule upon your father, a decent and honourable man whom I respect, and ruined his chances of success in politics and public life? Don't you see?

DARA: Yes, I do.

CHEDA: Well, then!

DARA: As far as I'm concerned, I tell you frankly, I think it would have been better if my father had never been made a minister.

CHEDA: There was no problem in your father becoming a minister, the problem was in your mother becoming a minister's wife. So, please listen to what I say, not what she says, and do as I do. In the end you'll see that I acted for the best, and you'll thank me. Only, stay beside me: I need you to give me courage.

SCENE 5

(Enter ZHIVKA *from outside, in a bad temper)*

ZHIVKA: Dara, I wish to have a serious talk with you in private. Will outsiders kindly leave the room.

CHEDA: Very well. *(Exeunt* CHEDA *and* DARA*, together.* ZHIVKA *watches them both go in astonishment, and then furiously throws down her hat and parasol)*

SCENE 6

(Enter PERA*, carrying a bundle of newspapers)* Good morning, Madam Minister! Here you are, I've bought six more copies – that makes another thirty-six so far.

ZHIVKA: Thank you. I know you've bought more than anyone

else, but I'm told that there are still lots more on sale. Tell me, are people reading them? – have you noticed whether many people are reading them?

PERA: Well … how shall I put it, madam? … yes, I'm afraid they are. Just now, as I was passing the "Paris" hotel, I saw a whole lot of people crowded round the tables, and one man was reading out loud from the newspaper.

ZHIVKA: Why on earth aren't there proper laws in this county? I went to see the Chief of Police to tell him to forbid publication of the newspaper, and all he could say was: "It can't be done, because of the laws relating to the Press." But, for goodness' sake, that's ridiculous! How can there be laws that give the police no powers?

PERA: It is probably because in this case they're not writing about you, but about things that happened in China …

ZHIVKA *(interrupting)* To hell with China!

PERA: … and perhaps because the police found that there was no defamation of character involved.

ZHIVKA: No defamation of character! Don't they say that I'm "a horrible old woman" – and isn't that defamation of character?

PERA: Yes, it is in a way.

ZHIVKA: Well, in what way is it not?

PERA: I suppose it could be said that it did not refer to you because it was supposed to have happened in China.

ZHIVKA *(seizing a copy of the newspaper)*: Here! Read this bit at the end – here …

PERA *(reads out loud*: "Perhaps it is not so surprising that such things should be happening in China, but what is really surprising is that the same things are happening in our own country, in the highest circles of society, in the home of one our mandarins." *(Speaks)* It's disgraceful!

ZHIVKA: It certainly is! It ought not to be allowed!

PERA: If we could only find out who wrote it.

ZHIVKA: Yes! But you said earlier …

PERA: Yes, I did. Madam, I have already asked. Believe me,

I've made enquiries all over the place, but it seems impossible to find out.

SCENE 7

(Enter VASA, *carrying a bundle of newspapers which he puts down on a chair)*

VASA: There! – I've bought these as well, but I can't get any more. The whole of today's edition has been bought up.

ZHIVKA: Yes, it's been bought up because you're useless!

VASA: I've not been useless! Including those I just brought in, I've bought a hundred and seventy copies.

PERA: And I've bought three hundred and six.

VASA: There!

ZHIVKA: If you weren't useless you'd have found out who wrote it.

VASA: Really, Zhivka! I've done my best. I've asked about everywhere, I've asked lots of people, but nobody knows, and that's that!

PERA: I've been asking, too, but it's no use.

VASA: It's just occurred to me, there might be one way of finding out. You remember that fellow who claimed to be a member of the family "through the female line"? – well, we might be able to find out who wrote it through the female line.

ZHIVKA: What are you thinking of?

VASA: Well, if the editor of the newspaper's married, he'll certainly have told his wife who wrote the article. All we've got to do is to find out who her best friend is, because she's sure to have told her, and then, if we can find out who *her* best friend's best friend is …

ZHIVKA: My God!

PERA: And that way, madam, we'll soon find out …

ZHIVKA: Right, then, off you go, Mr Pera! Get on to the female line and find out! Only do it quickly – at once – because I'm bursting with impatience. I'm desperate to know. And when I do find out who it is, he'd better look out! I'll give him something to remember! Go on, then, Pera, get on with it – and hurry!

PERA: Yes, madam! *(Exit)*

SCENE 8

ZHIVKA: Tell me, Vasa, do you know anything about the law?

VASA: To tell you the truth, Zhivka, the law and I are not very well acquainted with each other.

ZHIVKA: How can that be, when you were a Police Administrator for so many years?

VASA: Yes, I was but, frankly, while I was a Police Administrator I never felt any particular need to become acquainted with the law. But, if you were to ask my advice, I'd be perfectly capable of telling you the difference between right and wrong.

ZHIVKA: I'm not talking about right and wrong. I'm asking you how it is possible for the laws of this country to prevent the police from stopping the publication of a newspaper which insults the wife of a government minister?

VASA: Have you been to see the Chief of Police?

ZHIVKA: I've just come from there.

VASA: And what did he say?

ZHIVKA: He said that he could do nothing, because of the law. He said: "It's not legally a defamation, it's just an allusion." What's he mean: "just an allusion"? For God's sake, when they call me a horrible old woman – isn't that more than "just an allusion"?

VASA: Well, no, but it might be because they named Sima as the mandarin. That, I think, might be more than an allusion.

ZHIVKA: And if I break the scoundrel's nose who wrote it, will that be an "just an allusion"?

VASA: Oh, do stop talking like that, Zhivka! There seems to be a mania for breaking noses running through your family. Calm down, and let's discuss sensibly what we're going to do about it.

ZHIVKA: How on earth can I calm down, Vasa, you fool? They've insulted me and ridiculed me and painted me in the worst light in the newspapers, and you tell me to calm down! If I have to bite the very earth to do it, I'll find him, and when I do he'll scream for his mother and curse the day he learned to write! I'm going to strangle him, d'you hear? – I'm going to strangle him with my bare hands!

VASA: There! You've got into a bad temper again.

ZHIVKA: Well, why shouldn't I? What d'you expect me to get into?

VASA: It's just ... but I know how you feel.

ZHIVKA: Vasa, it's just occurred to me, do you know who I think it was that did it? – who the snake was that bit me?

VASA: No.

ZHIVKA: It was that Mrs Nata – that's who it was! I'm certain she was behind it all. I'll put my hand in the fire if she wasn't!

VASA: Why do you think it was her?

ZHIVKA: Because I got the better of her over him.

VASA: Got the better of her over who?

ZHIVKA *(trembling)*: Well, you know ... but only for form's sake.

VASA: I don't understand. How have you got the better of her "for form's sake"?

ZHIVKA: It's obvious – I got the better of her over the ministerial appointment and then everything else that goes with it.

VASA: The carriage?

ZHIVKA: It's not just the carriage, but lots of other things. You wouldn't understand.

VASA: Well, I still don't understand it when you say "for form's sake".

ZHIVKA: Of course you don't understand, because you've got no class. If you had any culture you would understand ...

SCENE 9

(Enter ANKA, carrying a letter)

ANKA: A letter for you, madam.

ZHIVKA: Who brought it?

ANKA: A messenger.

ZHIVKA: Thank you. *(Exit ANKA)*

SCENE 10

ZHIVKA *(having opened the letter and scanned it)*: Who can this be from? The signature's all scrawled, like a pattern on an Easter egg – I can't make it out.

VASA *(takes the letter and looks at it)*: Rista!

ZHIVKA: Who's Rista?

VASA: You know – Nicaragua.

ZHIVKA: As if I hadn't got enough troubles at the moment! What does he want?

VASA *(reads)*: "Dear Mrs Minister. In consequence of the unfortunate incident which occurred at your house …"

ZHIVKA: Hah! *That* coming from someone who got into the housemaid's bedroom!

VASA *(continuing to read)*: " … I had denied myself the pleasure of calling on you in person but now, in addition, and in view of the subsequent scandal which has been reported in the newspapers, I have to inform you that there is no further possibility of my becoming a member of your esteemed family."

ZHIVKA: Who cares if he becomes a member of the family! He can go to Hell! He can go to Nicaragua and get married there!

VASA *(continuing to read)*: "Also, having regard to the fact that the article in today's newspaper has tarnished my commercial reputation and has probably even brought into question my high position as an Honorary Consul, you will not be surprised to hear that I have spared neither effort nor expense in finding out the name of its author, in order that I may obtain satisfaction from him. Finally, I have managed to discover his name …"

ZHIVKA *(impatiently)*: Who is it? Who is it?

VASA: Wait a moment.

ZHIVKA: Read it! Read it!

VASA *(continues reading)*: " … and I consider it to be my duty to inform you … "

ZHIVKA *(boiling with impatience)*: Never mind all that, Vasa, read the name!

VASA: Oh my God!

ZHIVKA: Skip that bit – read the *name!*

VASA: Oh dear! *(Reads)* "That the author of that article in the newspaper was Uncle Vasa .. "

ZHIVKA *(Enraged, she rushes towards Vasa)*: Vasa, you bloody swindler! Vasa, you drunken old sot! … Vasa … *(She starts hitting him all over).*

VASA: Stop it! Wait! Oh Mother, I shall die – and I'm innocent!

ZHIVKA: So you write newspaper articles, do you, you filthy cur! Allusions, eh? … *(She picks up a chair)* Get out of my sight before I kill you, you drunken old pig! …

VASA: Zhivka, for God's sake, calm down and let me read the rest of it!

ZHIVKA: You've read out all that I wanted to hear.

VASA: Calm down! Listen! Why on earth should I have written it? It never entered my head to write anything. Anyway, seeing that I was discharged from government service for being illiterate, how could I have written an article like that, with allusions and all …

ZHIVKA: You did! You wrote it! I know you only too well, you old tosspot!

VASA: For goodness' sake let me read the rest of it.

ZHIVKA: Get on with it, then, read it!

VASA: I will, but please put that chair down. I can't read while you're brandishing a chair.

ZHIVKA: Read it!

VASA *(Reads)* " … the author of that article in the newspaper was Uncle Vasa, that is to say the gentleman who posed as Uncle Vasa, but was in fact your own son-in-law … "

ZHIVKA *(putting down the chair)*: What did you say?

VASA *(repeats)*: "… but was in fact your own son-in-law."

ZHIVKA *(astonished)*: What was that, again?

VASA *(reading again)*: " … but was in fact your own son-in-law."

ZHIVKA: Oh, oh, oh! It's too much! That son-in-law – he's done for himself this time! God damn and blast him in this world and the next! He's blackened my home, he's ruined my reputation! God grant that the hand he wrote that article with be paralysed!

Vasa: Control yourself, for goodness' sake!

Zhivka: How can I control myself when he's torn my nerves to shreds? He's ripped my life up like minced meat.! I'll not be calm – and, believe me, I'm going to shut *him* up for good! *(In fury)* Vasa, get me a gun, do you hear! Get me a gun so that I can shoot the brute! Get me a gun ... but don't ...

Vasa: I certainly will not!

Zhivka: All right then, go and buy me some rat poison! Do you hear what I say – go and buy me some rat poison! ...

Vasa: Zhivka, what on earth do you want rat poison for?

Zhivka: I'm going to kill him! I'm going to poison him like the vermin he is!

Vasa: Steady on, you can't do that! Don't talk like that. Let's think about this quietly and sensibly. In my opinion, Zhivka, you can simply have him prosecutcd.

Zhivka: Who?

Vasa: The son-in-law.

Zhivka: What, and let others judge him? Oh no, I want to judge him *myself*, d'you hear? Once I get him into *my* hands he won't slip out of them.

Vasa: All right then, what are you going to do?

Zhivka: I shall throw him out. I shall arrange for him to be thrown out this very minute.

Vasa: Where, to Ivanitsa?

Zhivka: To hell with Ivanitsa! Out of the country, d'you understand, deported! – like they do with vagrants and cardsharpers. And I'll do it this minute – I'll not give him a moment's grace. I'll have him deported ... now ... this instant! ... *(She picks up the telephone)* Hallo? Give me number 407, please.

Vasa: What are you doing?

Zhivka: I want to speak to Sima ... Is that you, Sima? Zhivka here. Listen to what I have to say. If you are the government and if you are a Minister, you'll do exactly what I tell you, and if you are a mandarin … *(She stops speaking and listens. As she does so her face loses colour)* Vasa, would you come and listen to this telephone? It sounds like someone cursing and swearing, and I don't understand it at all. Is it the telephone buzzing, or is it a buzzing noise in my ears? I can't make it out. You take it, please *(She gives the telephone to Vasa).*

VASA *(taking it)* Sima , it's me, Vasa. Yes, Vasa. Zhivka's got a buzzing noise in her ears … tell me … *(He listens)*

ZHIVKA: What's he saying? *(VASA motions to her to be quiet)* Tell me what he's saying.

VASA *(He replaces the receiver and shakes his head)*: He's angry. He's very angry indeed.

ZHIVKA: Well, didn't you tell him that I was angry too?

VASA: And he said that you were to stop your nonsense and leave him alone.

ZHIVKA: He said *what?*

VASA: He said that you had seriously disgraced him by the article that was published in the newspapers.

ZHIVKA: But I didn't write it.

VASA: He said there would be a Cabinet Meeting shortly, and the Minister of Internal Affairs had warned him that it would be discussed.

ZHIVKA: What would be discussed?

VASA: The newspaper article, of course.

ZHIVKA: Oh, I don't give a damn what they're going to discuss. What I want to know is why didn't you tell him … ?

VASA *(interrupts her)*: Hold on! He said something else. He said he feared that his own position would be brought into question, because today's article had aroused disquiet at the highest level and all his colleagues, the other ministers, were very unhappy about it.

ZHIVKA: What did he say … his own position in question? Just let him try! Vasa, go to the telephone and tell him that if he resigns I shan't let him into the house! If his colleagues are unhappy *they* can resign! Let them all resign, but don't let him *dare* to! … Tell him that!

SCENE 11

(Enter ANKA *from outside)*

ANKA: Mrs Nata Stefanovich wishes …

ZHIVKA: Who?

ANKA: Mrs Nata Stefanovich, the minister's wife.

ZHIVKA *(corrects her)* You mean the ex-minister's wife.

ANKA: Yes.

ZHIVKA: What does she want? Oh, she's chosen her moment to visit me, hasn't she just! The bitch has read that article in the newspaper and has come to have a good sniff around. I can't – I can't see her. Tell her to clear off!

VASA: Zhivka, you really must see her. It would never do to refuse.

ZHIVKA: Yes, I suppose I must, but my stomach's all churned up inside. What the hell? – she's here … Ask her to come in! *(Exit* ANKA. ZHIVKA *looks round the room)*: Oh Lord! – how can I receive her in here, with the room looking like a pigsty? Why in God's name did she choose this moment to come?

SCENE 12

(Enter NATA*)*

NATA: A very good morning to you, Madam Zhivka!

ZHIVKA: Oh, my dear Madam Nata, thank you so much for coming! It is such a long time since you last visited. Not having seen you, I was beginning to wonder if you had decided not to call.

NATA: No, not at all, but, believe me, I've hardly been able to draw breath between various meetings. You know, when I was a Minister's wife all the women's societies chose me to sit on their executive committees, and how I worked! … They wanted me to preside over so many meetings, debates, resolutions, and so on, that I almost had to give up looking after my own household. *(She looks at the trunk)* Oh! Who's doing all that packing?

ZHIVKA: That? Oh, er … oh, my daughter's getting ready to go to a Spa.

NATA: What, already, when the season hasn't started yet?

ZHIVKA: Well, yes, you see, she's got rheumatism and can't wait for the season to start.

NATA: Which Spa is she going to?

ZHIVKA: Which? … Oh, to Abbazia.[1]

NATA: Really? And, of course, she'll be travelling by wagon-lit? I always used to travel in a first-class sleeping carriage – it's so pleasant.

ZHIVKA: Yes, of course.

NATA: I'm surprised she's going to Abbazia. They don't have a cure for rheumatism there, do they?

ZHIVKA: Well, she's going to Abbazia first, on the way to Ivanitsa.

NATA: To Ivanitsa?

ZHIVKA: Yes. Do you know, they've just discovered a new spring of therapeutic water at Ivanitsa that's especially good for rheumatism.

NATA: Fancy that, I didn't know! *(She looks at the piles of newspapers)* My word! – what a lot of newspapers! It looks like an editor's office.

ZHIVKA: Oh, them! Yes, we paid for a whole year's subscription to the newspaper, so they've sent us a copy of every day's issue back to the beginning of the year. That's right, isn't it, Vasa?

VASA: Yes, back to the beginning of this year, and all last year's also.

NATA: I don't read the newspapers. Frankly, I don't like them … that is, unless there's something especially interesting in them.

ZHIVKA: Yes, yes! *(She looks knowingly at Vasa)* Vasa, would you make that telephone call that I spoke you to about, please.

---

1. Abbazia *(now Opatija)* The sea-side resort near Rijeka (then Fiume) on the Adriatic coast.

Tell him that he can't come home! *(Exeunt* Nata *and* Zhivka *to another room)*

SCENE 13

Vasa *(He takes some cigarettes from the box on the table and puts them into his own cigarette case, then he goes to the door, right)*: Dara! Dara! ... Is Cheda there? Ask him to come in here, please. I've got to have a few words with him.

(Enter Cheda*)*

Cheda: What is it, Uncle Vasa?

Vasa: Cheda, I wanted to speak to you ... Just a moment, what did I want to speak to you about? Oh yes! Just imagine, we've discovered who wrote that newspaper article.

Cheda: Oh?

Vasa: And who do you think it was?

Cheda: Goodness knows.

Vasa: It was you!

Cheda: Never!

Vasa: Oh yes it was – it was you!

Cheda: Who'd have thought it?

Vasa: And do you know how we found out?

Cheda: I'm curious.

Vasa: Nicaragua found out and told us.

Cheda: Is that Nicaragua still meddling in our family affairs?

Vasa: He's not meddling, but he has written a letter and is demanding satisfaction.

Cheda: Well, let Anka give him satisfaction!

Vasa: Oh, I have to admit that you cooked his goose nicely. However, in trying to cook Zhivka's goose by way of the newspapers you've gone too far.

Cheda: Yes, it was a bit overdone.

Vasa: It wasn't just a bit overdone, it was practically charred! And what's more, you've gone too far by uttering falsifications.

Cheda: What sort of falsifications?

Vasa: Well, for a start, you uttered a falsification concerning me.

CHEDA: Oh, really? I didn't know I had.

VASA: You knew – you knew all right! You pretended to that fellow that you were your Uncle Vasa, and that, my friend, is a falsification which nearly cost me my life just now! And not only that, but then, God forgive you, you uttered a falsification concerning Zhivka.

CHEDA: What, by pretending that she was a minister's wife?

VASA: No, but by describing her as a horrible old woman, and that is a further falsification!

CHEDA: Fancy! Who would have thought it?

VASA: And in doing so, my friend, you should know that you have committed the worst crime that a human being can possibly commit. If you kill somebody, the law will allow you to plead mitigating circumstances, and will take them into account in reduction of sentence. If you commit blasphemy, the same thing applies. If you burn down your neighbour's house, even then the law will allow you to plead mitigating circumstances. But there's no country in the entire world where the law would allow you to plead mitigating circumstances for the unpardonable crime of publicly calling your respectable mother-in-law a horrible old woman

CHEDA: How interesting! I never knew that.

VASA: No, you didn't. And you didn't know, either, that this whole affair is going to end very badly for you. Anyway, you and I have got to speak seriously.

CHEDA: Oh, I know. You're going to advise me to leave my wife.

VASA: It's nothing to do with your wife. There are much more serious things to talk about now than women. Leave aside what I've said so far – those things were said, as it were, in an official sense and so I had to say certain things – but what I want to talk to you about now is in accordance with my own sense.

CHEDA: Go ahead, then.

VASA: As you can see for yourself, this whole business with the newspapers must have far-reaching consequences. Sima himself has now been placed in a very difficult situation.

He telephoned a little earlier and said that the matter was going to be brought up at a Cabinet meeting today – this very morning.

CHEDA: Good!

VASA: And I've been thinking – entirely on my own account, you understand – I've been thinking about how we can smooth things over.

CHEDA: Well, you get on and smooth them over!

VASA: But how can I smooth things over? I can't do anything, but you might be able to. You might, for instance, have the newspaper publish a letter from you saying that you would lick up your own vomit.

CHEDA: Who'd lick it up?

VASA: You, my friend.

CHEDA: Oh, pardon me!

VASA: But, anyway, that's just in a manner of speaking. No, you could simply say: "Everything that I wrote in the newspaper was a lie."

CHEDA: Ah! But it was all true.

VASA: I know it was all true, but … my dear fellow, the truth can never be spoken openly, and it is certainly never printed in the newspapers! The truth is all right for gossip, but only like this, in private, between ourselves, within the family. When have you ever seen or heard of the truth being told publicly?

CHEDA: And did you think of all that yourself?

VASA: Yes, I did. And, look, I've thought of this, too – if you'd write something like that I could take it to Sima before the Cabinet meeting. And then, when they say to him: "What is all this in the newspapers, Mr Sima?" he could say to them: "Nothing! Please read this," and then he could produce your letter.

CHEDA (pretending to be pleased): But that would be marvellous!

VASA: Yes, I think so too. Because, just think, without it they'd say to him: "Brother Sima, you have brought shame on the whole Cabinet. Brother Sima!" they'd say, "To salvage our reputation you must hand in your resignation!"

CHEDA *(even more pleased)*: But that would be marvellous!

VASA: What would?

CHEDA: That!

VASA: That Sima should resign?

CHEDA: Yes.

VASA *(disappointed)*: Oh dear, oh dear! So I've been wasting my breath, talking to you, have I? And I, my friend, thought that I was talking to an intelligent man!

CHEDA: I thought the same about you but, obviously, we were both mistaken.

VASA: Very much mistaken!

SCENE 14

(Enter PERA KALENICH *from outside)*

KALENICH: Good morning, everyone, good morning!

VASA: Good morning.

KALENICH *(to* CHEDA*)*: May I have the honour of introducing myself – Pera Kalenich. *(To* VASA*)*: Is Aunt Zhivka in?

CHEDA: And this gentleman is? ...

VASA: Our relative.

KALENICH: Closest relative in the female line.

CHEDA: Oh, that's nice. I'm Aunt Zhivka's son-in-law.

KALENICH *(shaking hands with Cheda)*: You are? Well, fancy us not recognising each other! Actually, perhaps it's better that Aunt Zhivka isn't with us at the moment, so that we three, as male members of the family, can hold a more intimate family discussion.

CHEDA: Very well, what's on today's agenda?

KALENICH: The first matter on the agenda, of course, is the attack on Aunt Zhivka in today's newspapers. *(To* CHEDA*)*: You must have read it?

VASA: Oh yes, he's read it.

KALENICH: Well, I've prepared a reply in rebuttal because, I'm sure you'll agree, it is our duty as members of the family to defend Aunt Zhivka from such disgusting calumnies.

CHEDA: Of course!

KALENICH: Would you like to hear my reply? *(He takes a sheet of paper out of his pocket)* My reply is addressed to the ass who wrote that newspaper article. *(To* CHEDA*)*: Do you think I should call him an ass or a donkey – what do you advise?

CHEDA: It doesn't matter. I don't see that there's much difference. Only, have you taken into consideration that whoever it is that you are calling an ass or a donkey may come and break your nose?

VASA *(aside)*: Noses again!

KALENICH: Yes, I've thought of that, but the thing is, I'm not going to sign it.

CHEDA: Oh, that's all right, then.

KALENICH: I'll save you the trouble of listening to the whole thing. I can assure you that I have done it very cleverly. I have said that gentleman in question was the representative of a foreign government, Nicaragua, and that, as such, he came upon a visit to conduct some official negotiations which were intended, let us say, to lead to the conclusion of a commercial contract.

CHEDA: What, with Mrs Zhivka?

KALENICH: No, with our government. Then I have said that when he visited the house of the minister's wife in question the waiting room was temporarily unavailable and, as she was very busy, the gentleman in question was taken into the housemaid's room so that he could wait there, as if it were an ordinary waiting room.

CHEDA: And why did he take his coat off?

KALENICH: Oh, as to his taking his coat off, I've said that the room in question was very small and cramped.

CHEDA: You've certainly thought it out very well: that explanation would never have entered my head. That really was very clever of you.

KALENICH: D'you really think so?

CHEDA: I *am* pleased to know that I have such a clever relative!

Well, then, Uncle Vasa, we've nothing more to worry about –
no more problems! If what the gentleman has written is
published in the newspapers the whole affair will be
completely set to rights.

VASA: Unless it's too late.

KALENICH: Why should it be too late?

CHEDA: Well, it's quite possible that Mr Popovich may have
already tendered his resignation.

KALENICH *(unpleasantly surprised)*: What, Uncle Sima?

CHEDA: Yes, Uncle Sima.

KALENICH: But that's impossible!

CHEDA: And all on account of that article in the newspaper.

VASA: Yes, unfortunately, on account of that article.

KALENICH: But why, for goodness' sake? That would be awful!
Anyway, I don't see how he's to blame.

CHEDA: He isn't. But, you know, innocent people often get run
over, too.

KALENICH: Are you quite sure that he's going to resign?

CHEDA: No, I'm not, but that's what people are thinking and
saying.

KALENICH: Well, in that case, do you think that it might perhaps
be better if I delayed publishing this reply until the situation
becomes clearer because – it seems to me at least – if he resigns
and is no longer a government minister, then there's no point at
all in defending him any more, is there?

CHEDA: That's quite right. I agree with what you say. And it goes
further – if he resigns and is no longer a government minister,
then there's no sense in having a family relationship with him
any more, either.

KALENICH: That's true!

CHEDA: For instance, I'll tell you frankly that if he is no longer to
be a government minister I personally am going to sever my
relationship with Mrs Zhivka completely.

KALENICH: And do you really think he's going to resign?

CHEDA: To tell you the truth, I expect he has already resigned.

KALENICH: And, to tell you the truth, I'm not really such a close relative.

VASA: What's that? Only yesterday you were saying that you were!

KALENICH: Yes, that's so, but rather through the female line, you know, and a relationship traced through the female line is never very reliable.

VASA: But didn't you say yesterday that you would rather die than disown your family ties?

KALENICH: Yes, but I was only speaking figuratively. Perhaps you can't understand that, Uncle Vasa.

VASA: No, I can't.

CHEDA: Once upon a time, in the old days, kinship was kinship. Things are different nowadays – it's possible now for kinship to be just figurative.

KALENICH: You put it very well.

VASA: Well, I don't understand, and that's that!

CHEDA: Then there's no point in talking about it any more. Well now, my dear figurative relative, the best thing you can do is to put that manuscript in your pocket and go off round the business district, or tour the cafés, and ask people what's going on. If Uncle Sima's not going to resign, then you can come back here and read it out to Aunt Zhivka. If he does resign then there'll be no point in wasting any more time over it.

KALENICH: Yes! Exactly! You took the words out of my mouth. Right, then! – as soon as I know what the situation is I'll be back …

CHEDA: If necessary.

KALENICH: Yes, yes – if necessary. Goodbye, sir. Good bye, Mr Vasa! *(Exit)*

SCENE 15

CHEDA: Who was that, for goodness' sake?

VASA: God knows who he is. He made out that he was one of the family, but look at him now!

CHEDA: Well, now, Uncle Vasa, you accused me of falsification, but it seems as if you've been falsifying relatives!

VASA: It wasn't me doing it – he was the falsifier. And, anyway, did you see how quickly he threw his hand in as soon as he heard the word "resignation".

CHEDA: That's how things are, my dear Uncle Vasa. The rats all leave as soon as the ship looks like sinking. He wasn't the first and he won't be the last.

VASA: Well, he can go to hell! Anyway, it's time you answered my question – how are we going to smooth over this situation?

CHEDA: There's no point in talking about "smoothing", Uncle Vasa. Don't you see, the whole situation has got too rough even to be scraped down, let alone smoothed over?

VASA: Let's go and see your Dara, then. I want to talk to her. It's her mother, after all, and she's more likely to be heartbroken than you.

CHEDA: Certainly! – I've no objection. Perhaps she will be heartbroken. Come on!

(Exeunt CHEDA *and* VASA *into the room, right).*

SCENE 16

(Enter NATA, *followed by* ZHIVKA, *from the other room)*

NATA: I tell you, Madam Zhivka, you really mustn't take it to heart. It's just the way things are. As long as my husband was a government minister I was constantly surrounded by people. Oh, they were all my friends, weren't they! – oh, and how they all respected me, didn't they! – and wasn't my house always full of visitors! When I gave a party there were never enough chairs, and there were never enough teacups, even though I've got two dozen. And the women's clubs elected me to be their president, and the choral societies chose me as their patroness, and so on and so on. But as soon as your husband ceases to be a minister they all go as cold as the English. Then you see how things change! – even your relatives can't be bothered to visit. Three teacups are all you need! Some just stay away, others even pretend that they don't know you. I've been through it all, and I know. And I'm afraid you're going to find it out, too. But you really mustn't take it to heart.

ZHIVKA: To tell you the absolute truth, I wasn't all that keen for my husband to become a minister, but I really never expected it to turn out like this.

NATA: Oh, come now, Madam Zhivka! – let's be frank. It's marvellous! – you have your own carriage, cigarettes on the entertainment allowance, a complimentary box at the theatre, a first-class carriage on the train, and a dogsbody from the ministry to run errands. When you want to speak to somebody on the telephone you just tell the operators who you are and they fall over themselves to be the first to connect you! The officials all bow to you, and their wives are constantly calling on you. If you are at a luncheon, you take the place of honour, if you attend a ceremony you are given a bouquet, and when there's a parade you're given a place on the reviewing stand. It's marvellous – you can't deny it!

ZHIVKA: I suppose it is, if you look at it from that point of view.

SCENE 17

(Enter ANKA with a letter)

ANKA: For Madam!

(She gives the letter to ZHIVKA and exit. ZHIVKA holds it to her nose and sniffs it)

NATA: I wonder if you'd be so very kind as to let me smell that letter, too?

ZHIVKA: Really, Madam Nata, the very idea! Why should you possibly want to smell this letter?

NATA: Do please let me smell it.

ZHIVKA *(passes it to her)*: Very well, smell it, if it's so important to you.

NATA *(sniffing it)*: Ah, yes! The same scent and the same colour – pink! Go on, open it! I know exactly what's in it. I received letters just like that.

ZHIVKA: Why, what do you think it is?

NATA: Oh, come now – let's not pretend! You, too, learned to
play bridge, didn't you? – I wasn't the only one who did. Oh, I
know it all by heart! Go on – open it! You told me a little while
ago that there was a possibility that your husband might be
about to resign, didn't you? Well, I can assure you that, if that
is so, that letter may be very significant.

ZHIVKA: Significant? *(Nervously, she opens the letter and reads it.
Then, with an expression of disgust, she hands it to* NATA*)*.

NATA *(Reads the letter)*: Resignation! I told you! I received
exactly the same letter when *my* Cabinet resigned.

ZHIVKA: Oh, oh, oh! … I'm shocked!

NATA: Well, I'm afraid that's diplomatic love for you.

ZHIVKA: That fellow, Madam Nata, is a real diplomatic swine!

NATA: Take my word for it, Madam Zhivka, that letter is very
significant. That diplomatic swine never hands in his
resignation as a lover until he absolutely sure that the husband
in question has handed in his as a government minister.

ZHIVKA: What are you talking about? … Oh, God forbid! Has it
come to this?

NATA: I simply say that he's written that letter from certain
knowledge.

ZHIVKA *(very upset)*: Is it really possible?

NATA: Of course it's possible. The fall of a government, Madam
Zhivka, always comes unexpectedly, like thunder in a clear sky.
Oh, I'd made lots of plans – I was going to furnish my house,
I was going to take a holiday, I was going to visit a Spa this
summer, but . . suddenly . . bang! There was a clap of thunder –
the government fell, and all my plans were blown away. It hit
me hard. So, my dear Madam Zhivka, I know exactly how
you feel.

ZHIVKA: But, after all you said …

NATA: Oh, the sky clouded over somewhat, that's nothing
surprising, and where there are clouds there'll probably be
thunder. Anyway, I really must leave now. I don't want to add
to your troubles. You know how it is – it's always easier to bear

one's troubles without other people bothering you. So, good bye, Madam Zhivka. Don't take it too much to heart. Good bye! *(Exit)*.

SCENE 18

*(ZHIVKA, stunned, watches NATA's departure. After she has left, **enter** VASA from the other room)*

VASA: Has she gone?

ZHIVKA: Yes, she's gone, but I fear the worst. What do you think? Do you think he's going to resign? Do you think that it might really come to that?

VASA: Well … how shall I put it? … yes, it's possible. Cheda's just told me …

ZHIVKA: Oh, Cheda told you something, did he? I don't give a damn what Cheda told you. I'm going there myself – I shall go myself, in person, to that Cabinet meeting! I shall break in on them if I have to, and if he has already handed in his letter of resignation I shall tear it up, and I shall tell them, the other ministers, that they should clean up their own front doorsteps first, and *then* worry about the credibility of the government! And I shall tell them … I know exactly what I shall tell them! … Just wait till I get dressed! *(Exit, hurriedly, into the other room)*.

SCENE 19

VASA *(going to the doorway, left)*: Cheda! Dara! … Dara, come here, come quickly!

*(**Enter** CHEDA, followed by DARA)*.

CHEDA: What is it?

VASA: Wonders will never cease! Now she's going to force her way into the Cabinet meeting!

CHEDA: Let her!

VASA: But that would be dreadful! That would never do!

CHEDA: Well, what can we do about it?

VASA: You've got to help me stop her – by force if we have to.

SCENE 20

*(**Enter** RAKA and ANKA. RAKA emerges from one of the rooms holding a large kitchen knife, with ANKA trying to hold him back by clutching the back of his coat)*

RAKA: Let me go! Let me go, I say!

CHEDA *(blocking his path)*: Now, hold on, what are you up to?

RAKA: Let me go! I'm going to stab him!

CHEDA: Stab who, for God's sake?

RAKA: Sreta Matich.

CHEDA: Why?

RAKA: He insulted me, calling my father a Mandarin!

CHEDA: Well, didn't you insult his father?

RAKA: Yes, I did.

CHEDA: Then you're quits.

RAKA: But his father wasn't called a mandarin in the *newspapers*!

SCENE 21

*(**Enter** ZHIVKA from her room, dressed for outdoors. As she starts to hurry out, VASA and DARA try to restrain her)*

ZHIVKA: Get out of my way! *(She forces her way towards the outer door, but at that moment the door opens and SIMA **enters**, standing in the doorway. ZHIVKA recoils from him)*: What's happened? For God's sake, what's happened?

SIMA: They've accepted my resignation.

ZHIVKA *(She shrieks as though she had been wounded)*: Hell and damnation! Why did you give it in?

SIMA: Because of you! …

ZHIVKA: What's that!? Because of me? What the hell d'you mean "because of me", you idiot? The truth is, you weren't up to being a minister! That's the truth!

SIMA: No, I wasn't – not with a wife like you.

ZHIVKA: So now we aren't ministers any more?

SIMA: No, we certainly are not!

ZHIVKA: Oh, my sweet Saviour, why do you treat me as an enemy, when I've lit a candle to You every Friday? *(To SIMA)*:

So that's that! No more cars, no more boxes at the theatre, no more first-class sleeping carriages … it's all over, is it? … all gone, everything?

SIMA: Yes, everything!

RAKA *(loudly)*: Down with the government!

ZHIVKA *(picking up a bundle of newspapers and hurling it down)*: Shut up, you yapping little tyke! – not another sound from you! *(Exit RAKA, running. ZHIVKA then goes to SIMA and glares into his face)*: Because of me, eh? Because of me? Hah! If I'd been the Minister you wouldn't have seen *me* resigning because of *you*! *(Exit SIMA. She then stares at CHEDA, DARA, and VASA)*: And you three – nudging each other and laughing up your sleeves, are you? Well, Cheda, just you think about it – you and I are going to be at odds for ever and a day, and there'll be precious little ease or peaceful sleep for you from now on! *(Exit CHEDA)* And as for you, *(to DARA)* you get on with your packing! You'd better pack, if you can't get yourself away from that wretched creature. Pack for your journey, but you won't be travelling in a Pullman carriage, you know! Oh, no! it'll be third-class, d'you hear? – third-class! *(Exit DARA)* And you *(to VASA)* – what are you pulling a face for? Go on – clear off! Run round to the family and tell them that I'm not a minister's wife any more! Savka and Datsa and Soya will shriek with delight and say: "Oh, really! So Zhivka's had it, has she!" It'll make them feel better – I know them, and I know you too well! Go on – go and tell them! *(Exit VASA)*

*(*ZHIVKA *then approaches the front of the stage and addresses the audience)*: And as for you lot, having a fine time giggling over my misfortunes – don't forget that, since I'm not a minister's wife any more I don't have to be cultured and well-behaved any more either, so don't blame me if you get the rough edge of my tongue! Go home! Go on – go home! I'll not have you hanging about here and adding to my troubles. Clear off! – and may the Devil fly away with you if you start slanging me! Because, who knows, one of these days I may be a minister's

wife once more. After all, once these little minor difficulties have been passed over and forgotten I could be back, and don't say I didn't warn you! I'm telling you now – you'll see! Go on – get away with you now! Now! Clear off! Go home! …

Curtain